Sushi For Dummies®

Decoding the Sushi Bar Menu

The following Japanese words and dishes frequently appear on sushi bar menus. Stress each syllable equally, and you'll be ordering like a pro!

Types of sushi

Chirashi-zushi (chee-rah-shee-zoo-shee): Scattered sushi

Gunkan-maki-zushi (goon-kahn-mah-kee-zoo-shee): Battleship sushi

Maki-zushi (mah-kee-zoo-shee): Sliced rolls, in general, including the following two types:

> **Futo-maki-zushi** (foo-toh-mah-kee-zoo-shee): Thick (2- to 2 ½-inches wide) sliced rolls

> **Hoso-maki-zushi** (hoh-soh-mah-kee-zoo-shee): Thin (1-inch wide) sliced rolls

Nigiri-zushi (nee-gee-ree-zoo-shee): Finger sushi

Temaki-zushi (teh-mah-kee-zoo-shee): Hand rolls

Ura-maki-zushi (oo-rah-mah-kee-zoo-shee): Inside-out rolls

Seafood

Aji (ah-jee): Flavorful Spanish or horse mackerel, served as sashimi or on sushi. Ask for the fish skeleton served deep-fried and crunchy.

Amaebi (ah-mah-eh-bee): Raw shrimp, naturally sweet, usually served on top of finger sushi. Ask the chef to grill the heads, too.

Anago (ah-nah-goh): Glazed, barbecued saltwater eel.

Chu-toro (chooo-toh-roh): Deliciously buttery tasting fatty tuna belly meat.

Ebi (eh-bee): Cooked, butterflied shrimp, usually served on finger sushi.

Hamachi (hah-mah-chee): Japanese yellowtail, a very rich tasting fish, usually served raw.

Hirame (hee-rah-meh): Fluke, flounder, or halibut; usually served raw, thinly sliced as sashimi or on finger sushi, usually served with a ponzu dipping sauce.

Hotate (hoh-tah-teh): Delicately sweet sea scallops.

Ikura (ee-koo-rah): Fresh salted salmon roe; large, shiny, orange-red eggs, rich and wonderful, often served in battleship sushi.

Maguro (mah-goo-roh): The generic word for all types of tuna.

For Dummies: Bestselling Book Series for Beginners

Sushi For Dummies®

Cheat Sheet

Masago (mah-sah-goh): Fresh salted smelt roe with a crunchy texture.

O-toro (ohh-toh-roh): Extremely buttery tasting fatty tuna belly meat.

Sake (sah-keh): Salmon, rich and creamy tasting, delightfully chewy texture.

Sashimi (sah-shee-mee): Slices of pristinely beautiful raw fish.

Tai (tah-ee): A mild, white-fleshed fish eaten raw as sashimi or with sushi.

Unagi (oo-nah-gee): Glazed, barbecued freshwater eel.

Uni (oo-nee): Sea urchin roe, resembling tiny yellow tongues.

Sushi Bar Chit-Chat

If a Japanese-speaking sushi chef is behind the sushi counter, these ten brief Japanese expressions will come in handy and make you a very welcome guest. Stress each syllable equally, and you'll be set.

Hai (hah-ee): Yes.

Iie (eee-eh): No.

Konnichiwa (kohn-nee-chee-wah): Hello (in the afternoon).

Kombanwa (kohm-bahn-wah): Hello (in the evening).

Omakase ni shite kudasai (oh-mah-kah-seh nee shee-teh koo-dah-sah-ee): Please, you (the sushi chef) choose.

Kyo wa nani ga ii desuka (kyohh wah nah-nee gah eee deh-soo-kah)?: What's good today?

(Maguro) o kudasai (mah-goo-roh oh koo-dah-sah-ee): I'd like to have tuna, please. (Substitute other choices for maguro, the word for tuna.)

Oishii! (oh-ee-sheee): Delicious!

Kampai! (kahm-pah-ee): Cheers! (Said as a toast.)

Domo (dohh-moh): Thank you.

For Dummies: Bestselling Book Series for Beginners

Sushi

FOR

DUMMIES®

by Judi Strada and
Mineko Takane Moreno

WILEY

Wiley Publishing, Inc.

Sushi For Dummies®

Published by
Wiley Publishing, Inc.
111 River St.
Hoboken, NJ 07030-5774
www.wiley.com

Copyright © 2004 by Wiley Publishing, Inc., Indianapolis, Indiana

Published simultaneously in Canada

For general information on our other products and services or to obtain technical support, please contact our Customer Care Department within the U.S. at 800-762-2974, outside the U.S. at 317-572-3993, or fax 317-572-4002.

Wiley also publishes its books in a variety of electronic formats. Some content that appears in print may not be available in electronic books.

Library of Congress Control Number: 2004102331

ISBN: 0-7645-4465-9

Manufactured in the United States of America

10 9 8 7 6 5 4 3 2 1

1B/RX/QT/QU/IN

About the Authors

 **Mineko Takane Moreno,** born and raised in Tokyo, received her degree in French literature. Her love of food has inspired a lifelong education in many cuisines, including Japanese, Chinese, French, and Italian. Moving to San Diego in 1973, she began teaching Japanese cuisine, with a specialty in sushi. She currently teaches dozens of sushi classes a year at seven culinary schools, including Macy's, Williams-Sonoma, and Sur la Table. Mineko consults with restaurants wishing to put sushi and other specialties on their menu. Her culinary work has been featured in numerous print publications and on television and radio shows. She is a member of the International Association of Culinary Professionals.

Judi Strada has a bachelor's degree in Russian studies, which led her to study other cultures through their foods. She was the food consultant and spokesperson for *The Sheraton World Cookbook* and *The Culinary Festival Cookbook* and coauthor of *The Best of San Diego.* She is a frequent cooking guest on television and radio shows on both coasts. Judi, an award-winning writer, is currently food editor of *San Diego Magazine;* kitchen garden editor of *Garden Compass Magazine;* and a member of the Authors Guild, the American Federation of Television and Radio Artists, the International Association of Culinary Professionals, and the James Beard Foundation. She is founding president of Les Dames d'Escoffier, San Diego.

Dedication

From Mineko: With all my love to my husband, Manuel, for opening the doors of the world for me; and to my children, Veronica and Alexander, for their cherished support. In loving memory of my mother for encouraging me to introduce Japanese culture to others. To all my sushi students who taught me to be a better teacher. To my best friend, Judi Strada, who translated the world of sushi into such colorful and understandable language.

From Judi: To my husband, Randall Strada, my true love and champion since 10th grade; and to our remarkable children, Dominic and Catherine. To my mother and four sisters for cheering me on, no matter what. To Mineko Takane Moreno, my best friend, for such a delicious glimpse into your culture through sushi.

Authors' Acknowledgments

We're so grateful for all the support we received over the last two years as *Sushi For Dummies* took shape. Yukito Ota, owner and chef of Sushi Ota restaurant, San Diego, answered all our sushi-related questions. Mimu Tsujimura, Department of Linguistics, University of California, San Diego, created a pronunciation guide for this cookbook and answered Japanese language questions.

Linda Candler, V.P. Communications, National Fisheries Institute, provided invaluable seafood information. Heidi Wilkinson, formerly director of The Rice Foundation, addressed sticky rice questions. Shirley Cheng, professor of culinary arts, The Culinary Institute of America, Hyde Park, New York, lent insight into sushi's growing popularity. Roy Carver III, owner, and Bridgett Klinger, office manager, Pacific Farms, USA, fielded queries about wasabi. Bruce Gore, Triad Fisheries, answered salmon questions and explained the beauty of flash-frozen fish. Nijiya Market, San Diego, helped with sushi ingredients. Great News Discount Cookware offered advice about sushi equipment. Sushi chef Tim Johnson, Zenbu, La Jolla, California, gave insight into sushi bars. Marco Barat, American Wine and Spirits, and Bill Shepard, wine specialist, Jonathan's Market, La Jolla, California, offered tips on wines. Three other *For Dummies* authors, and friends, helped pave the way: Peter Economy, Carole Bloom, and Karen Ward. Coleen O'Shea, our literary agent, was most supportive. Photographer Gregory Bertolini graciously captured our images. And Maggie and Jerry Coleman saved the day, teaching us the difference between a baseball and softball's worth of rice.

A very talented team at Wiley Publishing ushered us through the publishing process: acquisitions editor Norm Crampton, whose early vision of *Sushi For Dummies* helped the book take shape; senior project editor Alissa Schwipps, whose cheerfulness and encouraging ways made it such fun; senior copy editor Tina Sims, who made the chapters read smoothly; technical editor Rich Hardesty, who certainly knows his sushi; recipe tester Emily Nolan, who tested each recipe; illustrator Liz Kurtzman, whose drawings bring sushi to life; nutritionist Patty Santelli for her careful analysis; Lesa Grant, publicist, who sees to it we take to the road with all the right materials in hand; to those whose names we don't know but who worked so hard to bring *Sushi For Dummies* into print — we wish you all perfect sushi rice. Thank you!

Publisher's Acknowledgments

We're proud of this book; please send us your comments through our Dummies online registration form located at www.dummies.com/register/.

Some of the people who helped bring this book to market include the following:

Acquisitions, Editorial, and Media Development

Senior Project Editor: Alissa D. Schwipps

Acquisitions Editor: Norm Crampton

Senior Copy Editor: Tina Sims

Assistant Editor: Holly Gastineau-Grimes

Technical Editor: Rich Hardesty, owner of H20 and ELEMENTS restaurants in Indianapolis, Indiana

Editorial Manager: Jennifer Ehrlich

Editorial Assistant: Elizabeth Rea

Cover Photos: © Paul Poplis/Getty Images/FoodPix

Cartoons: Rich Tennant, www.the5thwave.com

Production

Project Coordinator: Maridee Ennis

Layout and Graphics: LeAndra Hosier, Barry Offringa, Lynsey Osborn, Jacque Schneider, Julie Trippetti

Special Art: Liz Kurtzman

Proofreaders: David Faust, Andy Hollandbeck, Carl William Pierce, Brian H. Walls, TECHBOOKS Production Services

Indexer: TECHBOOKS Production Services

Special Help:
Laura K. Miller

Publishing and Editorial for Consumer Dummies

   Diane Graves Steele, Vice President and Publisher, Consumer Dummies

   Joyce Pepple, Acquisitions Director, Consumer Dummies

   Kristin A. Cocks, Product Development Director, Consumer Dummies

   Michael Spring, Vice President and Publisher, Travel

   Brice Gosnell, Associate Publisher, Travel

   Kelly Regan, Editorial Director, Travel

Publishing for Technology Dummies

   Andy Cummings, Vice President and Publisher, Dummies Technology/General User

Composition Services

   Gerry Fahey, Vice President of Production Services

   Debbie Stailey, Director of Composition Services

Contents at a Glance

Recipes at a Glance

Inside-out rolls

Pressed sushi

Scattered sushi

Sliced rolls

Sushi rice balls

Tofu pouch sushi

Desserts

Table of Contents

Introduction

● ●

Sushi may be the most recognizable Japanese word in the English language today, but its meaning is often misinterpreted. When we say "sushi," what do you think? Raw fish, right? Think again! Sushi actually means vinegared rice, which is the key ingredient in every sushi recipe. So if raw fish isn't your thing, never fear! You can use vegetables, cooked fish, and other tasty foods to create and enjoy fresh, flavorful, and fun sushi that tantalizes your taste buds at home or at a sushi bar!

Now, don't let the introduction of Japanese words, or the new-to-you ingredients, throw you off. They're all part of the sushi adventure, and we want you to have the fullest sushi adventure possible. To help you along, we give translations for Japanese words throughout the book, as well as offer a pronunciation guide for key sushi words on the Cheat Sheet in the front of the book. In Chapter 3, we introduce you to potentially unfamiliar sushi ingredients that likely will quickly find their place in your pantry and refrigerator. We also share with you my (Mineko's) easy, foolproof, sushi-making techniques, spelled out in a clear, concise way. The instructions make sushi doable for everyone; even kids succeed at making sushi when they use my tried-and-true techniques! To go with these easy-to-use methods are our delicious, very doable, favorite sushi recipes, so you can be wowing your friends and family in no time at all.

Just remember that you don't need to become an expert, or perform like a sushi chef, to do a really good job of making sushi. We've gone to great lengths to take the hassle out of sushi for you. You just need to keep *Sushi For Dummies* by your side, get ready for the fun, and start down the sticky rice road with us!

About This Book

After the information and recipes, the next best thing about this cookbook is how it's organized. Read the Recipes at a Glance in the front of the cookbook, and you'll know immediately which recipes you want to try. Within each part, you find chapters that contain complete information on the subject at hand, be it equipment, ingredients, or seafood. Within the chapters are bold headings and subheadings that clearly tell you what's coming next, making it a breeze to grasp *Sushi For Dummies*.

The following features make *Sushi For Dummies* great:

- ✔ **Truly good recipes you'll make again and again:** Ours are clear, concise, well tested, and encouraging.

- ✔ **No-fail versions of popular sushi techniques:** Brevity is best in recipes, but not if that means the cook's going to fail for lack of details. To help ensure that your sushi making is successful, Chapter 6 offers thorough explanations for the techniques used in *Sushi For Dummies*. After you read them, you can rely on the abbreviated techniques within each recipe, but we want you to get things right, so that's why we offer these full-blown versions of each technique.

- ✔ **Recipes organized with you in mind:** We organize our sushi recipes by lifestyle moments, giving you a heads up as to what recipes will fit what's happening in your life at the moment.

- ✔ **Practical advice:** We explain things like what to do with left-over ingredients and how to care for equipment so that it lasts a long time.

Conventions Used in This Book

Planning is key to saving time when making sushi. Read your chosen recipe all the way through, pulling out all the equipment and ingredients needed (except raw seafood, which should stay refrigerated until the last moment) before you begin making sushi. This way, you'll move smoothly through the recipe's steps without being interrupted to go get or do something you didn't plan on.

Here are some other non-recipe conventions you should keep in mind to get the most out of this guidebook:

- ✔ *Italic* is used for emphasis and to highlight new words or terms that are defined. We also use it when we mention Japanese words that haven't entered our conversational mainstream, such as *mirin* (sweet cooking sake).

- ✔ **Boldfaced** text is used to indicate the action part of numbered steps.

- ✔ Monofont is used for Web addresses.

- ✔ This little onion points out vegetarian recipes (including cheese). You find it next to the recipe titles.

- ✔ Traditionally, sushi chefs in Japan have always been men. Now, female sushi chefs are showing up behind sushi counters around the world. We refer to sushi chefs as "he" throughout the book, but clearly, women are very good at making sushi. After all, two women wrote this book!

We also use some standard conventions in the recipes:

✔ Our recipes serve four people, in general. Sushi is unique in that much of it is served in small bites, so you usually prepare more than one type of sushi for a meal. When we give a recipe for eight finger sushi, we assume that four people will have two each. We also assume that other sushi will be offered.

✔ Many recipes use very small amounts of rice that are impractical to make. We assume that you're making other sushi recipes in this book as well, or that you're using leftover frozen sushi rice (see Chapter 5).

✔ Preparation time is based on all equipment and ingredients being out, ready to go (fruits and vegetables well washed, under cold running water). Any measuring or chopping is included in the preparation time.

✔ "Sashimi-grade fish" is an industry term for the highest grade of seafood, suitable for eating raw.

✔ All eggs are large; butter is unsalted; flour is all-purpose; sugar is granulated sugar.

✔ Cheese is considered a vegetarian food.

✔ Regular Japanese (not Chinese) soy sauce is used in all recipes, unless the recipe states to use light (color) soy sauce.

✔ We list sea salt as an ingredient when it's key, such as in Hard-Boiled Quail Eggs with Matcha Salt in Chapter 13. Table salt is fine, but the clean, flavorful taste of sea salt is always preferred.

✔ Salt-cured fish roe is considered raw. Cold smoked salmon is considered raw fish. Marinated raw fish is also considered raw.

✔ Most people enjoy eating sushi with soy sauce and pickled ginger, but because the amounts vary according to individual tastes, the nutritional information at the end of each recipe doesn't account for these items. If you do decide to enhance your meal with these items, keep the following information in mind:

   • **1 tablespoon soy sauce:** Calories 10 (From Fat 0); Fat 0g (Saturated 0g); Cholesterol 0mg; Sodium 920mg; Carbohydrate 0g (Dietary Fiber 0g); Protein 2g.

   • **1 tablespoon pickled ginger:** Calories 15 (From Fat 0); Fat 0g (Saturated 0g); Cholesterol 0mg; Sodium 340mg; Carbohydrate 3g (Dietary Fiber 0g); Protein 0g.

What You're Not to Read

We think that all the information in this cookbook is absolutely fascinating, but not all of it is essential to making sushi at home:

- **Those spellbinding sidebars:** Throughout the book, shaded sidebar boxes appear that are filled with fun but skippable sushi-related information. We labored over every word, but you can skip these sidebars, if you like. Just don't tell us. We'd be heartbroken.

- **Those riveting pronunciation guides:** We thought you'd like to know how to pronounce common sushi words and expressions, so we provide pronunciation help on the Cheat Sheet and a few places in the cookbook. You can skip over these, but we suggest that you give them a try, especially wasabi (wah-sah-bee), before you head to the sushi bar.

- **Our extraordinary biographies:** You don't need to know who we are to know that this is the best sushi cookbook out there. After all, all *For Dummies* authors are considered experts in their fields. Still, aren't you curious?

Foolish Assumptions

We wrote this cookbook with some thoughts about you in mind:

- You know your way around the kitchen and enjoy cooking, but you don't know much about making sushi.

- You've made sushi, but the rice didn't turn out well, or the sushi wasn't up to your standards. You're searching for just the right sushi cookbook to solve your problems. This is it.

- You'd like to make sushi but aren't sure that it's easy to do (it is), that you can do it (you can), or that it will be fun to do (it is).

- You have basic kitchen equipment on hand, including pots and pans and measuring cups, which are some of the main items you need to make sushi, but you won't mind picking up a few affordable items to make your sushi adventure easier and more enjoyable.

- You've never been to a sushi bar and want a sushi bar guide to help you know what to expect, what to ask for, and how to ask for it.

- You live for sushi bars and want to know what special dishes you've been missing.

✔ You're tired of paying a fortune for sushi at sushi bars and ready to do it yourself with a little help (from us!).

✔ You received this cookbook as a gift. You have no idea what sushi is, but you're open-minded and ready to try new things. Welcome to an exciting new world of freshness, flavor, and taste!

Foolish of us, maybe, but we assume that you trusted us to do our very best when writing this cookbook, so that every time you open it, you'll enjoy reading it. Even more, we want you to enjoy the sushi you make from our recipes. Our promise to you is that you will!

How This Book Is Organized

Sushi For Dummies is your one-stop shop for the key things you need to know about making sushi, eating sushi, and ordering sushi at a sushi bar. We've organized everything into five distinct parts. Here's how it all shakes out.

Part I: Discovering the World of Sushi

Sushi has been around a very long time in Japan. Here, we tell you all about its past, plus its glorious present and future. Then we launch right into the equipment that's used to make sushi, and discuss the ingredients, like seafood, that are responsible for the wonderful tastes and textures of sushi.

Part II: Getting Ready, Getting Set

You can go nowhere in sushiville without the star player — properly prepared sushi rice. I (Mineko) have been teaching students how to make perfect sushi rice for many years. In this part, I share my secrets of sushi rice success with you, plus offer instructions on how to make the most popular types of sushi. Lastly, we cover a very important part of sushi preparation: how to cut those beautiful little pieces of fish and vegetables for sushi recipes.

Part III: Rock-and-Rollin' Sushi Recipes

Here they are — what you've been longing for: truly good sushi recipes! We cover sushi bar favorites first, in Chapter 8, because we know how much you crave them. Then we move on to chapters whose recipes are based on lifestyle moments. When you want quick satisfaction, turn to Chapter 9. If your goal is to make sushi ahead, Chapter 10 is for you. An important meal is on the horizon, and you want to pull out all the stops? Look in Chapter 11. In Chapter 12, you'll be surprised by how creative sushi can be.

Part IV: Enjoying Sushi Meals at Home and at the Sushi Bar

We knew that you'd want some savory start-up dishes, suitable drinks, and sweet conclusions to go with your sushi recipes, so they're here. If you want to throw a sushi party but would rather not do all the planning, we plan everything for you in a great hand roll sushi party in Chapter 14, giving you do-ahead advice and offering menus for side dishes and desserts. If you decide that you'd rather not set up a party at home but instead join everybody at a sushi bar, read Chapter 15. You'll probably know more about what to order and how to order it than anyone else!

Part V: The Part of Tens

Our two Part of Tens chapters are short and sweet, covering ten terrific tips for making sushi at home and ten etiquette do's and don'ts that will have you eating sushi with style.

Icons Used in This Book

We love sharing sushi in a way that makes it fun and informative! Enter the mighty sushi icons, those little pictures in the left-hand margin of this cookbook.

This icon highlights helpful hints and handy sushi shortcuts to make your sushi experience easy, tasty, fun, and hassle free.

These are the sticky notes you'd put on the fridge, if you could, because this icon highlights really important sushi information that we think is worth remembering.

This icon flags information that can keep you from goofing up a dish, or alerts you about potential health or safety issues.

If you want to be a sushi insider, this icon is for you. It clues you in about the secrets of sushi and sushi bars, correct sushi manners, and authentic sushi preparations and techniques, rocketing you to the level of a sushi expert.

Where to Go from Here

You'll notice how easy it is to jump from chapter to chapter in our book without feeling lost. That's intentional, so you can start enjoying *Sushi For Dummies* with any chapter you like. Even if you've made sushi before, we recommend that you start by reading two key chapters — Chapter 5, where you discover how to make perfect (and we do mean perfect) sushi rice, and Chapter 6, where we fully explain our easy-to-master types of sushi. If raw seafood is your thing, go directly to Chapter 4. If you're experienced at sushi and just want more great recipes, our triple-tested, most requested sushi recipes are in Part III. You want to know what's up with sushi bars, how to order, and what to say? Flip to Chapter 15, or check out the Cheat Sheet in the front of the book.

Wherever you start reading, start now, and enjoy!

Part I

Discovering the World of Sushi

"Get the plates ready."

In this part . . .

In this part, we briefly go over what sushi is and is not, and discuss how today's sushi has traveled from its humble beginnings 200 years ago as a street snack in Japan to the fanciest sushi bars all around the world. After we explore the history and diversity of sushi, we take you into the kitchen to show you what you need in the way of equipment — which is really very little — to make sushi at home. We also explain what ingredients you'll want to have on hand to make sushi for family and friends, plus we spell out the ABCs of working with fresh seafood.

Chapter 1

Embarking on the Sushi Adventure

Sushi is a world of tantalizing, clean, fresh flavors. Pristinely beautiful, plump, and chewy white rice, glistening with freshness and flavored with a fragrant vinegar dressing, is topped or mixed with fresh vegetables, cheese, tofu, or whatever you desire.

Notice we didn't say anything about raw fish. Why? Because there's a *huge* misconception that sushi means raw fish, when it really means vinegared rice or items served on or in vinegared rice. This inaccurate belief probably came to be because sushi bars, where most people first experience sushi, offer gorgeous sashimi (sliced raw seafood) dishes, and sushi is frequently topped or made with raw seafood.

We're not trying to take anything away from raw seafood — we love it! *Sushi For Dummies* offers great raw seafood information (see Chapter 4) and raw seafood sushi recipes. But when you consider that prepared sushi rice functions like bread in a sandwich, you begin to understand how versatile sushi is and how it can be a favorite food in any cook's repertoire, from vegetarians to fish, poultry, and meat lovers. We offer all kinds of sushi recipes made without raw fish, such as sushi bar favorites California Inside-Out Rolls, Caterpillar Inside-Out Rolls, and Cucumber Sliced Rolls, all in Chapter 8.

In this chapter, we demystify sushi, touching on its development over the last 2,000 years; what's involved in the way of ingredients, tools, and techniques to make all the satisfying sushi at home you could want; and how to get the absolute best experience out of a visit to a sushi bar.

Appreciating Sushi's Past, Present, and Future

Sushi can be over-the-top-chic at times, such as our Smoked Salmon Sushi Packages in Chapter 11, but that's not how it started out. It has a very humble past.

Over 2,000 years ago, Japan learned about preserving fish by packing or pressing it in salt and rice, a practice that was common throughout Southeast Asia at the time. An early type of pressed sushi, called *nare-zushi,* was held for months before the preserved fish was eaten, and the fermented rice thrown out. One of these early pressed sushi, *funa-zushi,* or preserved carp, developed around AD 700, is still enjoyed in Japan today — the pickled carp eaten, the fermented rice thrown out.

Fast forward to the fifteenth or sixteenth century, when the pressing process was substantially shortened, creating *nama-nare-zushi,* meaning partially fermented sushi. For the first time, the Japanese began to eat this freshly fermented, tangy rice with the pickled fish instead of discarding it. Pick up the pace and enter the seventeenth century, when a savvy Japanese sushi connoisseur thought to add vinegar to cooked rice to obtain the desired tangy rice taste, creating *haya-zushi,* or instant vinegared sushi rice. But the Japanese still pressed the vinegared rice with fish or other foods, waiting awhile before eating it. By the eighteenth century, *maki-zushi,* or rolled sushi, and *chirashi-zushi,* or scattered sushi, also began to appear.

By the early nineteenth century, *nigiri-zushi,* or finger sushi, came into being as sushi stalls popped up in Japan, offering these bite-sized vinegared rice treats to on-the-go customers. In 1824, a great moment in sushi history, a Tokyo (formerly Edo) sushi stall operator named Hanaya Yohei offered finger sushi topped with slices of raw fish, like our Tuna Finger Sushi in Chapter 8. Word quickly spread out from his stall, and now around the world, that raw fish and vinegared rice make a perfect pair!

Oshi-zushi, today's pressed sushi, is all about freshly cooked rice that is tossed with a rice vinegar dressing, cooled, then pressed with the freshest and best ingredients available, and eaten that same day (see our Crabmeat and Avocado Pressed Sushi with Wasabi Mayonnaise in Chapter 9). Many other types of sushi have developed over the years, and their origins are not always clear. Their taste and popularity are now well established, however, and they include such sushi as *temaki-zushi,* or hand rolls, and *inari-zushi,* or tofu pouches, both of which we offer in this cookbook.

Today, the names of sushi dishes, even the names of types of sushi, can vary for the same dish or same type of sushi, depending on the country you're in, the sushi bar you're in, who you're talking to, or for other reasons (see Chapter 6). After you read how sushi rice and types of sushi are made, you'll be able to work your way around this sticky rice name situation, and figure out what a sushi dish is by what's gone into it, regardless of what it's being called.

Today, sushi has lots going for it:

- ✔ **Sushi tastes good and makes you feel good.** Sushi doesn't contain big hunks of any food item. It's all small bites of flavorful foods that leave you feeling satisfied, but not stuffed or heavy.

- ✔ **Sushi is good for you.** It consists predominately of lowfat, high-protein, and complex-carbohydrate ingredients and is rich in vitamins and minerals. Sushi is the perfect food for a health-conscious nation.

- ✔ **Sushi exposes you to tastes and textures you may not have experienced before — it's an adventure!** Your first taste of lively pickled daikon radish *(takuan),* slippery and chewy longneck clam, or the buttery richness of raw tuna will wake you up to a whole world of exciting food choices!

- ✔ **Sushi is an incredibly well-designed food.** Rice vinegar, wasabi, pickled ginger, and soy sauce all have antibacterial properties, which are helpful when working with raw fish.

- ✔ **Sushi is frugal.** Nothing is wasted in Japanese cuisine, and sushi is proof of that attitude. When you order raw sweet shrimp *(amaebi)* at a sushi bar, not only do you enjoy the shrimp, but knowledgeable sushi lovers ask for the heads grilled (see the second menu in the sushi bar sidebar in Chapter 15). This sushi treat may sound weird and look strange, but it tastes terrific!

Sushi's future shines brightly. Chances are, if you can't find a sushi bar in every country in the world today, you will soon. Traditional techniques used in making popular types of sushi will still be around, but it's anybody's guess where *sosaku-zushi,* or creative sushi (see Chapters 11 and 12), will take us!

Enjoying Sushi at Home

Most people lead busy lives and have too little free time, yet they may want to eat exciting food such as sushi. Thankfully, sushi is not only delicious but also can be quick and easy to make at home. You just need fresh ingredients, a few tools, and this cookbook.

Gathering fresh ingredients

If ever a food culture treasured the high quality of its ingredients, it's the Japanese food culture.

To create the best sushi dishes, consider every single ingredient, and every single step when working with that ingredient (see Chapter 6). The best sushi includes ingredients so fresh that they're practically still growing in the ground or swimming in the sea. This means that you may spend more time carefully selecting your ingredients and cutting, combining, and properly arranging these ingredients than you do cooking — but it's worth it! Chapters 3 and 4 provide tips on purchasing the freshest ingredients either online or at a market in your area.

Remember the following ideas when selecting sushi ingredients:

- ✔ **Respect the integrity of each ingredient.** For example, in the Tuna Sushi Rice Balls in Chapter 9, nothing distracts from the beauty and pristine taste of the sashimi-grade raw tuna. Only three ingredients go into the rice balls: raw tuna, fresh-tasting sushi rice that complements the tuna's clean taste, and a dab of wasabi paste to heighten the flavors of the raw tuna and vinegared rice.

- ✔ **Reveal each ingredient's taste and texture.** Carefully evaluate every ingredient, from tofu to salmon roe, for the best way to preserve its unique qualities when used in a dish. For example, in Tofu Finger Sushi, found in Chapter 9, tofu's custardlike texture is a wonderful contrast to the chewy nature of sushi rice, just as its faintly nutty taste finds a perfect companion in the nutty flavor of the rice.

- ✔ **Let your ingredient choices follow the seasons.** Do this, and your sushi will take on a culinary character worthy of that time of year. For example, the Mexican Hand Rolls in Chapter 9, with their cooling sticks of mango, jicama, and cucumber, offer relief from summer heat.

Collecting a few tools

All you need to make most types of sushi at home is your own two hands and some basic kitchen equipment you probably already have. But, as you go down the sticky rice path, making all kinds of delicious sushi dishes, you're bound to want a few nifty sushi tools that make the process that much more pleasurable (see Chapter 2).

What's the only indispensable sushi tool you'll want to buy? An inexpensive, bamboo sushi mat that's required for making sliced sushi rolls. As your passion for sushi grows, you'll also want to pick up a rice cooker to take the guesswork out of this process; a *handai,* or beautiful wooden sushi rice tub, designed specifically for cooling down the rice for sushi; and an *uchiwa,* or flat fan, for creating a breeze to help cool off the hot rice, making your sushi rice experience all the more authentic.

The Japanese samurai, or warriors of old, carried a pair of fighting swords. Samurais are no more, but the tradition of making some of the world's finest knives (think of them as very short swords) continues. In Chapter 2, we go over the two Japanese knives that can help you achieve the even, smooth, sometimes transparently thin slices you want for our sushi recipes. Of course, you can use the sharpest nonserrated knives you have, but what a joy it is to own and use fine Japanese knives.

To finish off your sushi kitchen, and add finishing touches to your sushi, you'll want to pick up decorative vegetable cutters, which look like little cookie cutters, and a Japanese mandoline, for beautiful slivers and slices, both discussed in Chapter 2.

Mastering popular techniques

The techniques involved in making the most popular types of sushi aren't difficult at all. They may seem strange the first few times you try them, but they'll quickly become second nature to you, much as building a better cheeseburger becomes second nature. We explain each technique to you in detail in Chapter 6, so you should have no problems creating the sushi of your dreams. You need to read these instructions only once, and then you can simply follow the condensed, abbreviated version of the technique found in each sushi recipe.

But before you can make your first finger sushi or bowl of scattered sushi, you must first master the technique of making perfect sushi rice, the heartbeat of sushi. Making sushi rice that turns out fragrant, moist, and chewy is no big deal if you know what you're doing. So trust us when we say that if you want to make perfect sushi rice, all you need to do is follow the directions in Chapter 5, just once. After that, you'll be able to make sushi rice in your sleep (although we don't recommend it!). Please don't skip reading through that chapter, start to finish, or you may not get the perfect sushi rice you want.

What's the best way for a sushi beginner to get started? First, for the fun of it, and for the solid information, read Chapter 16. Doing so will take you all of five minutes. Then adopt the first principle: Relax! Sushi is as much fun to make as it is to eat.

Don't worry about lacking sushi skills. Start off with one simple technique and one simple recipe, such as the Smoked Salmon Sushi Rice Balls in Chapter 9. All you do is twist a small portion of sushi rice with smoked salmon into a round ball (using plastic wrap), unwrap it and top it with a caper. Anybody can do that, and the results are pretty and very tasty! Try this recipe, and you're on your way. Build on your success by adding a new technique from Chapter 6 each time you make sushi.

Sushi can look sloppy and still taste good, as long as your rice and ingredients taste good. So don't worry, be happy, make sushi!

Making up a sushi menu

When you're ready to make a full meal of sushi, select your recipes while keeping in mind that sushi doesn't have to be eaten in any specific order. Decide on the one, two, or three sushi you want to make from Chapters 8 through 12. We group our sushi recipes into what we call lifestyle moments so that you can flip to the chapter that meets your lifestyle needs at the moment. For example, if you're in a hurry and want to make finger-snapping fast sushi (in sushi time, that is), try out the recipes such as the Roast Beef and Watercress Hand Rolls in Chapter 9. Or if you want a menu that sidesteps the last-minute rush, turn to Chapter 10 for recipes such as Sweet Tofu Pouch Sushi or Teriyaki Chicken Sliced Rolls, which allow you to prepare several of the ingredients ahead of time so that you can assemble the sushi quickly when you're ready to sit down and eat.

If you want to begin a meal with an appetizer or add a delicious side item to the menu, then take a look at Chapter 13. Somewhere in that chapter is the perfect starter for you, perhaps Edamame (boiled soybean in their pods) or something dressier, such as the Hard-Boiled Quail Eggs with Matcha Salt. Dessert can be as easy as Fire and Ice Cream Sandwiches or Oranges in Plum Wine, which take very little time to make (both recipes are in Chapter 13).

 When creating a sushi meal menu for yourself or for a sushi party (see Chapter 14), go for a symphony of flavors. For example, if you start with a very singular taste, such as Salmon Roe Battleship Sushi in Chapter 9, move on to a more complex combination of tastes next, such as Grilled Shrimp and Thai Basil Inside-Out Rolls with Spicy Lime Dipping Sauce in Chapter 11.

Enjoying each and every piece

Sushi is not only delicious but beautiful, too. To get the most out of your sushi experiences, relish each piece of sushi with all your senses. When appreciating sushi, do the following:

- ✔ **Look:** See the beauty of the ingredients.
- ✔ **Taste:** Pay attention to the different flavors in the sushi and how they complement one another.
- ✔ **Feel:** Enjoy the different textures of sushi ingredients in your mouth.
- ✔ **Smell:** Savor the scent of the sea in fresh seafood, and the scent of the earth in vegetables.

Feeling at Home in a Sushi Bar

Walking into a popular sushi bar is always exciting. It's a gathering place to eat sushi, true, but if you sit at the sushi bar (and you should), it's also about camaraderie between you and the sushi chef and between you and the others at the sushi bar. This little tip — that the sushi chef welcomes your attention — is one of dozens throughout *Sushi For Dummies*. In fact, we devote Chapters 15 and 17 to helping you feel comfortable, know how and what to order, and practice perfect sushi etiquette. And the Cheat Sheet helps you figure out what's on the menu and how to pronounce the names of the dishes correctly. You'll be equipped to enjoy sushi from the finest sushi bars in Tokyo to the neighborhood sushi bar in Indianapolis. Here are a few pointers to get you started:

- ✔ **Make a reservation for seats at the sushi bar counter.** That way, you're guaranteed a seat, and you can observe and talk to the sushi chef while he's working.

- ✔ **Follow chopstick etiquette.** Japanese table manners focus on chopstick etiquette. For example, don't cross your chopsticks when you set them down. Instead, lay them down, tightly together, below your plate and directly in front of you. Chapter 17 contains more details about chopstick etiquette and other sushi manners.

- ✔ **If you're sitting at the sushi counter, order dish by dish rather than from the restaurant's standard menu.** If you don't know what to order, the sushi chef is there to help you. And you're sure to win the chef's favor if you tell him to prepare something his way when he asks how you want your sushi prepared. Chapter 15 has more details on ordering your meal.

- ✔ **Order sushi like a pro.** If you order in Japanese, the chef is sure to be impressed. The Cheat Sheet in the front of the book contains the Japanese pronunciation for many popular menu items as well as decodes many items on sushi bar menus.

Chapter 2

Outfitting the Sushi Kitchen

aking sushi is much more pleasurable if you have the right tools for the task. Although you don't absolutely need to have all the kitchen equipment and gadgets we discuss in this chapter, these specially designed tools can help you prepare sushi quickly, easily, and expertly. Yes, it's true that you can make sushi with basic kitchen equipment you probably already own. For example, if you want to make sushi rolls, the only indispensable equipment you need is an inexpensive bamboo mat. If you don't intend to make rolls, you don't even need that. You can make a whole world of hand-shaped finger sushi, scattered sushi, hand rolls, and creative sushi with the tools already in your kitchen.

Look in Japanese and Asian markets and better kitchenware stores for the special equipment discussed in this chapter, or check the online resources we provide at the end of this chapter.

Covering the Basics: Kitchen Equipment You Gotta Have

Chances are good that you already have most of the basic kitchen equipment you need to make sushi. But, to be sure that you don't get caught empty-handed, we list the necessities here:

✔ **Cutting boards:** Although you can get by with one cutting board, having two or three is even better. You need one board for raw meats, poultry, and fish you intend to cook; one for fruits and vegetables; and one for sashimi-grade seafood (which is suitable for eating raw). See Chapter 4 for information on sashimi-grade seafood.

We prefer wood cutting boards over plastic because wood is more resilient and therefore less likely to dull knives as quickly. Wood is also more beautiful.

✔ **Fine-mesh strainer:** In many recipes in this book, you place thinly sliced scallions and red onions in a fine-mesh strainer and rinse them under running water to improve their looks and soften their taste.

✔ **Fine grater:** Finely grated citrus peel, gingerroot, wasabi, and daikon radish show up in many recipes, so be sure that you have a fine grater on hand.

✔ **Liquid and dry measuring cups:** Measuring accurately is important when making sushi. Use glass or clear plastic liquid measuring cups (which have spouts). Judge the level by crouching down to look at the liquid at eye level. Measure dry goods, such as rice, level with the top of dry measuring cups.

✔ **Measuring spoons:** Sushi involves small amounts of ingredients. Keep several sets of measuring spoons on hand so that you don't need to keep washing one set as you go.

✔ **Nonstick frying pan:** A nonstick frying pan is helpful because you want as little oil as possible in sushi recipes and nonstick pans enable you to cook with a small amount of oil.

✔ **Plastic wrap:** You use plastic wrap to cover a bamboo mat for inside-out rolls (see the instructions later in this chapter) and to assist you in lots of other sushi preparations.

✔ **Tweezers:** Fish fillets can contain tiny bones. Remove them with tweezers, preferably ones that are broad tipped and ribbed on the inside to enable you to more easily grasp little bones.

✔ **Vegetable peeler:** If yours isn't sharp, toss it and consider buying a ceramic one. The ceramic peelers never rust and keep their edge. A vegetable peeler makes quick work of peeling vegetables and making pretty curls to decorate sushi plates (see Figure 7-3 in Chapter 7).

Acquiring the Right Stuff to Make Sushi Rice

Sushi rice is a combination of cooked short- (or medium-) grain rice and a vinegar dressing, which is then fanned and cooled until it takes on a beautiful sheen and divine chewy texture (see Chapter 5). The following sections explain what tools you need to make this tasty rice. We also suggest substitutions for this equipment in case you want to try your hand at sushi before you invest in new kitchen equipment.

Electric rice cooker

Electric rice cookers make cooking rice easy and almost foolproof. Some newer rice cookers even have a sushi rice setting. Rice cookers come in several sizes. We recommend that you buy one that holds 10 metric cups of dry rice, which means it will cook up to 6 U.S. cups of rice, plenty for any of our sushi recipes. We also recommend buying a cooker that has a nonstick inner pot (that holds the rice), which helps prevent the cooked rice from sticking to the pot and makes cleanup much easier. Take care not to scratch this inner pot because sticky rice just loves clinging to a scratched surface. Expect to pay about $70 to $80 for a sturdy 10-cup rice cooker that should last many years with proper care. High-end cookers can cost as much as $210, but you're safe to stick with a more barebones model.

If you don't have a rice cooker, you can cook sushi rice on your stove (we explain how in Chapter 5). Select a very heavy-bottomed pot, which helps ensure even heat distribution, and use a heavy lid to prevent steam from escaping. Be sure that the pot has room for the raw rice to expand about two and a half to three times in volume — for 2 cups raw rice, use a 2-quart pot; for 3 cups rice, use a 3-quart pot; for 4 cups rice, use a 4-quart pot. If the pot is too small, the water boils out, and the rice doesn't have room to expand. If the pot is too big, the rice spreads out too thin, the water boils too quickly, and the rice doesn't cook through properly.

Shallow wooden sushi rice tub

A Japanese wooden sushi tub *(handai* or *hangiri),* looking much like a very short barrel, is perfect for cooling down cooked sushi rice quickly and absorbing any excess moisture, which are requirements for finished rice that is moist yet still a little bit chewy. Most

Japanese sushi rice tubs are made of uncoated Japanese cypress or cedar wood and bound with copper bands (see Figure 2-1). They come in several sizes, but we recommend buying one that is roughly 16 inches in diameter and 4 inches high, just the right size for 10 to 12 cups of cooked rice. Tubs are expensive but worth it (expect to pay $110 to $120 for a good-quality tub). Mine (Mineko's) is 30 years old and still useful!

TOOLS FOR MAKING SUSHI RICE

FLAT FAN (UCHIWA) FOR COOLING DOWN THE HOT RICE

WOODEN SUSHI MIXING TUB (HANDAI)

WOODEN RICE PADDLE (SHAMOJI)

A KITCHEN TOWEL FOR COVERING THE COOLED SUSHI RICE

Figure 2-1: Tools for making sushi rice.

Before you use your rice tub, here are some things you need to know:

- ✔ **Break in a new tub by filling it with water and ¼ cup rice vinegar and then letting it soak overnight.** Dry it well the next day.

- ✔ **Before each use, fill the tub to the brim with water and let it soak while the rice cooks.** Doing so helps keep the rice from sticking to the tub, and it keeps the tub from soaking up too much of the rice vinegar dressing. (While you're at it, do what the pros do and soak the rice paddle and two or three kitchen towels, all discussed later in this section, in the tub at the same time.)

- ✔ **Empty the tub and wipe it out well with a wrung-out towel just before adding the hot, cooked rice.**

- ✔ **After each use, rinse the tub with warm water until clean.** Rinse it out by hand, not in the dishwasher.

- ✔ **After rinsing the tub, wipe it as dry as possible and then turn it upside down on the counter to completely dry before storing it.** Otherwise, it may develop mold spots. Tipping one side up on a clean, small bowl helps it dry faster. Don't dry the tub in the sun.

If you don't have a sushi tub, cool your rice in a wide, smooth, shallow, nonreactive container. A large salad bowl, lasagna pan, or large, nonstick cookie pan (with raised sides) works well. The nonstick coating on the cookie pan helps keeps the rice from sticking, but because the pan is metal, the rice turns cold quickly, so transfer the rice to a nonmetallic container right after cooling it down.

Rice paddle

A *shamoji,* or thin, smooth, flat wooden rice paddle (refer to Figure 2-1) has two functions when making sushi rice: It separates the hot, cooked rice from the side of its cooking pot, and it turns over and cuts through the cooked rice as it cools down in the sushi rice tub. It's purposely thin so that you smash or bruise as little of the rice as possible in this process. The handle can be short or long. I (Mineko) prefer a long handle because it keeps my hand farther away from the sticky rice.

Use your rice paddle for only sushi rice so that it doesn't pick up any off tastes or scents from other foods. If you don't have a Japanese rice paddle on hand, any thin, flat wood or plastic spoon works well.

Flat fan

The Japanese have a stiff, flat (not folding) lightweight fan *(uchiwa)* traditionally made of paper over bamboo ribs (refer to Figure 2-1). It's the perfect hand-held fan to create a breeze for cooling off hot sushi rice quickly, and such fun to use! Look for this flat fan in Japanese and Asian markets, especially during summer months. Bamboo *uchiwa* can cost $10 or more; plastic fans cost around $5.

Of course, you can use anything you have to create a breeze: an electric fan, a magazine, or a folded-up newspaper. In a pinch, I (Judi) use a stiff place mat. Use whatever works for you.

Lint-free kitchen towels

Who knew that your old cotton or flour-sack kitchen towels would find new life as sushi equipment! You'll dampen one or two of these towels, depending on the size of your sushi tub, to completely cover the top of the tub, keeping the prepared sushi rice moist and fresh. Keep another towel damp, by your side, as you make sushi.

What you want are well-washed, lint-free kitchen towels (no holes, please) to cover the finished sushi rice. New towels can contain lint and scents that you don't want to affect the taste of your sushi rice.

Knowing When to Mold 'Em: Tools for Shaping Sushi

Your well-washed, moist hands are the most valuable tools you have for shaping sushi, but you also may need a bamboo rolling mat and one or two sushi molds, depending on the type of sushi you plan to make.

Bamboo rolling mat

A bamboo mat *(makisu),* used for making sliced sushi rolls and inside-out rolls (see Chapter 6), is the one piece of equipment you can't fake. Believe me (Judi), I've tried lots of substitutes, including a kitchen towel and folded aluminum foil. They didn't work well, if at all. You can purchase mats for roughly $2 to $4 at larger grocery stores, kitchenware shops, Japanese and Asian markets, and online (we suggest online resources in the "Finding the Equipment You Need" section, later in this chapter).

Mats consist of thin strips of bamboo (about $\frac{1}{16}$ to $\frac{1}{8}$ inch wide) tied together with cotton string (see Figure 2-2). They come in several sizes, but most are about 9½ inches square. You need one this size to make the rolls in this book. If your mat has a flat side (usually green), use it flat side up. If it's knotted together at only one end, always lay it down with the knots on the end farthest away from you.

It's important to clean your mat thoroughly, immediately after each use, so that rice grains don't harden on the mat. To clean a bamboo mat, follow these steps:

1. **Wash it with a soft brush and hot, soapy water and rinse it well.**

2. **Stand the mat up on its side to drain and dry completely.**

   If you put it away damp, it will develop mold, which is difficult to get rid of. Discard a moldy mat and buy another one.

3. **Wrap and store it in a paper towel.**

Here's how to wrap a bamboo mat in plastic wrap for inside-out rolls:

1. **Lay a sheet of plastic wrap down, a little more than twice the length of the mat.**

2. **Lay the mat in the center of the plastic wrap.**

3. **Fold over the long sides of the plastic wrap and then the short sides, wrapping the mat completely.**

   Be sure that the plastic wrap fits snugly around the mat and that both sides of the mat are completely covered. Use the smooth-sheeted side to form your rolls.

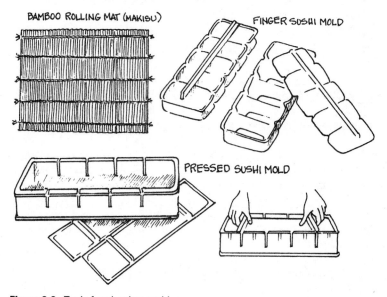

Figure 2-2: Tools for shaping sushi.

Sushi molds

We use two types of plastic molds in *Sushi For Dummies* (refer to Figure 2-2) to make two traditional shapes of sushi: one to make individual finger sushi and one to make pressed sushi that you finish cutting into pieces after the sushi is pressed. You can use just your hands to shape finger sushi, but you do need a mold to make pressed sushi (see Chapter 6 for substitutions). Here are descriptions of each:

  ✔ **Finger sushi mold:** Skilled sushi chefs would die rather than get caught using a plastic mold like this — it's too slow and not so chic. But for beginners, these plastic finger molds are a nifty way to get the shape you want. They're sold in several sizes; we prefer the five-piece size.

  ✔ **Pressed sushi mold:** Pressed sushi molds used to be made only out of wood that needs to be cared for as you would a wooden sushi rice tub. The newer plastic pressed sushi molds win us over because they're easy to use and clean. They're sold with and without knife grooves in the side. We use a plastic mold with four knife grooves (refer to Figure 2-2) to ensure even cuts. This mold holds one cup of rice (before pressing down), plus two thin layers of ingredients.

Although our recipes don't tell you to line the mold with plastic wrap, many people find it easier to lift sushi out of this mold if you first line it with plastic wrap. Fit a sheet of plastic wrap over the empty sushi mold and press the wrap into the mold before you add rice and ingredients.

Honoring Your Inner Samurai: Looking at Japanese Knives

What distinguishes Japanese knives from Western-style knives is that many types of Japanese knives are honed on only one side, the right side, to create the sharpest cutting edge possible, sharper than possible with a double-edged knife. (Left-handers need to special order their single-edged knives, honed on the left side.) Western-style knives are double edged, or honed on both sides.

Choosing a sushi knife

Sushi chefs primarily use three knives:

- ✔ A heavy duty cleaver *(deba-bocho)* for tough jobs, such as cutting through thick fish bones and filleting fish
- ✔ A sashimi knife *(sashimi-bocho)* to work with raw blocks of fish and fish fillets
- ✔ A vegetable knife *(usuba-bocho or nakiri-bocho)*

All three of these knives come in varying lengths and sizes and even slightly different shapes. Our recipes don't require the use of a cleaver because they call for precut blocks and fillets of fish, not whole fish, but we illustrate it, along with the sashimi and vegetable knife (see Figure 2-3) so that you know the physical differences when you go shopping for Japanese knives.

Many of my (Mineko's) Japanese knives are made by Kiya, a famous Japanese knife manufacturer. Manufacturers outside of Japan also craft Japanese-style knives that are very well made, among them Global, Wüsthof-Trident, and Kershaw Knives.

THREE TYPES OF USEFUL JAPANESE KNIVES

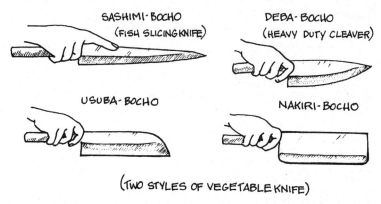

Figure 2-3: Types of useful Japanese knives.

You may wonder whether you should buy a carbon steel knife that takes an extremely sharp edge but requires the most maintenance and can rust; stainless steel knives that never rust but don't take as sharp an edge as carbon steel; or one of the new composite metal knives that take a sharper edge than stainless steel and are less susceptible to rust but are expensive. We leave that choice up to you. We own Japanese knives made of carbon steel, stainless, and the new composite metals. Depending on the task at hand, we enjoy working with all three kinds. Just be sure that any knife you select feels balanced and comfortable, like an extension of your hand.

We use the following two knives in this book. Chapter 7 describes how to hold and use these knives when cutting fish and vegetables.

- ✔ **Sashimi knife:** A single-edged Japanese sashimi knife *(sashimi-bocho)* is an extremely long, thin, and sharp fish-slicing knife (refer to Figure 2-3). Raw fish cut with this knife is used in almost all types of sushi, but most conspicuously on top of finger sushi. It's also the knife you use to cut sashimi, which is precisely sliced, best-quality raw fish that's accompanied by a dipping sauce.

- ✔ **Vegetable knife:** You can choose from two styles of Japanese vegetable knives (refer to Figure 2-3): a single-edged one *(usuba-bocho),* used primarily by sushi chefs, that looks like a flat-nosed French chef's knife, or a double-edged one *(nakiri-bocho),* used by home cooks, that looks like a small, thin, rectangular-shaped Chinese cleaver. The Japanese vegetable knife is prized for cutting razor-thin pieces of food, as well as making quick work of chopping or mincing. Buy whichever style of vegetable knife suits you.

If you don't want to invest in new knives right away, you can use your thinnest, sharpest, nonserrated knives for sushi, but you'll enjoy your sushi-making experience so much more with Japanese sashimi and vegetable knives.

Using and caring for knives

Here are some basic tips to ensure that you stay safe and enjoy using your fabulous Japanese knives for many, many years.

Being safe, not sorry

A good knife can be a treasured kitchen companion for years to come if you use it correctly and treat it with respect.

- **Go slow.** If you've never used extremely sharp knives for specific tasks, take your time developing a feel for the knife.

- **Always use a cutting board when using a knife.** A cutting board helps your knife keep its edge, and it gives you a surface that's easily cleaned. Place a damp, wrung-out towel under the board so it doesn't slip.

- **Always set your knife down gently.** Don't bang it around; gentle handling saves the blade and you from harm.

- **For safety's sake, lay your knife down above your working area, not to the left or right of you, with the sharp edge away from you.** That way, it's not in your working area, where it's more likely to get knocked off the work surface.

- **Keep knife handles and your hands clean and dry to prevent the knife from slipping.**

Cleaning and storing knives

These basic tips help ensure that your knives have long lives:

- **Wash your knives well in soapy water and rinse and dry them well.** Carbon steel knives in particular rust and pit if left wet. Never put knives in the dishwasher.

- **Dry the knives well immediately after washing them by running the flat back of the knife through a towel.** Never wipe it with the blade's cutting edge down in the palm of your hand.

- **Store knives in the case they came in, in a wooden rack, or in their own space in a drawer, individually and completely well wrapped.** Doing so protects the blade and you.

Using a whetstone to sharpen Japanese knives

You can use the right techniques to slice your fish or vegetables, but if your knife is dull, the results won't be good. Dull knives tear delicate foods, such as raw fish, and create opportunities for accidents.

Don't use electric knife sharpeners or any other sharpeners designed for double-edged knives or you'll ruin your cherished single-edged knives.

Use what the Japanese have been using for ages to keep their knives sharp: a water-lubricated whetstone. They're made of natural stone or ceramic stone, in rough, medium, or fine densities, and are appropriate for all knives. If you buy just one, buy a medium-density stone. Follow your Japanese knife manufacturer's instructions for using a whetstone.

Sharpen your knives at the end of the day, giving them the night to cool down and rest, too. If you use them too soon after sharpening, they could lend a subtle but undesirable metallic taste to your ingredients, especially raw fish.

Adding Other Handy Sushi Equipment

In addition to the tools discussed earlier in this chapter, four other items are very handy to have when making sushi:

- **Bamboo skewers:** You use these items to keep boiled shrimp straight for our Shrimp Finger Sushi in Chapter 8. Look for 6- to 8-inch bamboo skewers in most supermarkets.

- **Wooden cooking chopsticks:** After you master eating with chopsticks, you'll want to move on to cooking with chopsticks because of the ease with which you can pick up and mix ingredients. Cooking chopsticks *(saibashi)* are made of wood with ribbed or plain tips and are usually 12 to 14 inches long to keep your hands away from hot pans and oils.

- **Decorative cutters:** The cutters are thicker and tougher than cookie cutters, capable of cutting through hard vegetables such as carrots (see Figure 7-3 in Chapter 7). The best ones are made of rustproof stainless steel. With little effort, these cutters give a dish a finished look, like we do in Ground Turkey and Vegetable Osaka-Style Scattered Sushi in Chapter 10.

✔ **Japanese mandoline, or vegetable slicer:** Mandolines are fixed-blade vegetable slicers that make thin, precise cuts hard to achieve by hand (see Figure 7-3 in Chapter 7). They're available in tabletop or hand-held versions. Plastic Japanese mandolines with ceramic blades are affordable, rust free, and user friendly. Some Japanese mandolines, like our favorite by Benriner, come with exchangeable blades for thin or thick slices and slivers.

Finding the Equipment You Need

You should be able to find everything you need to prepare sushi at the stores and Web sites listed in this section. But first, check locally for Japanese or Asian markets to save shipping costs and to see firsthand what your choices are. Be aware that a store's stock changes often, so shop around if you don't find the tool of choice at your first stop, and be sure to acquire the equipment you need well before you host a sushi party (see Chapter 14).

✔ **Great News Discount Cookware and Cooking School:** Lots of sushi equipment is sold in this San Diego store, including a great selection of Japanese single-edged knives, rice cookers, sushi rice tubs, rice paddles, bamboo mats, and finger and pressed sushi molds. Phone: 888-478-2433. Web site: www.great-news.com.

✔ **The House of Rice Store:** This Scottsdale, Arizona, store carries bamboo mats, finger sushi and pressed sushi molds, and Japanese knives. Phone: 877-469-1718. Web site: www.houserice.com.

✔ **Katagiri & Co.:** This well-respected Japanese market in New York City offers extensive kitchenware, including well-priced knives, bamboo mats, rice cookers, tableware, and Japanese ingredients. Phone: 212-755-3566. Web site: www.katagiri.com.

✔ **Pacific Rim Gourmet:** The last time we visited this online site, it offered eight different electric rice cookers in all price ranges, three sizes of pine sushi rice tubs, finger and pressed sushi molds, bamboo mats, and Japanese ingredients. Phone: 800-910-9657. Web site: www.i-clipse.com.

✔ **Williams-Sonoma:** This nationwide chain of fine cookware stores offers a great selection of cutting boards and Japanese-style knives made by Global and Kershaw. It also sells springform cake pans, such as the one used in our Birthday Cake Pressed Sushi in Chapter 11. Phone: 877-812-6235. Web site: www.williams-sonoma.com.

Chapter 3

Getting Familiar with Sushi Ingredients

In This Chapter

▶ Browsing a store, catalog, or Web site for sushi ingredients

▶ Selecting pantry items

▶ Making space in the fridge and freezer for sushi staples

This chapter covers the Japanese ingredients used in our cookbook, categorized by where they're stored when you get them home. But, be adventuresome! Broaden your sushi horizons and pick up ingredients we don't mention that interest you.

Shopping for Sushi Ingredients

Chances are, even if you've never eaten sushi, you've seen a few sushi staples in your local grocery store, such as Japanese short-grain white rice, Japanese soy sauce, miso, rice vinegar, sesame seeds, and fresh gingerroot. For other ingredients, you may need to visit a Japanese or Asian market or shop online.

Shopping in a Japanese or Asian market for the first time can be challenging, but trust us, it's fascinating and fun to do. The produce aisle by itself is a trip, with its dozens of special Japanese vegetables, such as refreshingly sharp daikon radish, and fragrant herbs, such as shiso, both of which we describe in this chapter.

Figuring out what vegetable is what isn't as hard as figuring out what's in the bottles and packages. Although imported products can have content information printed entirely in Japanese, usually an English label is stuck somewhere on the packaging after the fact. Either way, your best bet is to ask someone for help identifying what you want. Take this book to the store to compare our ingredient illustrations with what's available and to show the clerk what you want. Keep product packaging to help you identify the ones you like, or don't like, for future shopping trips.

If you don't have a Japanese or Asian market in your hometown, don't worry! The phone and the Internet can bring sushi ingredients to you overnight. We suggest a few helpful resources in the following list. Remember, businesses close, stock can change, and different companies carry different things, so if you're planning an important sushi meal, prepare days ahead so that you're sure to find the ingredients you need. Shopping around reveals the best prices, too. And don't forget about shipping costs; they can elevate the cost of your out-of-town orders.

- ✔ **Amazon.com:** Some of the companies we mention here and in other chapters have hooked up with online retailer Amazon. com (www.amazon.com). Visit the Gourmet Food link and then link to Japanese food or sushi and you may find what you need.

- ✔ **AsianFoodGrocer.com:** Check here for pickled daikon radish *(takuan),* tofu, nori, wakame, and many misos, including all-natural and low-salt varieties. The Web site is www.asianfood grocer.com, or call 1-877-867-3101.

- ✔ **EthnicGrocer.com:** On our last visit to this Web site (www. ethnicgrocer.com), we found black sesame seeds, *dashi konbu,* mirin, pickled ginger, dried shiitake mushrooms, and wasabi powder and paste.

- ✔ **Katagiri & Co.:** As we explain in Chapter 2, this well-respected Japanese market in New York City offers Japanese ingredients as well as kitchenware and tableware. Visit online at www. katagiri.com or call 212-755-3566.

- ✔ **Quality Natural Foods:** At this site (www.qualitynatural foods.com), you can find pickled plum *(umeboshi),* pickled daikon radish, pickled ginger, bonito flakes *(katsuobushi),* nori flakes *(ao-nori), wakame, dashi konbu,* and dozens of misos. The phone number is 1-888-392-9237.

- ✔ **Melissa's:** Melissa's (www.melissas.com) is synonymous with the finest in fresh produce and vegetable products, especially hard-to-find exotic or ethnic items. Visit this site for Japanese cucumbers, daikon radish, daikon radish sprouts, edamame, dried shiitake mushrooms, and much more. The site offers a complete explanation of each item's seasonality, selection, and storage. Call for special orders, 1-800-588-0151.

- ✔ **Sushi Foods Co.:** As we explain in Chapter 4, this company, based in San Diego, California, is a great resource for some of the ingredients listed in this chapter as well as the sashimi-grade fish and other fish items (such as barbecued *unagi,* or barbecued freshwater eel) needed for our sushi recipes. You can order online at www.sushifoods.com or call 1-888-817-8744.

✔ **Uwajimaya:** This Japanese and Asian grocery store is located in Seattle and Bellevue, Washington, and Beaverton, Oregon. Orders are taken by catalog (request one online), or call for sashimi-grade fish, lots of fresh vegetables, Japanese staples (such as soy sauce and seaweeds), and true wasabi paste. To order, call 1-800-889-1928 or visit online at www.uwajimaya.com.

Buy the smallest amount of each ingredient you need, especially if sushi is to be an occasional thing, so that your supplies don't go stale or spoil and you end up throwing money away.

Stocking the Sushi Pantry

The fun begins as you find out what dry goods you need to make our sushi recipes. This section covers rice and other pantry goods necessary to make hand rolls, sliced rolls, and finger sushi, to name just three variations of sushi covered in this cookbook. After you open these items, some of them are best kept in the refrigerator or freezer, as we indicate.

Dry ingredients

A cool, dry, dark pantry or cupboard is best for all dry food ingredients (see Figure 3-1), especially sushi ingredients such as nori (sheets of dried seaweed), which quickly deteriorates if exposed to heat, moisture, or light. Most of these dry goods are best used within 6 months of opening, unless we suggest otherwise.

White short- or medium-grain rice

There is no one grocery item known as sushi rice, per se, but many varieties of premium-quality short- or medium-grain white rice are suitable for sushi. (Chapter 5 has details on selecting and cooking short- or medium-grain white rice.) Long-grain white rice, a favorite in the Western world, isn't suitable because it cooks up dry and fluffy, not sticky, a sushi requirement. Arborio rice, used in risotto, isn't suitable, because it cooks up too creamy.

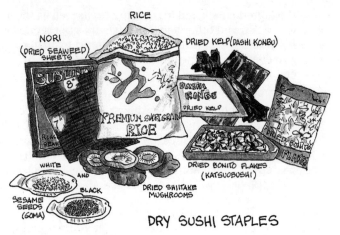

Figure 3-1: Dry sushi staples.

Although medium-grain white rice is good for beginners because we think it's a little less sticky and therefore easier to work with, everyone's goal should be to make sushi with a premium-quality Japanese short-grain white rice, such as *koshihikari* and *akita komachi*. Japanese short-grain rice lends the most authentic taste and texture to sushi.

One pound of raw rice equals about 2 cups. Short- and medium-grain white rice is usually sold in bags by the pound, or loose in bins. Tightly seal opened bags of rice to keep it clean and dry, or transfer the raw rice to a sealed container.

If you need only a small amount of cooked rice for sushi, you'll be delighted to know that you can buy cooked short-grain white rice (labeled *gohan*), either frozen or in shelf packaging. If you're planning to make just a little sushi, follow the manufacturer's reheating instructions and then toss the hot rice with our rice vinegar dressing, following the instructions in Chapter 5. For more information on rice, visit the USA Rice Federation at www.usarice.com.

Dashi konbu (dried kelp)

Dashi konbu, or dried kelp, resembles broad, leathery, wrinkly ribbon. The darker green the leaves, the better the quality of *dashi konbu*. A piece of *dashi konbu* is always added to the rice we cook for sushi recipes, infusing the rice with a faint sea taste (see Chapter 5).

Dashi konbu is often coated with a natural, white powdery substance that blossoms out in the drying process. Look for *dashi konbu* in transparent cellophane bags. Reddish brown *dashi konbu* is often old and not desirable. Like all seaweed, you should buy the highest quality possible. If you keep *dashi konbu* tightly sealed, it will keep up to one year.

Katsuobushi (dried bonito flakes)

Looking like pale salmon-colored wood shavings, *katsuobushi* are in fact shaved flakes of steamed or boiled, smoked, and then dried bonito (a type of tuna). It sounds strange to some of us to cook with dried fish flakes, but after you taste our Clear Soup with Tofu, Wakame, and Shiitake Mushrooms (see Chapter 13), you'll get it. *Katsuobushi* is sold in small packets as well as in larger cellophane bags. Once opened, or if not used within a month or so, store it in the freezer, tightly sealed against moisture.

Matcha (powdered green tea)

Matcha, or powdered green tea, is a special tea used in the Japanese tea ceremony. This powdered tea also makes a dynamite seasoning when combined with salt, as in our Hard-Boiled Quail Eggs with Matcha Salt in Chapter 13, and when combined with sugar, as in our Sake Brownie Soufflés with Matcha Sugar, also in Chapter 13. Store opened packages of *matcha* in the freezer.

The higher the quality of *matcha* you buy, the better it will taste, but we use it combined with salt or sugar, so you needn't go overboard in cost.

Nori (sheets of dried seaweed)

Nori is one of the most recognizable components of sushi. It's a laver, or seaweed, that's been processed into thin sheets. It's aromatic and crisp, like a potato chip, the result of drying, not frying. Chapter 6 illustrates nori's many uses. The best-tasting nori is dark green verging on black. (Reddish brown nori is often old and not desirable.)

Sheets of nori are sold in several sizes, including the most common and the one we use, 7 inches x 8 inches. Nori is crisp enough to break by bending it into pieces, or you can cut it with scissors or a knife. It's sold unroasted or roasted. For our recipes, you want roasted (sometimes called toasted) nori, but you'll reroast the nori again before using it in our hand roll recipes to ensure its crispness and bring out its flavors. Here are two ways to reroast nori:

  ✔ If you have a gas stove, pick up a sheet of nori with your fingertips and pass the nori back and forth through a low flame for 5 to 10 seconds.

Don't hold the nori still over the flame, or it will quickly burn. Also, the nori is big enough that you shouldn't burn your fingers, but be careful.

✔ Place the nori on a clean oven rack and bake it in a preheated 350-degree oven for 30 seconds.

Most nori is sold in transparent cellophane bags. Nori softens rapidly, so pull out only what you need and tightly reseal the bag. We keep nori in sealed plastic bags in the freezer.

Shiitake mushrooms, dried

Brown-capped shiitake mushrooms are one of the oldest cultivated mushrooms, and for good reason. They're filled with fragrance and a highly desirable meaty flavor. Soaking dried shiitake mushrooms in cool water results in plumper, smoother, and softer reconstituted mushrooms than when done in hot water. The caps are eaten, and the stems can be discarded or saved for stock. We use the caps in our Ground Turkey and Vegetable Osaka-Style Scattered Sushi in Chapter 10.

Dried shiitake mushrooms are usually sold in transparent cellophane packages. Look for whole, not broken, caps, with turned-under edges. They last almost indefinitely when stored in a tightly sealed container or plastic bag. Freeze them once opened.

Tempura mix

Sometimes prepared mixes are great. Tempura batter mix is one of these because it makes crispy-perfect tempura. We use tempura mix in our Shrimp Tempura Inside-Out Rolls in Chapter 8. Brands we like are Nissin and Showa. Store opened tempura mix in a sealed plastic bag for a few months, or freeze up to 6 months.

Wakame (dried seaweed)

Wakame is a subtly sweet, thin, deliciously smooth, and chewy seaweed that's a dream to eat. It's in our Cucumber and Wakame Salad in Chapter 13. This classic Japanese salad, or a variation thereof, is served in many sushi bars.

We use ready-to-use *wakame,* meaning precut into bite-size pieces and ready to eat after just 5 minutes of soaking in cold water. Dried, it looks like black, curly shreds of confetti, but when soaked it multiplies many times in size into green wavy ribbons. Avoid dried reddish brown *wakame* because it may be old. As with all seaweeds, buy the best you can afford and keep it in a cool, dark place, well sealed, up to one year.

Bottled ingredients

Many of the bottled ingredients used when making sushi and its side dishes are probably familiar to most of you. Japanese soy sauce is found in grocery stores everywhere, as are rice vinegar and sake. Better grocery stores and Japanese and Asian markets have the rest. These bottled ingredients keep, unopened and in a cool dark pantry, for many months, unless noted otherwise.

 Refrigerate opened bottles of ingredients, such as soy sauce or rice vinegar, so that they taste good and last longer.

Thick chili sauce

Even though chili sauce didn't start out as a Japanese ingredient, sushi bars would have to close their doors if they ran out of it! People love chili sauce in their sushi, and we do, too. Our favorite is Sriracha Hot Chili Sauce, the same thick chili sauce that many sushi bars favor, but you can use whatever thick chili sauce you like. It's the punch in our spicy soy mayonnaise recipe in Chapter 14.

Mirin (sweet cooking sake)

Mirin, a slightly syrupy, sweet cooking sake (about 8 percent alcohol), adds not only heightened sweetness but a lovely sheen as well, as in our Glazed Barbecued Eel in Chapter 8. Once opened, mirin will keep refrigerated for several months.

 Mirin and rice wine vinegar look similar, both faintly golden. Be careful that you don't mix the two up, or you'll have peculiar-tasting dishes!

Plum wine

True Japanese plum wine *(umeshu)* is made with unripened plums, rock sugar, and *shochu* (a strong distilled spirit), making it more of a sweet, fruity liquor than a wine. A good brand to try is Choya, bottled with plums in it. Just as good for our purposes is a plum wine made of sweetened white wine flavored with plum essence. Use either in our refreshing Oranges in Plum Wine in Chapter 13.

Ponzu sauce

Authentic ponzu sauce derives its unusual fragrance and zip from *yuzu,* a lemon-colored, tangerine-shaped citrus grown for its zest, not pulp. Use ponzu when you need a lighter, brighter soy sauce for delicate fish such as tai (see Chapter 4) or sushi such as our Tofu Finger Sushi with Ponzu Sauce in Chapter 9.

Since *yuzu* is hard to get and very expensive, we based our Ponzu Sauce recipe on a combination of three fresh citrus juices — lemon, lime, and grapefruit — added to soy sauce. Commercially, we like the brand Otafuku, which contains *yuzu*. Opened ponzu sauce keeps its fresh flavors for a couple of months when refrigerated.

Rice vinegar

Mild but full of flavor, rice vinegar is what gives prepared sushi rice its clean, almost crisp taste. Buy the best rice vinegar (no salt or sugar added) you can afford. Its pleasant flavor and scent will linger in the rice for hours. We both use Mitsukan Gold. In a pinch, apple cider vinegar is a good substitute. Refrigerate opened vinegar and use it up within several months for the freshest flavor.

We don't care for bottled seasoned rice vinegar, sometimes called sushi vinegar, because it tastes too sharp to us in comparison to homemade vinegar dressing. Plus, it takes only two minutes to make our fresh, fragrant rice vinegar dressing (see Chapter 5).

Sake (Japanese rice wine)

Sake is primarily consumed as a beverage (see Chapter 13), but it's also used in cooking, such as in our Carrots, String Beans, and Lemon Zest Tofu Pouch Sushi in Chapter 10. You needn't invest in expensive sake for cooking purposes, but do buy one that is drinkable. Those labeled cooking sakes don't taste as good to us and we think can take away from — not add to — your dish. Refrigerate opened sake, using it up within a month or two.

Sansho (Japanese pepper)

Sansho, called Japanese pepper, is actually the dried and ground pods of the prickly ash tree. The result is a fragrant, finely ground pale spice that's more minty-citrusy or tangy than spicy hot. We use it to play off the rich taste of barbecued *unagi* (freshwater eel) in our Caterpillar Inside-Out Rolls in Chapter 8. It's always delicious on fried foods and in vegetable dishes. Add *sansho* at the end of any preparation to preserve its fresh scent and flavor. It's sold in small spice bottles. Freeze open bottles if you don't use it frequently.

Soy sauce (shoyu)

Soy sauce was introduced to the Japanese by the Chinese centuries ago. The Japanese took this fermented soy bean sauce and ran with it, tweaking its taste to suite their palates. Japanese soy sauce is sold in several variations:

- ✔ **Regular *(koikuchi shoyu)*,** meaning standard soy sauce, used in our recipes unless we specify otherwise. (The word regular isn't always printed on the label.)

> ✔ **Light color (*usukuchi shoyu*),** meaning lighter in color, to be used in dishes where the darker color of regular soy sauce would mar the dish's appearance. It's lighter in color but actually saltier in taste, too salty to be a dipping sauce by itself.
>
> ✔ **Lite,** meaning reduced salt.

The best-tasting soy sauces are naturally brewed. Kikkoman makes very good naturally brewed soy sauces. My (Judi's) favorite brand of soy sauce for dipping is Higeta Honzen. Refrigerate opened bottles of soy sauce.

Shichimi togarashi (seven spice chili seasoning)

Buckle up and get ready for some really great chili seasoning that's so good it has jumped out of sushi bars and into the kitchens of professional chefs and good cooks all around the world!

Shichimi togarashi traditionally contains fresh chili flakes, black and white sesame seeds, poppy seeds, *sansho* (see the reference earlier in this section), *ao-nori* (see Chapter 13), and Mandarin orange peel. We use it in our Shrimp Tempura Inside-Out Rolls in Chapter 8. *Shichimi* is delicious on any sushi that needs a spicy taste, on Japanese noodles, and especially on fried rice. This reddish seasoning is usually sold in small spice bottles.

Dark sesame seed oil

The roasted, nutty fragrance of dark sesame seed oil is enough to make anyone hungry! We use it in our Grilled Shrimp and Thai Basil Inside-Out Rolls with Spicy Lime Dipping Sauce in Chapter 11. It's sold in small bottles. Refrigerate it after you open it.

Spicy sesame seed oil (rayu)

Take dark sesame seed oil, heat it up with chili, and you have *rayu*. A drop or two adds just the right combination of warmth and flavor to sushi, such as our Spicy Tuna Hand Rolls in Chapter 8. Use it in soups, sauces, or wherever you want a toasted, nutty flavor with kick. It's sold in small bottles. Refrigerate it after you open it.

Filling the Sushi Fridge

Refrigerators of avid sushi lovers contain not only opened pantry items but also goodies such as pickled ginger, wasabi, and pickled daikon radish. We discuss fresh seafood in Chapter 4.

You gotta have these

Sushi lovers wouldn't be caught without the following two items in their refrigerator.

Pickled ginger (amazu shoga)

Sweet and tart at the same time, sliced pickled ginger plays a major role in sushi. At the sushi bar it's referred to as *gari,* but it's sold as *amazu shoga.* Nibbling on a piece refreshes and cleanses the palate, preparing you for that next bite of sushi. Look for naturally beige or pink pickled ginger, often called sweet pickled ginger, to eat as a condiment. It's sold in jars and small plastic containers. Red pickled ginger *(beni shoga)* is sour and pungent, used mostly as a garnish. Keep pickled ginger refrigerated and well sealed.

Be careful not to introduce bacteria into products by taking pickled ginger and other ingredients out of containers with your fingers.

Wasabi paste and powder

Wasabi paste (made with wasabi powder or purchased in tubes) has a fresh, hot taste that complements and highlights the taste of raw seafood and all kinds of sushi. We also use wasabi paste to make Wasabi Mayonnaise (Chapter 9), Wasabi Oil (Chapter 12), and Wasabi Vinaigrette (Chapter 13). Read about fresh wasabi root later in this chapter.

True wasabi, Wasabia japonica, is hard to find in powdered or paste form. Some labels say "Japanese horseradish" under the word wasabi. Pungent horseradish root has less floral fragrance and less complex taste than true wasabi root. If you want true wasabi powder or paste, look for labels that say "genuine wasabi" or "100% real wasabi."

To make wasabi paste from powder, follow these steps:

1. **Combine equal parts wasabi powder and water in a small bowl and stir until it's the consistency of thick mayonnaise.**

   Add water to the powder little by little if you're making more than 2 tablespoons paste.

2. **Cover the bowl with plastic wrap, or do as the Japanese do and turn the bowl over.**

   If the mixture is the proper thickness, it won't drip down if you turn the bowl over. Let the wasabi paste rest about 10 minutes to develop flavor before eating.

Cover and refrigerate leftover, reconstituted wasabi. Opened tubes of wasabi should stay refrigerated. Always freeze genuine wasabi paste if not used right away.

To order true wasabi paste and small wasabi rhizomes to grow your own, contact Pacific Farms USA LP, P.O. Box 51505, Eugene, OR 97405; phone 1-800-927-2248; Web site www.freshwasabi.com.

You're gonna want these

Clear some space in the fridge for very tasty sushi ingredients. You may be familiar with some of them, such as tofu, but some ingredients, such as barbecued *unagi,* may be new to you.

Deep-fried tofu pouches (abura-age)

Tofu pouch sushi *(inari-zushi),* shown in Figure 3-2, is huge in Japan as a home-style sushi, but it's just now making its way into the United States. *Abura-age* are puffy little squares or rectangles of golden fried tofu, usually sold 2 to 4 to a package in the refrigerated section of Japanese or Asian markets. The individual pieces are cut in half, opened as you'd open pita bread, and then stuffed with sushi rice, as in Sweet Tofu Pouch Sushi in Chapter 10.

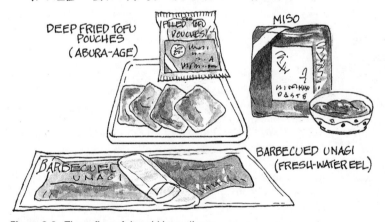

THREE FLAVORFUL SUSHI INGREDIENTS

Figure 3-2: Three flavorful sushi ingredients.

In our recipes, we use the square *abura-age* that are 3 inches x 3 inches. *Abura-age* are oily, so they must be briefly boiled in water before stuffing to rid them of excess oil. Packaging may refer to *abura-age* as *age,* or fried tofu pouches. Freeze *abura-age* if not using them within three days.

Barbecued unagi (freshwater eel)

Barbecued (or grilled) freshwater eel *(unagi)*, shown back in Figure 3-2, is the rich, flavorful fiiling in the center of internationally famous Caterpillar Inside-Out Rolls in Chapter 8. Butterflied, precooked glazed eels, about ¼ to ⅓ inch thick, are sold in cellophane packages in the freezer section or fresh fish section of Japanese and Asian markets. Weights range from about 6 to 11 ounces. A 7-ounce barbecued *unagi* is the perfect size for a Caterpillar Roll. Although barbecued *unagi* is sometimes sold with extra glazing sauce, we find our quick and easy sweet glazing sauce far fresher tasting.

Kani kama (imitation cooked crabmeat)

Don't turn up your nose at the thought of imitation crabmeat *(kani kama)* until you've tried a really good brand, such as Osaki or Yamasa. Also try to understand the beauty of straight ingredients when you're trying to roll up sliced or inside-out rolls, such as our Rainbow Inside-Out Rolls in Chapter 8.

Kani kama is usually made of cooked pollock (a white-fleshed, mild fish) and crab flavoring. It's pressed into many different shapes, but the best for your purposes are leg-shaped pieces, which are 3 to 4 inches long and about 1 ounce each and sold in packages of six or more individually wrapped pieces. These pieces pull or shred apart like string cheese, making it easy to lay them straight out in sushi rolls. Freeze *kani kama* if you're not using it right away.

Certain brands of *kani kama* contain true crab extract, something those with shellfish allergies should check for.

Miso

Miso (fermented soybean paste), shown back in Figure 3-2, is deeply rooted in Japanese cuisine. It's used to flavor soups, such as our Miso Soup with Manila Clams in Chapter 13, and sauces, such as our Grilled Peppers and Eggplant Inside-Out Rolls with Miso Dipping Sauce in Chapter 10.

Miso comes in light and dark colors, and its taste varies from nutty to complex, from slightly salty to very salty. Its fragrance is a bit like ale. Use light-colored miso when you want a more delicate flavor in your food, and darker miso for stronger flavors. Ultimately, you should buy and use the miso that suits your palate. Look for miso in the refrigerated section of stores. Kept cold, it's good for several months. Use clean spoons to dip into miso to keep the remaining product pristine.

Miso doesn't dissolve easily when stirred into hot stock. Thin the miso first with a little hot stock and then add it to the pot. Miso's flavor will be "off" if it's boiled or heated for too long, so add it at the end of preparations.

Tofu

Tofu (soybean curd), like miso, is sold all across the country now. Its popularity is based on its high-protein, lowfat profile, plus its ability to soak up the flavors around it, such as in our Chilled Seasoned Tofu in Chapter 13. Faintly nutty, custardlike tofu comes in two primary textures:

- **Soft or silken:** A texture like a smooth, creamy custard
- **Regular or firm:** A firmer, more porous texture than soft or silken

 Tofu is sold many different ways, including packed in water and vacuum-packed. We recommend that you buy tofu packed in water. Use it before the expiration date on the package. Keep leftover tofu covered with fresh water and refrigerated for up to 3 days, changing the water daily. We don't recommend freezing tofu because its texture changes.

Quail eggs

Dainty, one-bite-sized quail eggs are such a kick to serve and eat! Everybody likes their looks, and how yummy they are served as Hard-Boiled Quail Eggs with Matcha Salt in Chapter 13. Japanese markets stock fresh quail eggs, usually ten to a 5-inch-long plastic package. They're popular in soups, salads, and sushi. Use quail eggs within three to four days of purchase. If you can't find quail eggs, you can substitute chicken eggs in our recipe. One hard-boiled chicken egg, quartered, equals four quail eggs.

Sushi-loving fresh veggies

Prepared sushi rice goes with almost all vegetables. The ones in this section, favorites of sushi lovers, are used in our recipes.

Japanese cucumber

We're being specific about using Japanese cucumbers (see Figure 3-3) for four good reasons: Their skin is thin and delicious; they're not watery, so they won't make your sushi soggy; they have almost no seeds; and they're very tasty. In other words, they're perfect for sushi! In a pinch, use English or hothouse cucumbers.

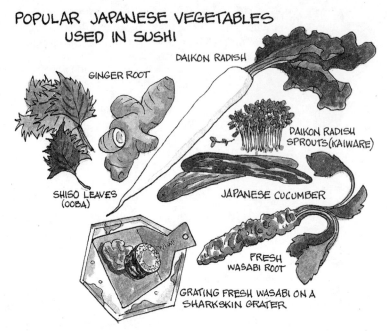

POPULAR JAPANESE VEGETABLES
USED IN SUSHI

DAIKON RADISH

GINGER ROOT

DAIKON RADISH
SPROUTS (KAIWARE)

JAPANESE CUCUMBER

SHISO LEAVES
(OOBA)

FRESH
WASABI ROOT

GRATING FRESH WASABI ON A
SHARKSKIN GRATER

Figure 3-3: Popular Japanese vegetables used in sushi.

Most Japanese cucumbers are sold about 1 inch thick and 8 to 9 inches long. Always select firm cucumbers, with no soft spots.

Before you use these cucumbers in sushi, such as in our Cucumber Sliced Rolls in Chapter 8, you want to salt-scrub them to clean and soften their skin and bring up their color:

1. **Sprinkle ¼ teaspoon salt on a cutting board.**

2. **Rinse the cucumber and then roll it thoroughly, all over, in the salt.**

3. **Rinse off the cucumber, removing all the salt, and wipe all the salt off the cutting board.**

4. **Cut both ends off the cucumber.**

5. **Rub the cut surface of each end against the cut surface of the cucumber until it foams (Mineko swears this action removes any bitterness).**

6. **Rinse and dry the cucumber — it's ready!**

Daikon radish

Refreshingly sharp daikon radish (refer to Figure 3-3), a mainstay in the Japanese kitchen, looks like a giant white carrot. It's used in soups, stews, sauces, and salads, such as our Shredded Daikon and Carrot Salad with Sweet Citrus Dressing in Chapter 13. It's shredded as a side dish for sashimi and grated as a condiment with deep-fried foods like tempura. Grate it with chiles, as we do in Red Snapper Finger Sushi with Spicy Daikon Relish in Chapter 9, and you've created a classic Japanese condiment called *momijioroshi*. Once grated, daikon radish begins developing a very pungent odor, so keep all daikon dishes well covered in the refrigerator.

Look for firm, smooth, whole daikon radishes or chunks of daikon radish. Cut off and then peel the amount you need. Wrap the remainder in paper towels and then in plastic wrap. It keeps, refrigerated, up to a week.

Daikon radish sprouts (kaiware)

Packages of alfalfa sprouts are common in stores across the country. We're sure that daikon radish sprouts *(kaiware),* shown back in Figure 3-3, aren't far behind, because their sharp, peppery taste one-ups alfalfa sprouts, adding zip to whatever they're in, such as our Shrimp Tempura Inside-Out Rolls in Chapter 8. To clean the sprouts, rinse, pat them dry, and *then* cut off their roots. If you cut off their roots first and rinse them, you'll have sprouts everywhere, not in one bunch. In a pinch, use Zesty Sprouts (an alfalfa and onion sprout mixture) or alfalfa sprouts for our recipes.

Gingerroot

Knobby-looking gingerroot (refer to Figure 3-3) is a fabulous flavor enhancer if ever there were one. For example, we use it grated in Ginger Beef and Lettuce-Wrapped Sliced Rolls in Chapter 10. Look for plump ginger with skin that's shiny, not wrinkled and dry. Fresh gingerroot keeps a week or more in the refrigerator if you wrap it first in a paper towel and then loosely in plastic wrap.

Scallions

Scallions, or green onions, are more than bit players in sushi. We use them over and over for their looks and taste. We lightly sprinkle them on Tofu Finger Sushi with Ponzu Sauce in Chapter 9 and generously add them to Tuna Sliced Rolls in Chapter 9. Thinly sliced scallions take on a shiny, translucent look and milder taste when they've been properly rinsed:

1. Place the sliced scallions in a fine-mesh strainer.

2. Run cold water through the strainer, for 10 seconds or so until the scallions are no longer slimy, gently tossing them with your fingers.

3. Gently squeeze the scallions dry in a paper towel.

Shiso leaves (ooba)

Such a pretty little notched-leaf herb, so fragrant and full of flavor! Shiso (refer to Figure 3-3), also called perilla, is nicknamed Japanese basil because of its similar taste, but it's really a mint. Yet, neither mint nor basil can adequately replace this aromatic leaf in recipes.

Red-leafed shiso is used to color pickled vegetables and as garnish. But green-leafed shiso is what we covet for all kinds of sushi, such as Spicy Hamachi Hand Rolls in Chapter 9, where it's rolled up and cut into slivers. *Shiso* is sold in little bundles of up to ten leaves, tied at their base, usually in small Styrofoam trays. Look for leaves that are clearly fresh, not wilted or turning dark on their edges.

Wasabi root, if you're so lucky

You lucky duck, you, if you can get your hands on expensive fresh wasabi root (refer to Figure 3-3) to grate as a condiment for your sushi. A root usually weighs about 4 ounces and is about 4 to 6 inches long. Here's what to do with it:

1. Trim leaves down to the crown, or top of the root.

2. Moments before you want to eat it, pare a little skin off and grate the wasabi root, in a circular fashion, from the crown end down, creating just a teaspoon or so.

   A small, sharkskin grater is traditional, but you can use any small, fine-tooth grater.

3. Eat the grated wasabi right away, before its fragrance and flavor fade.

   Wasabi root is one of Mother Nature's most wonderful, ephemeral experiences!

Grate more, in small portions, only as you need it. Wrap leftover wasabi root in paper towels and then in plastic wrap and refrigerate.

Puckeringly good pickled veggies

Fresh vegetables are great, but pickled vegetables lend just that right pop of color, texture, and flavor that sushi sometimes cries out for. We use three favorites in *Sushi For Dummies*.

Pickled daikon radish (takuan)

Bright yellow, salty-sweet-sour, crunchy daikon radish (see Figure 3-4) is a flashy showstopper in sushi (read about fresh daikon radish earlier in this chapter). We use it as a sharp accent flavor in Avocado, Cucumber, and Pickled Daikon Radish Sliced Rolls in Chapter 10. Pickled daikon radish is usually sold in cellophane packages, either whole or in pieces. If tightly sealed and refrigerated, they keep for months.

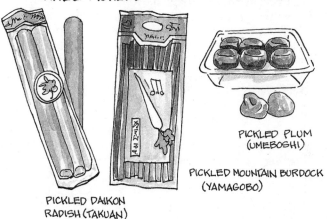

THREE PICKLED SUSHI INGREDIENTS

PICKLED PLUM
(UMEBOSHI)

PICKLED MOUNTAIN BURDOCK
(YAMAGOBO)

PICKLED DAIKON
RADISH (TAKUAN)

Figure 3-4: Three pickled sushi ingredients.

Pickled mountain burdock (yamagobo)

Mountain burdock (refer to Figure 3-4), often referred to simply as burdock, is a long, skinny root whose strong, earthy flavor makes it a perfect pickling candidate. Usually dyed sunset orange (don't get the pickling juice on you or it will stain your clothes), we use pickled burdock in Ginger Beef and Lettuce-Wrapped Sliced Rolls in Chapter 10. *Yamagobo* is usually sold whole in cellophane packages. If tightly sealed and refrigerated, they keep a few weeks.

Pickled plums (umeboshi)

Ume, small, round fruits likened to plums, are pickled when unripened. Over time, *umeboshi* (refer to Figure 3-4) soften into a pleasantly acidic, salty, "I don't know what that is, but I like it" flavor. To prepare them, you push the pit out of the preserved fruit and then mash or chop the flesh for recipes such as our Spicy Hamachi Hand Rolls in Chapter 9. Divine! *Umeboshi* are usually sold in small plastic containers. If tightly sealed and refrigerated, they keep for months.

Delving into the Sushi Deep Freeze

These two inexpensive but prized sushi ingredients should always be in your freezer.

Edamame (soybeans in their pods)

Pull a 1-pound bag of edamame out of the freezer, follow our recipe in Chapter 13, and in under 10 minutes, you have a pretty, healthy, fun-to-eat appetizer. Edamame look like fat sweet peas, holding two or three soybeans per pod. You strip the beans out of the pods with your teeth. Once boiled, they'll keep, refrigerated, up to a week. They're great to snack on.

Sesame seeds

Black and white (unhulled preferably) sesame seeds are staples in the sushi kitchen. They're used individually, such as in our Tuna, Cucumber, and Black Sesame Seed Pressed Sushi in Chapter 9, or together, as in our colorful Grilled Peppers and Eggplant Inside-Out Rolls with Miso Dipping Sauce in Chapter 10. Black sesame seeds taste a little nuttier than white. Always keep sesame seeds in the freezer because of their high oil content. Roast them to bring out their flavor before using, even if the label says they're already roasted. Here's how:

1. **Pour the amount of sesame seeds you need for your recipe into a small frying pan and place over medium heat.**

2. **When hot, roast for 2 minutes or so, until the fragrance of the seeds rises.**

   Sometimes they pop or jump in the pan, and sometimes not.

Roast just before you use them, but they'll keep their reroasted flavor for a week or so if stored tightly sealed.

Chapter 4

Chilling Out with Fresh Seafood

· ·

In This Chapter

▶ Selecting, handling, and storing fresh seafood

▶ Looking at the best seafood for your sushi

▶ Discovering the sexy world of fish roe

· ·

Saltwater fish and shellfish are the rock stars of sushi. Centuries of practice have made Japanese cooks wise in the ways of preparing raw and cooked seafood, such as the seafood favored for use in sushi (vinegared rice items) or sashimi (slices of raw fish).

Pristinely fresh seafood not only tastes divine but also is a high-quality protein filled with vitamins and minerals. Becoming wise about selecting, handling, and refrigerating highly perishable seafood is crucial to enjoying the best seafood has to offer. This chapter contains seafood information to make you fish-wise, especially if you're new to sashimi-grade raw fish.

Those who become hooked on sashimi-grade raw fish, an industry name for high-quality fish suitable for eating raw, will tell you that freshly caught, properly handled raw fish has the most wonderful, true taste to it. They describe the taste, depending on the fish, as ranging from mild and faintly sweet to buttery and full flavored. We use sashimi-grade raw fish in some of our recipes.

Although many edible varieties of seafood are for sale, in this chapter we focus only on the fish and shellfish called for in our recipes, whether eaten raw or cooked. They're among the most popular seafood items in sushi bars and among sushi cooks. Although a lot of saltwater fish and shellfish are from aquaculture farms and ocean pens, most seafood available is still harvested wild. The best season for fishermen to catch certain fish varies depending on the part of the world, so being knowledgeable and flexible in your choices is important.

Practicing Safe Seafood

If you keep your kitchen work area clean, recognize the hallmarks of fresh seafood, and do your part to ensure that seafood gets home good and cold and is handled correctly, you'll be on your way to enjoying the best of seafood sushi. You also should know the concerns about consuming raw seafood. We cover these topics in this section.

Taking cleanliness to heart

Keeping your food preparation area clean is part of any good cook's marching orders. This advice is especially important when you're working with raw fish. Take these precautions:

- ✔ **Wash your hands well with hot, soapy water.**

- ✔ **Wash your knives well in hot, soapy water.**

- ✔ **Use a smooth cutting board made of hard wood or plastic, free of any deep scratches or cracks that can trap bacteria.** Consider having three cutting boards: one for raw meats and fish you intend to cook, one for fruits and vegetables, and one for sashimi-grade raw fish you intend to eat raw.

- ✔ **Wash cutting boards well with hot, soapy water.** Occasionally sprinkling the board with salt and then scrubbing it well with a cut lemon is good for cleanliness and a pleasant, fresh smell. Rinse and dry the board well.

- ✔ **Be careful of cross-contamination.** Work with raw fish separately from cooked seafood and other ingredients. Use paper towels, not cloth towels, to clean up work surfaces.

Being aware of potential raw seafood risks

Sashimi-grade seafood is an industry term that means the seafood is considered suitable for eating raw. Sashimi-grade seafood tastes as fresh as an ocean breeze and loses none of its nutritional value through cooking. But fish and shellfish, like other animal protein, can contain bacteria and parasites, causing potential health risks for some when consumed raw. Please be aware of the following:

- ✔ Not all varieties of seafood are suitable to eat raw. Only select saltwater fish and shellfish should be consumed uncooked, and we discuss some of these later in this chapter.

✔ Properly handled saltwater fish carries little risk of harmful bacteria. Cooking seafood thoroughly kills any bacteria.

✔ Most seafood vendors ensure that their sashimi-grade seafood is parasite free, eliminating most of the risk. If you're concerned, purchase only *flash-frozen* (a quick-freeze commercial process that kills any parasites while preserving the high quality of the fish) sashimi-grade raw seafood. We don't recommend freezing fresh sashimi-grade raw seafood at home to be eaten raw.

✔ Certain medical conditions, pregnancy, and at-risk health situations may make it unsafe to eat raw or undercooked fish or shellfish. People with sensitive systems should consult with their physician for an opinion. For further information on seafood safety, visit these Web sites:

• **The U.S. Food and Drug Administration's Center for Food Safety and Applied Nutrition:** vm.cfsan.fda.gov or 1-888-723-3366

• **National Fisheries Institute, Inc.:** www.nfi.org or www.aboutseafood.com

• **Seafood Network Information Center:** http:// seafood.ucdavis.edu

Find out all you can about raw seafood, and then make an educated decision as to what's right for you.

Making sure the seafood is fresh

Don't walk into just any seafood market and buy just any fish, especially to eat raw. Do your homework. Find out if there's a first-rate Japanese market or other trusted fish market in your area. Also look into the possibility of ordering sashimi-grade raw seafood, cut to your specifications, from a respected sushi bar in your neighborhood. Or you can rely on companies who ship high-quality seafood overnight (see the sidebar "Swimming into the Net: Ordering fish online," later in this chapter). Let the fishmonger know if you want sashimi-grade seafood to eat raw.

We don't offer recipes that use whole fish in *Sushi For Dummies,* so the following tips involve blocks of fish and fillets. But if you're in a fish market and the whole fish looks fresh, it's a good sign that the cut fish is fresh, too. In a nutshell, whole fish should have clear, bright eyes; shiny, firmly attached scales; bright red gills; and a fresh, cool scent. A good fish market, just like a good sushi bar, doesn't smell fishy — it smells cool and clean.

Sashimi's frozen secret

Much of the sashimi-grade fish on the market today was flash-frozen almost as soon as it was caught, to ensure quality and for the food safety reasons mentioned in this chapter. When the fish is defrosted in the refrigerator, the outcome is excellent, making it hard for most people to tell the difference between flash-frozen and fresh. I (Mineko) use flash-frozen sashimi-grade raw fish all the time to enjoy raw. If you're buying fish still frozen, be sure that it is frozen solid, has no freezer burn or dry edges, and shows no evidence of ice crystals around it. Defrost the fish in the refrigerator, not at room temperature. It's easiest to slice while still very cold, almost frozen.

Some ways to determine whether fish is fresh include

- ✔ The fish doesn't have any odor, just a cool, clean smell.

- ✔ The flesh has a clean, vibrant, almost translucent look; firm texture; no tears or soft-looking spots in the flesh; and no off colors or dryness showing on the edges.

- ✔ The fish doesn't have any liquid around it in the fish tray or, if it's prepackaged, in its packaging.

- ✔ If the raw fish is prepackaged, you can't smell it, so look for a packaged-by or use-by date.

We use a variety of shellfish in our recipes. It's best to eat live shellfish the day it's purchased. Shrimp is usually sold frozen or defrosted. We explain how to handle shrimp in each recipe.

We use the following shellfish in this book:

- ✔ **Oysters:** Purchase live oysters that are shut tight and don't have any nicks or cracks in their shells. If overly cold, they may open a little but shut when tapped. Use any variety of oysters you like for Oysters on the Half-Shell with Tempura Sushi Rice Balls in Chapter 12. (Figure 4-1 shows you how to shuck oysters.)

- ✔ **Hard-shell clams:** Purchase live clams that are shut tight or that close up when tapped, indicating they're alive. Make sure that they don't have any nicks or cracks in their shells. We recommend Manila clams, but small littlenecks do nicely in our Miso Soup with Manila Clams in Chapter 13.

- ✔ **Mussels:** Purchase live mussels that are black- or green-lipped, can be slightly opened but shut when tapped, and have no nicks or cracks in their shells. For our Sake-Steamed Mussels in Chapter 13, use the smallest mussels available.

✔ **Fresh sea scallops:** In our Spicy Scallop Hand Rolls in Chapter 8, we indicate that you can use sashimi-grade shucked scallops. There's a definite difference in taste and looks between scallops sold *wet,* or treated with a solution to preserve freshness, and *dry,* which means in their natural state. Dry scallops have a truer, slightly sweeter taste, and are less watery, so they're preferred for sushi. They should smell fresh, clean, and cool.

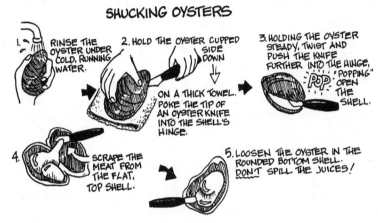

Figure 4-1: Opening, or shucking, an oyster.

Bringing seafood home

After you purchase high-quality fresh seafood, it's up to you to keep it that way until you eat it raw or cooked. If you intend to eat sashimi-grade fish raw, pick it up the day you intend to eat it, as close as possible to the time you'll serve it.

If you purchase frozen seafood, keep it frozen until the night before, or the morning of the day you intend to eat it. It's best to defrost frozen seafood in the refrigerator, which can take five or more hours for a 1-inch-thick piece of fish.

Always use a cooler, filled with either ice or frozen gel packs, to bring raw seafood home. You want to maintain an even, cold temperature for the seafood up until the moment you're ready to prepare it. Live shellfish need air, so be sure that the bag or container they're in isn't sealed shut.

Remember that your hands and all equipment that comes into contact with raw seafood should be washed with hot, soapy water and then rinsed well. But hot hands and equipment harm delicate, highly perishable raw seafood, so be sure that your hands are cold and the equipment is at room temperature when actually handling it. Dip your hands into a bowl of ice water and then dry them off before you start handling raw fish.

Storing fish at home

When you get the raw fish home, here's what do to:

- ✔ **Immediately put the fish in the coldest part of your refrigerator, which is usually the bottom portion of the refrigerator (a drawer, if your fridge has one), until you serve it.** Don't stack anything on top of the fish.

- ✔ **Handle the fish as little and as gently as possible to prevent smashing or bruising the flesh.**

- ✔ **Quickly rinse blocks of fish and fillets in a bowl of lightly salted cold water (2 teaspoons to 5 cups ice cold water) just before preparing it to eat.** Pat it dry with paper towels.

Storing shellfish at home

These tips will keep shellfish safe until serving time:

- ✔ **As soon as you get live or shucked shellfish home, refrigerate them until just before you prepare your sushi.**

- ✔ **Live shellfish need air.** Keep them in the refrigerator in a open dish or bowl covered with damp paper towels. It's best to eat shellfish the day they're purchased.

- ✔ **Scrub live oysters, clams, and mussels just before preparing to eat them, until their shells are clean.** Mussels often have filament, called a *beard,* hanging out. Pull it off (see Figure 4-2). If any mussels, clams, or oysters fail to shut when tapped, they're dead, so throw them out.

- ✔ **Shucked scallops to be eaten raw should be eaten the day they're purchased.** If you're going to cook the scallops, they'll keep in a tightly sealed container in the refrigerator up to two days.

SCRUBBING AND DEBEARDING MUSSELS

Figure 4-2: Cleaning live mussels.

Reeling In Six Fabulous Fish for Sushi

This section introduces you to our six fabulous-finned star players. Three types of tuna, or *maguro,* lead off the list. These are always a favorite of raw fish lovers. You can use any one of these three tunas in our recipes, depending on availability and your wallet. As of this writing, sashimi-grade yellowfin and big eye tuna cost about half as much as bluefin, which is about $40 to $60 a pound, depending on the cut. The fattier the cut of bluefin, the more prized and costly it is.

- **Bluefin tuna:** Called *kuro maguro* (black tuna) or *hon-maguro* (true tuna), this tuna is huge, up to 10 feet long and up to 1,500 pounds. It's the most prized of all tuna for sashimi and sushi. The following are the cuts of bluefin tuna:

    - *Akami:* This pure red meat, with a taste and texture almost like very rare filet mignon, is found near the top or back of the fish. Until about 80 years ago, it was more prized in Japan than *chu-toro* and *o-toro.* It's sold in blocks.

    - *Chu-toro:* This cut is choice, marbled, milky-pink meat, due to a desirably high fat content. It has a very rich taste and buttery texture and comes from the belly of the fish. It's sold in blocks.

    - *O-toro:* Most choice of all tuna meat, this is the fattiest part of the belly, up near the head. It's a very pale pink, and it melts on the tongue. *Negi-toro,* a hand roll mentioned in the sidebar "Raw fish items to order at a sushi bar," later in this chapter, is made with the over-the-top, fattiest, richest part of this belly meat. It's sold in blocks.

- **Big eye tuna:** *Mebachi maguro,* a chunkier tuna, up to 6½ feet long and 400 pounds, is named for its unusually large eyes. It's considered a milder-tasting tuna than bluefin tuna. Although belly cuts of big eye tuna are sometimes sold as *chu-toro* and *o-toro,* the best *chu-toro* and *o-toro* is considered to come from bluefin tuna. It's sold in blocks.

- **Yellowfin tuna:** *Kihada maguro,* a more streamlined tuna, gets its name from the yellowish color of its skin and fins. This smaller tuna, up to 6 feet long and 300 pounds, is found in tropical waters. Called *ahi* in Hawaii, yellowfin possesses a mild flavor and firm texture. It's deep pink to reddish in color, depending on the size of the fish. It's sold in blocks.

- ✔ **Tai:** *Tai,* red sea bream (red snapper is often used in the United States), is a very popular fish to eat raw. This white-fleshed fish has a very mild, delicate taste yet still has some bite, or texture, to it. It's a refreshing fish to eat after the richness of *chu-toro* or *o-toro*. It's sold in fillets.

- ✔ **Hamachi:** *Hamachi,* sometimes called Japanese yellowtail, is fattier than the yellowtail caught off the coast of California. *Hamachi* is a young fish, very luscious and buttery in texture, almost oily, possessing a desirable bold flavor, some say with a tangy finish. It's sold in blocks and fillets.

- ✔ **Salmon:** Raw salmon is a favorite at sushi bars, especially in recipes such as our Rainbow Inside-Out Rolls in Chapter 8. *Sake* (spelled like the rice wine), or salmon, has gorgeous peachy orange to deep-red flesh, prized for its rich and flavorful taste. Salmon should have been flash-frozen if you're going to eat it raw.

Roe, Roe, Roe Your Sushi

Just as the Japanese eat all kinds of seafood new to neophyte sushi lovers, they really get into different kinds of fresh roe, or fish eggs, exotic to most people. Depending on the fish, roe can be as small as sand grains and bright yellow, or the size of green peas and translucently red, like jewels of the sea.

Swimming into the Net: Ordering fish online

Thank goodness for the Internet. It brings the world to our doorsteps, in this case the sashimi-grade fish required for our sushi world. At the time of this writing, the three companies listed here do a bang-up job of providing absolutely fresh or flash-frozen saltwater fish suitable for eating raw. Availability of a particular fish is always subject to the season and the seas. Ordering on Thursday for Friday delivery usually sees a great selection of fish.

- ✔ **Sushi Foods Co.** (www.sushifoods.com): Sushi Foods Co. in San Diego, California, carries most of the sashimi-grade fish as well as other fish items, like *kani kama* (cooked imitation crabmeat), barbecued *unagi* (freshwater eel), and wasabi *tobiko* (seasoned flying-fish roe) needed for our sushi recipes. All fish listed on the Web site is flash-frozen if not listed as fresh. The company also stocks Japanese ingredients. Place your order by noon Pacific standard time for overnight delivery. The phone number is 888-817-8744.

✔ **Catalina Offshore Products Inc.** (www.catalinaop.com): Located in San Diego, California, this company is a well-known purveyor of sashimi-grade fresh and flash-frozen blocks and fillets of fish trimmed specifically for sushi and sashimi preparations, as well as sashimi-grade jumbo sea scallops and live *mirugai* (geoduck clams). The company is especially well known for its *uni* (sea urchin roe) and also carries real wasabi paste. Order by 10 a.m. Pacific standard time for overnight delivery. The phone number is 619-297-9797.

✔ **Browne Trading Company** (www.browne-trading.com): This Portland, Maine, company offers impeccably fresh fish suitable for sushi, as well as red, orange, and wasabi *tobiko*. It's famous for its oysters, including Winterpoints and Pennaquids from Maine. Visit the Web site to see what's in that week. Orders are taken over the phone. Order by noon eastern standard time for overnight delivery, depending on fish availability. Call 800-944-7848, option 4.

Most roe is rich, so it's served in small portions, such as in battleship finger sushi, where a strip of *nori* (dried seaweed) around the rice holds in the loose roe (see Chapter 6). But roe takes to all kinds of sushi, especially as a garnish. Japanese and Asian markets carry roe; also look for them at the companies mentioned in the "Swimming into the Net: Ordering fish online" sidebar in this chapter. Keep all fresh roe in the coldest part of the refrigerator, which is usually the bottom portion.

We use the following fresh fish roe in our recipes:

✔ **Salmon roe:** We're talking about fresh, lightly salted salmon roe, not the pasteurized kind sold in jars at some grocery stores. *Ikura,* or fresh salmon eggs, are translucent orange-red beauties the size of green peas, and they explode in your mouth with a creamy richness. It's the topping in our Salmon Roe Battleship Sushi in Chapter 9. It's usually sold in dated packages. Use it within a few days.

✔ **Smelt roe:** *Masago,* or fresh smelt roe, the size of large sand grains, is used extensively in sushi bars and by home cooks for its bright orange color and sweet, crunchy taste. It's usually sold in dated packages. *Masago* is an optional ingredient in our California Inside-Out Rolls in Chapter 8. Use within a few days of purchase.

✔ **Seasoned flying-fish roe:** *Tobiko,* or fresh flying-fish roe, is slightly larger than smelt roe. It has a wonderfully crunchy texture and salty taste. Its natural color is a translucent pale orange, but it's frequently colored and seasoned. We use lime green wasabi *tobiko* on top of our Birthday Cake Pressed Sushi in Chapter 11. *Tobiko* is usually sold in dated packages. Use within a few days of purchase.

Raw fish items to order at a sushi bar

One main reason to eat in a sushi bar is to enjoy the vast variety of sashimi-grade fish and shellfish that only sushi chefs have access to. Another is to watch them create delicious little masterpieces, using these very same fish and shellfish for delicacies such as the following five sushi bar specialties. The first one is a sashimi (slices of raw fish) dish, and the remaining four are sushi preparations. For more sushi bar specialties, see Chapter 15.

✔ *Hirame no usuzukuri* (thinly sliced flounder served with ponzu sauce): The delicate-tasting white flesh of flounder is sliced transparently thin and then fanned out on a colorful plate that shows through the slices of fish. Pick up a paper-thin slice of flounder with your chopsticks (see Figure 15-1 in Chapter 15) and dip it in just a touch of ponzu sauce (see our recipe in Chapter 9), a refreshing-tasting citrus-based soy sauce. Then eat. Sheer ecstasy!

✔ *Engawa no nigiri-zushi* (flounder gristle finger sushi served with ponzu sauce): *Engawa* is the thin, narrow strip of gristlelike meat that runs all around the edge of this flat fish. Many fishmongers throw out this strip — tragic but true. Sushi bar chefs and their devoted clients prize this gristle for its rich, fatty taste and delightfully chewy texture. Order this for an over-the-top adventure.

✔ *Mirugai to wasabi no temaki-zushi* (longneck clam and slivered wasabi hand roll): The combination of slivered raw longneck clam and slivered fresh wasabi leads to an amazing taste experience that's so much more than just these two parts. The sweet, full flavor of the clams and their chewy texture combines with the pungent and lingering taste of fresh wasabi to create an explosion of goodness in your mouth.

✔ *Negi-toro no temaki-zushi* (fatty tuna and scallion hand roll): The most expensive and rarest of the raw tuna specialties, *o-toro* is the pale pink, meltingly rich, fatty belly meat of the bluefin tuna. In *negi-toro no temaki-zushi, o-toro* is gently scraped or spooned off the belly, mixed with a touch of finely minced scallions, and used as a filling with prepared sushi rice in a hand roll.

✔ *Katsuo no nigiri-zushi* (seared bonito finger sushi with freshly grated ginger): The shimmering silver skin of bonito (a member of the mackerel family) is left on in this sushi dish. The fish is briefly seared but not cooked through, to bring out the flavor of the fat under its skin, and then it's cut into slices to top the sushi rice. A small amount of freshly grated gingerroot is served as the perfect counterpoint to the seared richness of the fish.

Part II
Getting Ready, Getting Set

The 5th Wave   By Rich Tennant

"I didn't have time to cut the radishes into matchsticks, so I just used matchsticks."

In this part . . .

The "big three" building blocks of all sushi recipes are in this part. The first is making perfect sushi rice, which is no big deal when you follow our tried-and-true methods. The second building block is knowing what to do with all that sticky rice, so we show you different types of sushi and their techniques, cracking the kingdom of sushi wide open in all its delicious and varied splendor. The third is letting your inner samurai out, happily cutting, slicing, and dicing with sharp Japanese knives so that you capture the best tastes and textures possible and create beautiful sushi that's a joy to make and eat. *Hi-Yah!*

Chapter 5

Cooking and Seasoning Sensational Sushi Rice

*W*e'll let you in on a little secret — this is really a rice cookbook. Without fragrant, vinegared sushi rice *(su-meshi),* we'd have no sushi recipes to share with you. *Sushi* means vinegared rice, not raw fish, a common misconception.

People who come to my (Mineko's) sushi classes often say, "My rice never turns out the way I want." You can make sloppy sushi that tastes good if the rice tastes good. But if the rice doesn't taste good, you're in trouble.

It's our joy to show everyone how to make no-fail, fragrant, and flavorful sushi rice. Think of preparing sushi rice as a sport much like football that takes about 1½ hours from start to finish, with most of that time spent letting the rice soak or cook. We give you the playbook to perfect sushi rice in this chapter.

Understanding the Object of the Game

Before you can set out making sushi rice, you need to know what perfect sushi rice looks, smells, and tastes like.

When making sushi rice, your goal is to end up with the following:

- **Sticky rice that is moist, not wet:** Perfect sushi rice is cooked short- or medium-grain white rice that's a little sticky in texture, not gummy or wet in the least. The rice is plump and has a smooth, almost porcelain sheen to it, the result of the rice's holding in just the right amount of moisture.

- **Each rice grain whole, not smashed:** The cooked grains cling together but remain whole, a result of tender treatment throughout the preparation process explained in this chapter.

- **Rice grains that are still slightly springy or chewy:** We're not talking about a creamy exterior and firm interior, like the Italian arborio rice dish called risotto. Properly prepared sushi rice has a pleasantly chewy texture through and through.

- **Rice that's white, full of fragrance and flavor:** Well-made sushi rice has a pleasantly sharp, bright taste and smell that results from a rice vinegar dressing (see the section "Introducing the Rice Vinegar Dressing," later in this chapter) added to the rice while it's hot. The dressing doesn't overpower the rice's fresh taste, but adds interest to it. The beautiful white color of well-made sushi rice results from using good rice and rinsing it well.

Gathering the Equipment

Preparing sushi rice is a pleasure if you have the right equipment on hand, including an electric rice cooker; a wooden sushi tub *(handai or hangiri)*; a flat, wooden rice paddle *(shamoji)*; a flat fan *(uchiwa)*; and a damp kitchen towel.

If you love sushi, we recommend that you acquire these items (see Chapter 2 for where to get this equipment). However, if you want to first try your hand at sushi rice before you invest in new kitchen tools, we also offer substitution ideas for the standard equipment in Chapter 2.

Introducing the Star Player — Rice

You can't make good sushi rice without the star player: short- or medium-grain white rice. Here's what you need to know about the rice.

Selecting the rice

You can make sushi rice with any premium short- or medium-grain white rice sold by the bag in most supermarkets across the country and for sure in Asian markets. We recommend California-grown, short- or medium-grain rice, like short-grain *koshihikari* and medium-grain Calrose. (Don't use Arborio, long-grain, or parboiled white rice; they're not suitable for sushi rice.) Labels on short- and medium-grain rice bags don't always state their length, so look for labels that say Japanese rice or sushi rice. Ask the grocery clerk to help you determine the grain of the rice. (See Chapter 3 for more information on rice and where to purchase it.)

Both short- and medium-grain white rice are sticky, but medium-grain white rice seems less sticky, making it easier for beginners to work with. Try both and see which one suits you best.

Make sure the rice is of premium quality, which means it's whole in shape and the kernels are uniform. Thanks to modern machinery, most rice that comes to the market today is not broken up, but be aware that you want rice that consists of whole kernels for the best sushi rice results. The raw rice also should have a shiny, translucent look; it shouldn't appear completely milky or chalky in color.

The best rice for sushi is about six months old. By then the rice has had a chance to dry out a bit, creating a cooked sushi rice texture that is chewier than if it were made with moist, newly harvested rice. Granted, we're talking a subtle difference, but each little difference counts to some sushi lovers.

Store open bags of rice tightly sealed in a cool, dry place to keep out moisture and other contaminants. After you open the bag, we think it's best to use it up within six months.

If you're in a hurry and need just a little cooked rice to make sushi for one or two people, you can use the microwaveable, individually packaged portions of cooked Japanese (short-grain) rice labeled *gohan*. We've seen the precooked rice only in Asian markets, but it likely will be widely available soon. Simply follow the reheating directions on the package and then skip to the "Introducing Rice Vinegar Dressing" section, later in this chapter. Scale down the amount of dressing to match the amount of rice you're making.

Measuring the rice

Rice expands about two and a half to three times when cooked. Its cooked volume varies depending on the raw rice's ability to absorb water. To figure out how much raw rice to cook for your recipe, see Table 5-1.

Rice cookers usually come with a small plastic measuring cup that's marked for the metric system. This cup, when full, equals about ¾ cup of rice in U.S. units, not the 1 cup in U.S. units our Table 5-1 relies upon. Don't use this plastic cup to measure rice for our recipes; use a standard U.S. unit measuring cup. Measure raw rice accurately by leveling off the rice even with the top of the measuring cup.

Table 5-1	Raw Rice-to-Water Ratios	
Raw Rice	*Water*	*Cooked Rice*
2 level cups	2 cups	5 cups to 6 cups
3 level cups	3 cups	7½ cups to 9 cups
4 level cups	4 cups	10 to 12 cups

Preparing the Rice for the Big Game

Before you can get into the game — cooking the rice — you need to rinse and soak it well and then add *dashi konbu* (dried kelp) and *sake* (rice wine) for flavor. (Chapter 3 tells you where to get these ingredients.) Preparing the rice for cooking takes about 35 minutes. In this section we tell you how.

Rinsing the rice

Rinsing the rice leads to pure white cooked rice possessing the desired fresh scent and flavor. Very fine rice flour billows up in white clouds when you first begin rinsing the rice. Although some people rinse the rice like crazy until the water is absolutely clear, we think four to six times is fine, stopping when the water is almost clear. Here's how you do it:

1. **Remove the inner pot from the rice cooker, placing the amount of raw rice called for in your recipe into it (or a bowl or pan big enough for your hand to move around in).**

2. **Fill the inner pot with enough cold water to cover the rice.**

3. **Swirl the rice around in the pot, using an opened hand, for 5 or 6 seconds.**

   As silly as it sounds, rinse the rice gently. Don't crush it in your hands or against the side of the pot. Dry rice grains are brittle. If you break a lot when rinsing them, the finished rice is too sticky and won't be as attractive or tasty as you want.

4. **Wait a second or two until the rice settles down and then carefully pour off the cloudy water.**

   Don't use a strainer to drain the rice, or you may break some grains. But it's a good idea to put a strainer in the sink to catch any grains that escape. And never let the rice soak in this milky water or the cooked rice won't taste fresh.

5. **Rinse the rice three or more times, until the water is almost clear.**

If you use rice advertised as rice that you don't have to rinse, rinse it anyway, three to four times. Rinsing this rice a few times results in better-looking and better-tasting rice than not rinsing it at all.

Giving the rice a good, long soak

After you rinse the rice, it's time to soak it before subjecting it to heat. Soaking softens and plumps up the rice grains, ensuring a nice, chewy, finished-throughout texture.

If you like the taste of your tap water, use it to soak the rice. If not, use purified or bottled water. Rinsing the rice with less-tasty tap water is okay because the rinsing is done quickly, preventing the rice from soaking up much of the tap water.

Here's how to soak the rice:

1. **Put the rinsed rice in the inner pot of the rice cooker or in a heavy pot with a lid.**

   Be sure that your pot has room for the raw rice you're cooking to expand about two and a half to three times in volume — for 2 cups raw rice, use a 2-quart pot; for 3 cups rice, use a 3-quart pot; for 4 cups rice, use a 4-quart pot. If the pot's too small, the water boils out, and the rice doesn't have room to expand. If the pot is too big, the rice spreads out too thin, the water boils too quickly, and the rice doesn't cook through properly.

2. **Add the water called for in Table 5-1, earlier in this chapter.**

Don't measure the cooking water for the rice from the directions on rice bags. Sushi rice is made with less water to achieve a chewier texture than everyday rice. The rice should be level in the pot and completely covered with the water.

3. **Set the rice aside to soak for 30 minutes.**

If you're using a rice cooker, don't plug it in yet. Many rice cookers turn on to the warm setting when plugged in, resulting in soft, not chewy, rice.

Preparing the Rice Vinegar Dressing

Rice vinegar dressing adds a vibrant, faintly sweet taste to the cooked rice, making this seasoned rice, or sushi, a perfect partner for many other ingredients. Making the rice vinegar dressing before cooking the rice ensures that the sugar and salt in the dressing are completely dissolved before the rice is done.

The proportion of rice vinegar dressing to cooked rice is important so that the subtle taste of the cooked rice is highlighted, not overcome, by the dressing. Table 5-2 helps you get the measurements just right. The first column notes how much rice you plan to make; the next three columns tell you how much vinegar, sugar, and salt to use to make your dressing. Sea salt is preferred for its clean flavor, but table salt is fine.

Table 5-2	Rice Vinegar Dressing Measurements		
Cooked Rice	*Rice Vinegar*	*Sugar*	*Salt*
5 to 6 cups	¼ cup	1 tablespoon	1½ teaspoons
7½ to 9 cups	6 tablespoons	4½ teaspoons	2 teaspoons
10 to 12 cups	½ cup	2 tablespoons	1 tablespoon

Commercially prepared seasoned sushi vinegars *(sushi-zu* or *shari-zu)*, made of rice vinegar, sugar, and salt, are available, but their taste is too sharp compared to a rice vinegar dressing you make yourself. Making your own dressing takes just 2 or 3 minutes and allows you to adjust the amount of sugar and salt to your taste and even vary the vinegar for creative or extreme sushi recipes, such as the Tarragon Vinegar Dressing we use in our Smoked Salmon Sushi Packages (see Chapter 11).

The dressing is as easy as 1-2-3 to prepare. Here's how:

1. **Combine the rice vinegar, sugar, and salt in a small bowl.**

2. **Stir it continuously for a minute or two, until the mixture goes from cloudy to clear, indicating that the sugar and salt have dissolved.**

3. **Set aside at room temperature until the rice is cooked.**

   You can refrigerate this mixture for several days, but you don't want to pour cold dressing over the hot rice, so return it to room temperature before using.

Kicking Off! Cooking the Rice

At last it's time to get off the sidelines and into the game — cooking the rice! First you give it a little flavor and then you turn on the heat.

Adding sake and dashi konbu to the soaked rice

You add a piece of *dashi konbu* and a splash or two of sake after the rice is soaked for 30 minutes, just before you turn on the heat. You can skip the sake if you need to for health reasons, but you really should use the *dashi konbu* (see Chapter 3).

 ✔ **A 2-inch or 3-inch square piece of *dashi konbu* is just enough to lend a gentle sea breeze flavor to 2 to 4 cups of soaked rice.** Wipe off the konbu with a damp paper towel or run it quickly under tap water. Cut a few slits in the sides of the konbu to help release its flavors.

 ✔ **A tablespoon or two of sake lifts the spirits of the rice.** But don't use so much sake that you make the rice soggy or drunk! Just a splash or two is all you need.

Turning up the heat

You've done all the preparations, and now it's time to get in the game and cook the rice! You can cook your rice in a rice cooker or on the stovetop — we explain how in the following sections.

In a rice cooker

Nothing could be easier than cooking rice in a rice cooker. Depending on how much rice you're making, it takes 25 to 35 minutes. After you soak your rice in the inner pot and add the *dashi konbu* and sake, all you do is place the inner pot in the cooker base, plug in the cooker, and turn it on — it's that easy. The rice cooker takes it from there, turning off, or down, at the appropriate time. When the rice is done, let it rest for 15 minutes. Don't remove the lid!

Be sure that the inner pot is completely dry when you insert it into the rice cooker to avoid corroding the heating element in the bottom, shortening the life of the rice cooker.

Although some rice cookers advertise that the rice can stay warm in its pot up to 5 hours without a loss in quality, for sushi rice that's way too long because the bottom gets too brown and the rice too soft; 3 hours is max. If possible, move the cooked rice out of the inner pot 15 minutes after it's through cooking.

Right after you turn the cooked rice out of the inner pot, fill the inner pot with water to prevent any sticky rice left in the pot from hardening on it, making cleanup more difficult.

When you're done cooking the rice, store the rice cooker's plug in a plastic bag, in the cooker. That way, the plug won't scratch the pot, and you'll always know where it is.

On the stovetop

Cooking the rice in a heavy pot on the stovetop does require a little attention. Depending on how much rice you're making, this cooking method takes 25 to 40 minutes. After you've made a batch or two, cooking rice on the stovetop becomes second nature. Until then, hang around the kitchen, watching the time.

After you soak your rice in the pot and add *dashi konbu* and sake, here's what to do next:

1. **Place the lidded pot over medium heat and bring slowly to a boil.**

2. **After the rice starts boiling, without removing the lid, lower the heat, and simmer the rice for about 15 to 20 minutes.**

3. **After 15 to 20 minutes, reduce the heat to its lowest possible point and barely simmer for about 5 minutes.**

4. **Raise the heat to the highest level for about 7 seconds, and then turn off the heat completely.**

   This is a tried-and-true Japanese method of finishing the rice, ridding it of any excess moisture.

5. **Turn off the heat and let the rice rest for 15 minutes (either on the cooling burner or on the countertop).**

   Don't remove the lid! No peeking, which allows steam to escape. Wait it out — it's worth it. If you peek, the rice isn't ruined, but leaving it covered is still your best bet.

Finishing the Rice — It's a Winner!

The final steps of the sport of sushi rice preparation may feel a little awkward to you the first few times you perform them, but they're fun to do, and the rice is better for it. These steps (shown in Figure 5-1) involve turning out your hot, cooked rice, seasoning it with rice vinegar dressing, and then tossing and fanning it at the same time. If you have a friend nearby to fan the rice for you, it's double the fun! The whole process takes about 5 minutes after you get the hang of it.

Turning out the rice

Sometimes rice browns a little bit on the bottom when it cooks. This isn't a bad thing. The color disappears as you spread the rice out, cooling it, as explained later in this section. If a little brown still peeks through, that's okay. By the time you top or toss the rice with other ingredients, you won't even notice it. Here's how you *turn out* hot rice (which means seasoning it with rice vinegar dressing, tossing, and fanning it until it's glistening and cool).

1. **Moisten the sushi paddle and the sushi tub with water to help keep the cooked rice from sticking.**

2. **Remove the *dashi konbu* from the rice.**

   It's edible, so you can mince it for use in soups or salads or you can discard it.

3. **Run the damp paddle down and around the rice pot to loosen the rice (refer to Figure 5-1). Then invert the rice pot over the sushi tub, causing the cooked rice to fall into it.**

   Sometimes the rice falls out in a perfect cake form, and other times, it crumbles. It doesn't matter which way it comes out.

TURNING OUT AND FINISHING UP THE SUSHI RICE

1. INSERT THE PADDLE BETWEEN THE RICE AND THE POT TO HELP THE RICE SLIP OUT.

2. TURN THE RICE OUT INTO THE SUSHI TUB.

3. POUR THE VINEGAR DRESSING OVER THE RICE PADDLE ON TO THE HOT RICE. MOVE THE PADDLE ALL OVER THE RICE AS YOU GO

   SHAMOSI

   HANDAI

4. GENTLY BREAK UP AND SPREAD OUT THE SUSHI RICE EVENLY.

5. TOSSING, TOSSING, TOSSING AND FANNING, FANNING, FANNING THE SUSHI RICE.

6. COVER THE SUSHI RICE WITH A DAMP, WRUNG-OUT TOWEL TO KEEP IT MOIST. LEAVE AT ROOM TEMPERATURE. DON'T REFRIGERATE!

Figure 5-1: Turning out and finishing up the sushi rice.

Pouring on the rice vinegar dressing

Apply the dressing while the rice is hot and eager to absorb it.

We just know that you have your rice vinegar dressing prepared, ready to pour over the hot rice. No? Then do this: Combine the rice vinegar mixture in a small glass bowl and microwave it for 15 to 30 seconds to warm up the vinegar. Stir for 30 seconds or so until dissolved. Don't let the vinegar boil or the flavors change. This shortcut should cut at least 1 minute off the process.

Add the rice vinegar dressing as explained in these steps (and as shown earlier in Figure 5-1):

1. **Slowly pour the rice vinegar dressing over the rice paddle onto the hot rice, moving the paddle around over the rice as you do so.**

   Wait a few seconds, giving the rice time to absorb most of the rice vinegar dressing. A little of the dressing may puddle out under the rice. This is fine.

2. **Begin spreading the rice into a thin, even layer by using the rice paddle in a cutting motion, separating the chunks of rice.**

   Don't stir it. Simply cut through it, trying not to mash the rice. This process takes about 1 minute.

3. **After the rice is spread out, start turning it over gently, in small portions, allowing steam to escape, for about 1 minute.**

By now the rice vinegar dressing is well absorbed, and you're ready to start fanning the rice while you continue turning it over.

Fanning the rice until it's cool

Fanning while you turn over the seasoned rice (refer to Figure 5-1) speeds the cooling process, helping to create the chewy texture you're after. It takes just a few minutes to do.

1. **Continue turning over the rice, but now start fanning as you do so.**

   If these two actions are hard to do at once, fan a little, turn the rice over a little, and then fan again. Don't toss the cooked rice like you would a salad; just turn it over gently. As the rice cools and the steam evaporates, the rice should take on a lovely sheen.

2. Stop fanning when there's no more visible steam.

The rice should still feel a little warm, but it's done!

If it happens (and it does) that you've measured correctly from a new bag of rice but the cooked rice seems a little too dry or wet when it's finished, don't fret. It still tastes good and can be used for sushi. Next time you make sushi rice from the same bag of rice, add a little more water if your rice seemed too dry, or a little less if it seemed too wet.

Keeping the rice moist

Now that your sushi rice is moist, chewy, and delicious-tasting, you want to keep it in good shape. Here's how:

✓ **Cover the sushi tub with a damp, wrung-out towel to prevent the rice from drying out (refer to Figure 5-1).** A plain white cotton or linen towel is suggested, but whatever you have is fine. Check the towel every so often. If the towel dries out, wet it with warm water, wring it out, and re-cover the rice (see "The art of the damp — not dripping wet — towel" sidebar in this chapter).

✓ **Never refrigerate prepared sushi rice or it dries out, hardens, and loses its fresh scent and flavor.** Keep it covered in a draft-free, cool corner of the kitchen.

✓ **Enjoy your sushi rice the day you make it.** If you make it a day ahead, it loses most of its luster, flavor, and taste.

✓ **Freeze any rice not used that day in 1-cup portions, sealed tightly in plastic wrap and freezer bags, for up to three months.** Microwave each portion about 2 minutes to reconstitute it.

The art of the damp — not dripping wet — towel

Surprise, surprise. There's actually a right way to squeeze water out of a kitchen towel. This method gives you a damp, not dripping wet, towel to lay over your prepared sushi rice to keep it moist, or to wipe your hands on while making sushi dishes. What you do is soak a kitchen towel in water, pick it up, fold it in half, and twist it tightly, your hands going in opposite directions, several times, until it releases no more water. Of course, you can squeeze your kitchen towel anyway you want, but this way works best.

Chapter 6

Introducing Popular Sushi Types and Techniques

*I*n this chapter, we show you how to make the ten different types of popular sushi found in *Sushi For Dummies*. To keep things simple, we group these sushi types into five main categories (with popular variations included): hand-shaped, rolled, pressed, scattered, and stuffed sushi. Plus, we tell you about creative sushi, not so much a type as a no-boundaries sushi phenomenon that's taking the sushi world by storm.

Begin mastering your own sushi universe by following our tried-and-true techniques that you can find in this chapter.

Getting Organized: Gathering the Essential Tools

Every time you make sushi, you need three things by your side:

✔ **Sushi rice:** The rice (see Chapter 5) should be prepared that same day and kept covered with a damp kitchen towel. Leave your sushi rice out at room temperature in a cool, draft-free place. Never place it in the refrigerator, where it dries out and hardens. When you're ready to make the sushi, pull the damp cloth back to expose only as much rice as you need to work with, re-covering the rice if you take a break.

✔ **Vinegared water:** A bowl of vinegared water, called *tezu*, is an indispensable part of your sushi repertoire. Moisten your hands with it each time you pick up some rice and the rice won't stick to your hands. The rice vinegar (see Chapter 3) flavors the water and, more importantly, helps sanitize your hands. The recipe is simple: 1 part rice vinegar to 4 parts water (for example, ¼ cup, or 4 tablespoons, rice vinegar to 1 cup water). You need about 1 cup vinegared water to work with 5 to 6 cups prepared sushi rice. If you have large hands, you may find that you want more vinegared water than this. Just keep the proportion of rice vinegar to water the same. The vinegared water will get messy as you continue to dip your rice-flecked hands in it. Make a new bowl when you think it's necessary.

In a pinch, you can substitute apple cider vinegar for rice vinegar.

✔ **A damp kitchen towel:** You want to keep your hands moist, not dripping wet, so do the "sushi two-step" each time you wet your hands. The sushi two-step goes like this:

1. Dip your hands into the vinegared water, making sure the insides and back of your fingers are damp.

2. Tap your fingertips a few times on a damp, wrung-out towel, placed next to the vinegared water, to remove any excess water.

Dripping wet hands make soggy sushi. Moist is best.

Hitting the Ground Running with Hand-Shaped Sushi

Watching sushi chefs show off their skills is one of the big draws at a sushi bar. They're culinary actors who shine the brightest when hand-shaping sushi — especially finger sushi — in their flashy, professional way. Fortunately, we provide easier ways to achieve the same results with finger sushi and battleship sushi (which is finger sushi with a little band of nori, or dried seaweed, around it). The third kind of hand-shaped sushi offered in this section, sushi rice balls, is a beginner's favorite because it's the easiest of all three hand-shaped sushi to make.

Finger sushi

Nigiru means "to gently squeeze," which is what you do when you pick up a bite-size portion of sushi rice and gently squeeze it into a slender oval ball, forming finger sushi *(nigiri-zushi).* (See the sidebar "When sushi is zushi," later in this chapter.) Sushi chefs do this hundreds of times a day, quickly shaping the rice by using the palm and fingers of only one hand. Next, with lightning speed, they press the rice ball onto some delectable topping, like tuna or butterflied shrimp. Only after each finger sushi is complete do they set it down on the counter. They do this aerial act over and over, perfectly it seems, with no mess anywhere, all day long.

Don't worry about emulating the speed of a sushi chef the first few times you make finger sushi. Your family and friends will understand if you don't produce a perfect piece of finger sushi on your first try. Instead, enjoy the fun of working with sushi rice at your own pace.

If you're a fan of shortcuts, use a mold to make finger sushi, as we show you in the "Molding finger sushi" section, later in this chapter. When you master the art of shaping finger sushi — whether by hand or by mold — try the recipes in Chapters 8, 9, 11, and 12.

Hand-shaping finger sushi

Shape all the finger sushi you want first and then dab seasonings, such as wasabi (see Chapter 3), and add toppings, such as in our Shrimp Finger Sushi (see Chapter 8), instead of making one complete finger sushi, topping and all, at once, like sushi chefs do.

Don't be surprised if you feel a bit klutzy at first; crafting hand-shaped sushi takes a little practice. Just eat your first few sloppy ones and keep going, following this routine:

1. **Prepare your sushi rice (see Chapter 5) and toppings and pull out or prepare any seasonings called for in your recipe.**

2. **Dip your hands in a bowl of vinegared water before shaping each piece of finger sushi (see the section "Getting Organized: Gathering the Essential Tools," earlier in this chapter).**

   Tap your fingertips on a damp, wrung-out towel, placed next to the vinegared water, to remove any excess water.

3. **Pick up and gently squeeze and roll a bite-size portion (about 2 tablespoons) of sushi rice into a slender oval ball, about 2 inches long x 1 inch wide, using the palm**

and fingers of one hand, aided by the other hand if necessary (see Figure 6-1).

Try not to smash the rice together. Just press firmly enough so that the rice grains cling together, creating a delicate piece of finger sushi. If you squeeze too hard, you'll get a heavy wad of sushi rice.

4. **Gently press the bottom of the finger sushi with your thumb to give it a slightly humped look and place the finger sushi on a damp cutting board or plate.**

5. **Continue making finger sushi, rewetting your fingers (see Step 2) as necessary and placing the sushi on the cutting board or plate.**

Don't let the sushi touch each other, or they'll stick together. At this point, you can cover the sushi with plastic wrap, and they'll keep at room temperature in a cool, draft-free place (not the refrigerator) for several hours.

6. **Dab on any seasonings and toppings called for in your recipe.**

HAND-SHAPING FINGER SUSHI

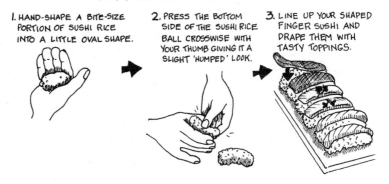

1. HAND-SHAPE A BITE-SIZE PORTION OF SUSHI RICE INTO A LITTLE OVAL SHAPE.

2. PRESS THE BOTTOM SIDE OF THE SUSHI RICE BALL CROSSWISE WITH YOUR THUMB GIVING IT A SLIGHT 'HUMPED' LOOK.

3. LINE UP YOUR SHAPED FINGER SUSHI AND DRAPE THEM WITH TASTY TOPPINGS.

Figure 6-1: Hand-shaping finger sushi.

Molding finger sushi

What a revelation! If you don't want to try shaping finger sushi by hand, you don't have to. Use a mold (see Figure 6-2) to make finger sushi. The difference in the appearance and texture of molded versus hand-shaped finger sushi is slight, with no difference in taste. You need a mold made just for finger sushi, preferably one that makes five pieces of finger sushi at a time (see Chapter 2 for information about where to buy molds). We show you how to make molded finger sushi by placing plastic wrap inside the mold. Using the plastic wrap makes the job cleaner and quicker in the long run — no washing the mold between each use. Here's how you do it:

1. **Prepare your sushi rice (see Chapter 5) and toppings and pull out or prepare any seasonings called for in your recipe.**

2. **Set the bottom portion of a finger sushi mold on the counter and lay a piece of plastic wrap several inches larger than the mold over it, pressing it down inside the mold's individual depressions and against the sides.**

   A few inches of plastic wrap should be hanging over the edges of the mold when you're done.

3. **Dip your hands in a bowl of vinegared water (see "Getting Organized: Gathering the Essential Tools," earlier in this chapter) before touching the sushi rice.**

   Tap your fingertips on a damp, wrung-out towel, placed next to the vinegared water, to remove any excess water.

4. **Pick up a bite-size portion (about 2 tablespoons) of sushi rice with your fingers and fill one of the depressions in the mold.**

   You want the rice to come just to the top of the mold, not much higher. That way, when you press down with the lid (in Step 6), you don't pack the rice too tightly together, making it too dense.

5. **Continue rewetting your fingers (see Step 3) and filling the depressions one by one until the mold is full.**

6. **Fold over the loose plastic wrap and press down with the lid.**

7. **Remove the lid, fold back the plastic wrap, and pull up on the plastic wrap, lifting the finger sushi out of the mold.**

8. **Place the finger sushi on a damp cutting board or plate, flat side down.**

   Don't let the sushi touch or they'll stick to each other. At this point, you can cover the sushi with plastic wrap, and they'll keep at room temperature in a cool, draft-free place (not the refrigerator) for several hours.

9. **Continue making finger sushi until you have all you need.**

10. **Dab on any seasonings and then add the toppings called for in your recipe.**

When sushi is zushi

We're not misspelling *sushi* when we spell it *zushi*. Sometimes in Japanese, when you combine two nouns, like *nigiri* and *sushi,* the second word's pronunciation and English spelling changes, leading to *nigiri-zushi.* Know this, and you'll sound like a pro the next time you're in a sushi bar ordering finger sushi by its Japanese name, *nigiri-zushi.* Of course, whichever way you say it, the sushi chef will know that you mean finger sushi, but how cool you'll appear when you say it correctly — with a *z* sound.

MOLDING FINGER SUSHI

1. LAY PLASTIC WRAP OVER THE FINGER SUSHI MOLD.

2. STUFF THE SUSHI MOLD ONE BY ONE.

3. PRESS DOWN ON THE SUSHI RICE WITH THE LID.

4. TAKE THE MOLDED FINGER SUSHI OUT OF THE MOLD.

Figure 6-2: Molding finger sushi.

Battleship sushi

Sometimes you'll want to make finger sushi that's topped with very loose or finely chopped ingredients, such as salmon roe or spicy guacamole, as in our battleship recipes found in Chapters 9 and 11. These luscious toppings would fall off the rice if it weren't for a tiny collar of nori (see Chapter 3) that's wrapped around the rice ball (see Figure 6-3). In the process, the rice ball takes on the look of a tiny battleship. The rice ball used in battleship sushi is the same shape rice ball used in finger sushi, made by hand or with a mold.

Hand-shaping battleship sushi

Here's how to hand-shape battleship sushi:

1. **Prepare your sushi rice (see Chapter 5) and toppings and pull out or prepare any seasonings called for in your recipe.**

2. **Cut sheets of nori into as many 1-x-7-inch strips as you need.**

3. **Dip your hands in a bowl of vinegared water before shaping each piece of battleship sushi (see the section "Getting Organized: Gathering the Essential Tools," earlier in this chapter).**

   Tap your fingertips on a damp, wrung-out towel, placed next to the vinegared water, to remove any excess water.

4. **Pick up and gently squeeze and roll a bite-size portion (about 2 tablespoons) of sushi rice into a slender oval ball, about 2 inches long x 1 inch wide, using the palm and fingers of one hand, aided by the other hand if necessary.**

5. **Continue making finger sushi, rewetting your fingers (see Step 3) as necessary, until you have all you need.**

6. **Place the sushi on a cutting board or plate, and don't let the sushi touch or they'll stick to each other.** At this point, you can cover the sushi with plastic wrap and they'll keep at room temperature in a cool, draft-free place (not the refrigerator) for several hours.

7. **Dry your hands if they're wet.**

   Damp hands will cause the nori to go limp.

8. **Wrap a 1-inch-wide strip of nori around the sides of each finger sushi, shiny side out, creating a tiny collar all around the rice (see Figure 6-3).**

   Use a grain of sticky rice to stick the underside of the nori strip to itself if it doesn't stick by itself.

   The nori collar should extend above the rice by ¼ inch or so.

9. **Delicately dab on any seasonings and then fill with the loose ingredients called for in the recipes in Chapters 9 and 11.**

10. **Serve immediately while the nori is still crisp.**

MAKING BATTLESHIP SUSHI

1. CUT A 7-INCH BY 8-INCH SHEET OF NORI INTO 8 STRIPS, 1-INCH BY 7-INCH EACH.

2. GET READY FOR BATTLE! WRAP THE SUSHI RICE BALL WITH A 1-INCH BY 7-INCH STRIP OF NORI.

3. FILL THE BATTLESHIP SUSHI WITH LOOSE TOPPINGS.

Figure 6-3: Making battleship sushi.

Molding battleship sushi

Molded battleship sushi is made in the same type of mold and the same way that molded finger sushi is made (see the section "Molding finger sushi," earlier in this chapter), only you take it a step further by wrapping each piece of sushi with a strip of nori (see Steps 2, 7, and 8 in the "Hand-shaping battleship sushi" section, earlier in this chapter). After you wrap as many molded finger sushi pieces as you want, fill with loose ingredients and serve immediately.

Sushi rice balls

Sushi rice balls *(temari-zushi)* are popular because they're as easy as child's play to make. In fact, *temari* refers to what they look like: tiny toy balls. Sushi rice balls are shaped by twisting a golf-ball-size amount of sushi rice in a piece of plastic wrap until the rice forms a perfect ball (see Figure 6-4). Ingredients can be mixed into or placed on top of the rice, like in our Tuna Sushi Rice Balls recipe in Chapter 9. You can make them smaller or bigger — whatever you want. Here's how:

1. **Prepare your sushi rice (see Chapter 5) and toppings and pull out or prepare any seasonings called for in your recipes.**

2. **Lay a 10-inch square piece of plastic wrap on a smooth, clean surface and place any ingredients you'd like to see wind up on the top of your finished rice ball in the center of the plastic wrap.**

3. **Wet a ¼ cup measuring cup with vinegared water, tapping off any excess water (see the vinegared water recipe in the section "Getting Organized: Gathering the Essential Tools," earlier in this chapter).**

4. **Dip your hands in a bowl of vinegared water before shaping each sushi rice ball.**

   Tap your fingertips on a damp, wrung-out towel, placed next to the vinegared water, to remove excess water.

5. **Gently pack the moist cup with sushi rice.**

6. **Invert the ¼ cup rice onto the toppings on the plastic wrap.**

7. **Gather the corners of the plastic wrap together; using both hands, twist the plastic wrap and the rice ball in opposite directions until a firm ball shape is formed.**

8. **Unwrap and place the rice ball, topping side up, on a damp cutting board or plate.**

   If the sushi rice balls don't contain anything perishable, they'll keep for several hours in a cool place (not the refrigerator), covered with plastic wrap, before serving.

SHAPING SUSHI RICE BALLS

1. PLACE THE TASTY TOPPING AND SUSHI RICE ON A SHEET OF PLASTIC WRAP. LIFT THE CORNERS OF THE PLASTIC WRAP UP.

2. TWIST THE PLASTIC WRAP, ROUND AND ROUND, TO SHAPE THE SUSHI RICE BALLS.

3. UNWRAP AND SERVE THE PLUMP LITTLE SUSHI RICE BALLS, TOPPING SIDE UP ↑.

Figure 6-4: Shaping sushi rice balls.

Tumbling into Rolled Sushi

Sushi rolls are kind of like sandwiches: The sushi rice acts as the bread, and almost anything goes on the inside — or outside. *Sushi For Dummies* is filled with sliced roll, inside-out roll, and hand roll recipes because we enjoy them as much as the rest of the world does! You can make rolls out of an endless variety of ingredients, dictated by what you think would taste good with vinegared rice, but keep a balance of flavors or tastes in mind.

Sliced sushi rolls

Here's where sushi's popularity really takes off. Everybody loves making and eating sliced sushi rolls *(maki-zushi)*. Medium-size rolls are the easiest for beginners to tackle because they're big enough to get a comfortable grip on. Thin rolls with just one filling ingredient or thick rolls with four or five filling ingredients can require a little more practice to handle well.

Sliced sushi rolls are traditionally made in three different sizes, or diameters: thin 1-inch rolls *(hoso-maki);* medium 1½-inch rolls *(chu-maki);* and thick 2- to 2½-inch rolls *(futo-maki)*. Figure 6-5 illustrates these rolls. The thickness you want determines whether you use one half sheet of 7-x-8-inch nori (for thin rolls) or a whole sheet (for medium and thick rolls) and how much sushi rice you use. (See Chapter 3 for nori information.) Thin, medium, and thick rolls are all made by using a small, flexible bamboo mat *(makisu),* described in Chapter 2, and all three sizes use the same rolling method explained later in this section.

One of the biggest mistakes of beginners is overstuffing sliced rolls, making them too difficult to roll and causing the nori to split and fall apart. Keep that in mind as you make your first few rolls.

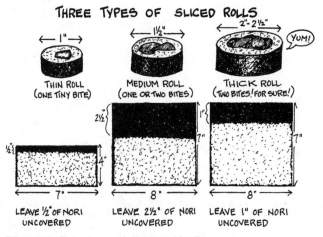

Figure 6-5: Three types of sliced sushi rolls.

Table 6-1 describes these three different sizes of rolls and explains the ingredients you need for each size. You can find sliced sushi roll recipes in Chapters 8, 9, 10, and 11.

Table 6-1	Three Types of Sliced Sushi Rolls	
Type of Sliced Roll	**Description**	**Ingredients**
Thin	1-inch-wide, one-bite sliced sushi; perfect cocktail fare	Half sheet of nori, 4 inches x 7 inches; about ½ cup, or 3 ounces, of prepared sushi rice; a single ingredient, such as cucumber or tuna, in the center
Medium	1½-inch-wide, one- to two-bite sliced sushi; the preferred size to make at home because it's the easiest to roll	One whole sheet of *nori,* 7 inches x 8 inches; about 1 cup, or 5 ounces, of prepared sushi rice; two or three ingredients in the center
Thick	A big, plump, 2- to 2½-inch-wide, two- or three-bite sliced sushi, splashy looking and fun for parties	One whole sheet of *nori,* 7 inches x 8 inches; about 1½ cups, or 8 ounces, of prepared sushi rice; four or more ingredients inside

Select the amount of ingredients you need to make your recipe's type of sliced sushi roll, based on Table 6-1. You're ready to start rolling sushi (see Figure 6-6):

1. **Place a bamboo mat in front of you, with the bamboo slats parallel to the edge of the table or countertop, so that the sushi rolls away from you.**

2. **Place the nori lengthwise, shiny side down, on the edge of the mat closest to you.**

3. **Dip your fingers in a bowl of vinegared water before picking up the sushi rice for each roll (see the section "Getting Organized: Gathering the Essential Tools," earlier in this chapter).**

   Tap your fingertips on a damp, wrung-out towel, placed next to the vinegared water, to remove excess water.

   Be particularly careful that your hands are moist, not dripping wet, or you may drip water on the nori in the next step, making it soggy.

4. **Spread the rice out evenly over the nori, gently pressing it into place with your fingertips, leaving a ½-inch- to 2½-inch-wide (refer to your recipe) strip of nori, not covered with rice, on the edge farthest away from you.**

   The nori softens and shrinks a little when it comes into contact with the moist rice. If you don't leave a bare strip of nori on the far edge, your roll may rip or pop open.

5. **If you're using wasabi paste (see Chapter 3) or other flavoring, spread it in an even line across the center of the rice.**

6. **Place the fillings across the middle of the rice, on top of any flavorings and close together, spanning the length of the nori.**

   If you spread the fillings out too far apart, you'll have trouble tightening the roll in Step 8.

7. **Lift the edge of the mat closest to you by placing your thumbs under the mat and the rest of your fingers over the fillings. Roll the mat over, pressing the fillings into the rice as you go. Stop rolling when the edge of the mat touches straight down onto the far edge of the rice, making sure that the bare border of nori is still exposed.**

   Lift and roll in a nonstop motion that's as fluid as possible. The slower you go, the more likely the fillings will slide out.

8. **Tighten this partial roll before you complete rolling it by gently pulling the mat-covered roll toward you with one hand while tugging three times on the free edge of the mat with your other hand — first in the center, then on one side, and then on the other side (see Figure 6-6).**

9. **Lift up the edge of the mat off the sealed partial roll, lay the mat down on the counter, and bring the sushi roll back to the edge of the mat closest to you.**

   This is a unique move that I (Mineko) find helps beginners make a pretty, firm roll. You can lift the edge of the mat off the partial roll and keep rolling to finish it, as is commonly done, but try it my way — moving the roll back to the edge of the mat closest to you — and you'll see how this move improves your chances of finished, firm, pretty rolls.

10. **Lift the edge of the mat again with both hands, placing your thumbs back under the mat and your fingers over the partially rolled sushi, and finish rolling it all the way over onto the last of the nori.**

ROLLING A SLICED ROLL

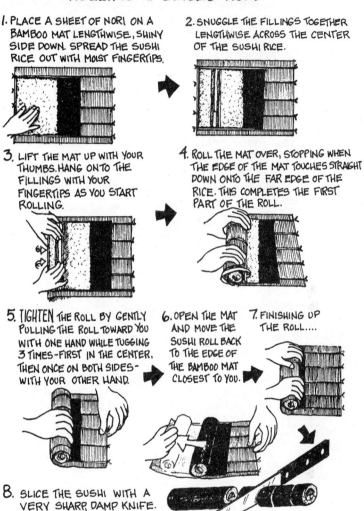

1. PLACE A SHEET OF NORI ON A BAMBOO MAT LENGTHWISE, SHINY SIDE DOWN. SPREAD THE SUSHI RICE OUT WITH MOIST FINGERTIPS.

2. SNUGGLE THE FILLINGS TOGETHER LENGTHWISE ACROSS THE CENTER OF THE SUSHI RICE.

3. LIFT THE MAT UP WITH YOUR THUMBS. HANG ON TO THE FILLINGS WITH YOUR FINGERTIPS AS YOU START ROLLING.

4. ROLL THE MAT OVER, STOPPING WHEN THE EDGE OF THE MAT TOUCHES STRAIGHT DOWN ONTO THE FAR EDGE OF THE RICE. THIS COMPLETES THE FIRST PART OF THE ROLL.

5. TIGHTEN THE ROLL BY GENTLY PULLING THE ROLL TOWARD YOU WITH ONE HAND WHILE TUGGING 3 TIMES - FIRST IN THE CENTER, THEN ONCE ON BOTH SIDES - WITH YOUR OTHER HAND.

6. OPEN THE MAT AND MOVE THE SUSHI ROLL BACK TO THE EDGE OF THE BAMBOO MAT CLOSEST TO YOU.

7. FINISHING UP THE ROLL....

8. SLICE THE SUSHI WITH A VERY SHARP, DAMP KNIFE.

Figure 6-6: Rolling a sliced sushi roll.

11. **Using both hands, give the finished sushi roll a final squeeze or two with the mat.**

    If it seems loose, give it three more pulls, as in Step 8, to further tighten it.

12. **Take the sushi roll out of the mat, and if the outside edge of the nori is still a little loose, rest the roll on its seam for a few minutes.**

    The moisture from the rice will come through and finish the job.

    If the roll's shape is a little off, place the mat back over the top of the roll and squeeze gently along the length of the mat with both hands, creating a rounder or more squared-off shape.

13. **Cut the roll into 8 equal pieces by cutting halves into halves, wiping your knife with a damp cloth between each slice to prevent the knife from sticking and pulling the sushi roll apart.**

14. **Serve immediately or, if nothing perishable is in the filling, cover the sliced rolls with plastic wrap and keep them in a cool place (not the refrigerator) for a few hours.**

Inside-out rolls

Sushi rolls that expose the sushi rice on the outside are called inside-out rolls *(ura-maki-zushi)*. They're perfect do-ahead sushi if you use cooked seafood, meats, or vegetables, as in our recipes in Chapters 8, 10, and 11. And they're actually easier to make than other sliced sushi rolls discussed earlier in this chapter. In those rolls, the nori is on the outside of the sticky rice, but in the inside-out rolls, the exposed sushi rice helps stick everything together when you roll it up (see Figure 6-7). Here's how:

1. **Prepare your sushi rice (see Chapter 5) and fillings and pull out or prepare any seasonings called for in your recipe.**

2. **Cover a bamboo mat (see Chapter 2) with plastic wrap (it keeps the rice from sticking to the mat) and place the covered mat in front of you, with the bamboo slats parallel to the edge of the table or countertop.**

    Place a half sheet of nori (measuring 4 inches x 7 inches) shiny side down, lengthwise, on the edge of the wrapped bamboo mat closest to you.

    Some beginners find it easier to use a 5-x-7-inch piece of nori for the same amount of rice. Try it both ways and see which you prefer.

3. **Dip your hands in a bowl of vinegared water before touching the sushi rice (see the section "Getting Organized: Gathering the Essential Tools," earlier in this chapter).**

Tap your fingertips on a damp, wrung-out towel, placed next to the vinegared water, to remove excess water.

4. **Spread approximately 1 cup sushi rice (5 ounces) evenly over all the nori, pressing it out with your fingertips.**

   Rewet your fingertips as necessary (see Step 3).

5. **Pick up the rice-covered nori, turn it over, and place it rice side down, nori side up, lengthwise, back on the edge of the mat closest to you.**

   Don't worry — even if you want it to, the rice won't fall off.

6. **Put the chosen seasonings and fillings across the length of the nori, not quite centered on it but a little closer to you.**

7. **Lift the edge of the mat closest to you with both hands by placing both thumbs under the mat and the rest of your fingers over the fillings.**

   Be sure to hold on to the fillings with your fingertips to keep them in place while rolling the sushi.

8. **Begin rolling the mat and its contents away, stopping when the edge of the mat you're rolling touches straight down onto the nori, enclosing the fillings completely.**

9. **Lift up the edge of the mat you're holding, and continue rolling the inside-out roll away from you until it's sealed.**

   If you don't lift up the edge of the mat, you'll roll the mat into the sushi roll!

10. **Seal the roll by gently pulling the mat-covered roll toward you with one hand while tugging three times on the free edge of the mat with your other hand — first in the center, then on one side, and then on the other side (see Figure 6-7).**

11. **Pick up and place the roll on a damp, clean, smooth surface.**

    If the roll's shape is a little off, place the mat back over the top of the roll and squeeze gently along the length of the mat with both hands, creating a rounder or more squared-off roll.

12. **Cut the roll into 6 equal pieces with a sharp knife, wiping the knife with a damp cloth between each slice to prevent sticking and pulling the sushi apart.**

Some beginners like to lay a piece of plastic wrap over the completed roll and then slice it with a damp knife because the plastic wrap helps hold the roll together while you slice. After slicing, peel off the individual pieces of plastic.

ROLLING AN INSIDE-OUT ROLL

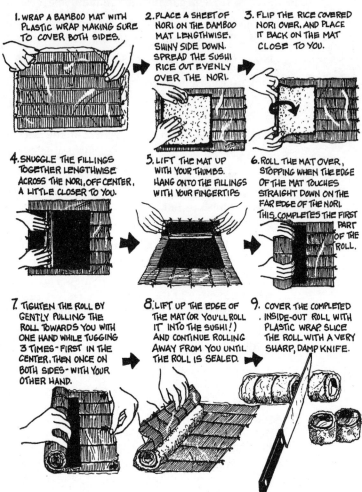

1. WRAP A BAMBOO MAT WITH PLASTIC WRAP MAKING SURE TO COVER BOTH SIDES.

2. PLACE A SHEET OF NORI ON THE BAMBOO MAT LENGTHWISE, SHINY SIDE DOWN. SPREAD THE SUSHI RICE OUT EVENLY OVER THE NORI.

3. FLIP THE RICE COVERED NORI OVER, AND PLACE IT BACK ON THE MAT CLOSE TO YOU.

4. SNUGGLE THE FILLINGS TOGETHER LENGTHWISE ACROSS THE NORI, OFF CENTER, A LITTLE CLOSER TO YOU.

5. LIFT THE MAT UP WITH YOUR THUMBS. HANG ONTO THE FILLINGS WITH YOUR FINGERTIPS

6. ROLL THE MAT OVER, STOPPING WHEN THE EDGE OF THE MAT TOUCHES STRAIGHT DOWN ON THE FAR EDGE OF THE NORI. THIS COMPLETES THE FIRST PART OF THE ROLL.

7. TIGHTEN THE ROLL BY GENTLY PULLING THE ROLL TOWARDS YOU WITH ONE HAND WHILE TUGGING 3 TIMES - FIRST IN THE CENTER, THEN ONCE ON BOTH SIDES - WITH YOUR OTHER HAND.

8. LIFT UP THE EDGE OF THE MAT (OR YOU'LL ROLL IT INTO THE SUSHI!) AND CONTINUE ROLLING AWAY FROM YOU UNTIL THE ROLL IS SEALED.

9. COVER THE COMPLETED INSIDE-OUT ROLL WITH PLASTIC WRAP. SLICE THE ROLL WITH A VERY SHARP, DAMP KNIFE.

Figure 6-7: Rolling an inside-out roll.

13. **Serve immediately, or if nothing perishable is in the rolls, you can cover them with plastic wrap and keep them in a cool place for a few hours.**

Hand rolls

Our Mexican friends call hand rolls *(temaki-zushi)* Japanese tacos. They look more like pointed ice cream cones made out of crisp nori and filled with sushi rice, fresh fish, vegetables, or whatever you like to eat (see Figure 6-8). We offer hand roll recipes in Chapters 8 and 9. You hold hand rolls upright in your hand like an ice cream cone and munch away.

Hand rolls are made as you eat them because the moist sushi rice filling softens the crisp nori quickly. But this is no big deal because hand rolls are so easy to make. Why not have a sushi buffet party starring Japanese tacos at your house (see Chapter 14)? Your guests can get into the act by filling and rolling their own roll!

If filling the nori while holding it in your hand feels awkward, start by laying the nori down on a smooth, clean surface and filling it there. Then pick it up and roll it into a cone. You'll quickly get the hang of it. For these steps, we assume that you're placing the nori in your left hand:

1. **Prepare your sushi rice (see Chapter 5) and fillings and pull out or prepare any seasonings called for in your recipe.**

2. **Pinch or cut nori sheets in half to form 4-x-7-inch sheets. (See Chapter 3 for nori information.)**

3. **Place the half sheet of nori in the palm of your open hand, shiny side down, with the nori running at a slight angle across your palm, most of its length jutting off your hand (see Figure 6-8).**

4. **Dip your right hand in a bowl of vinegared water (see the section "Getting Organized: Gathering the Essential Tools," earlier in this chapter).**

   Tap your fingertips on a damp, wrung-out towel, placed next to the vinegared water, to remove excess water.

5. **Place a golf-ball-size amount (about ¼ cup) of sushi rice on the nori, up toward the top portion of the nori, patting the rice out in a diagonal, from the top area of the nori toward the heel of your palm (see Figure 6-8).**

   Don't place rice on the bottom left corner of the nori (near your thumb) or on any of the nori jutting off your hand.

6. **Dab any seasonings down the length of the rice.**

7. **Place the fillings lengthwise in the center of the rice, with a little of their tips showing over the top edge of the rice and nori for looks.**

8. **Fold the exposed, left corner of nori over the rice and fillings up toward the right and continue rolling to the right until you have a cone-shaped roll.**

Eat hand rolls right away, while the nori is crisp.

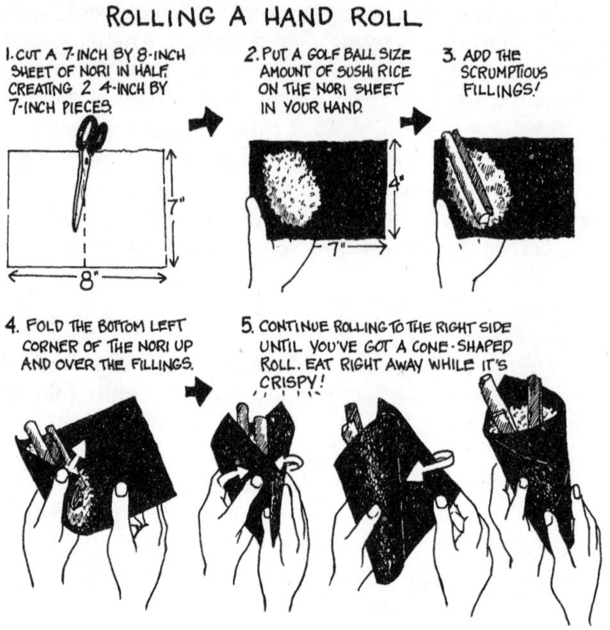

ROLLING A HAND ROLL

1. CUT A 7-INCH BY 8-INCH SHEET OF NORI IN HALF, CREATING 2 4-INCH BY 7-INCH PIECES.

2. PUT A GOLF BALL SIZE AMOUNT OF SUSHI RICE ON THE NORI SHEET IN YOUR HAND.

3. ADD THE SCRUMPTIOUS FILLINGS!

4. FOLD THE BOTTOM LEFT CORNER OF THE NORI UP AND OVER THE FILLINGS.

5. CONTINUE ROLLING TO THE RIGHT SIDE UNTIL YOU'VE GOT A CONE-SHAPED ROLL. EAT RIGHT AWAY WHILE IT'S CRISPY!

Figure 6-8: Rolling a hand roll.

Building Up to Pressed Sushi

If you've ever wondered how the Japanese make some of their fanciful shaped little servings of sushi, here's one of their secrets — they use molds.

Although pressed sushi is usually made by using a rectangular wooden or plastic mold (see Chapter 2), you can use almost any nonreactive container, such as a small glass baking dish, to lend shape, as long as you can easily remove the pressed sushi from the dish. A cut-out piece of heavy cardboard, covered with plastic wrap, that fits just inside your improvised sushi mold can serve as a lid to press down on the rice and ingredients.

Our pressed sushi recipes, such as the Crabmeat and Avocado Pressed Sushi with Wasabi Mayonnaise in Chapter 9 have two layers of sushi rice, one layer of filling, and a final layer of toppings, but you can make them with as many or few layers as you like. Pressed sushi is served in little bites as appetizers or in larger portions for more of a meal.

Here, we assume that you have a plastic sushi mold that holds approximately 1 cup of sushi rice in volume. This mold has convenient knife grooves in its side to ensure even cuts, as seen in Figure 6-9. Although we don't line the mold with plastic wrap, some beginners find that doing so is helpful because it makes lifting out the pressed sushi easier.

1. **Prepare your sushi rice (see Chapter 5), fillings, and toppings and pull out or prepare any seasonings called for in your recipe.**

2. **Wipe all three parts of the mold with a damp towel.**

3. **Dip your hands in a bowl of vinegared water before touching the sushi rice (see the section "Getting Organized: Gathering the Essential Tools," earlier in this chapter).**

   Tap your fingertips on a damp, wrung-out towel, placed next to the vinegared water, to remove excess water.

4. **Pick up and spread about ½ cup (about 3 ounces) sushi rice evenly into the mold and then press down with the lid.**

5. **Remove the lid and wipe it off with a damp towel.**

PRESSING SUSHI

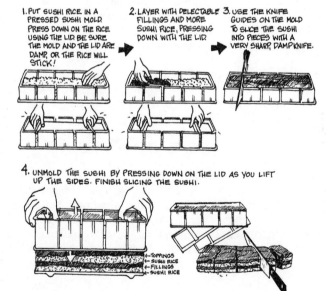

1. PUT SUSHI RICE IN A PRESSED SUSHI MOLD. PRESS DOWN ON THE RICE USING THE LID. BE SURE THE MOLD AND THE LID ARE DAMP, OR THE RICE WILL STICK!

2. LAYER WITH DELECTABLE FILLINGS AND MORE SUSHI RICE, PRESSING DOWN WITH THE LID.

3. USE THE KNIFE GUIDES ON THE MOLD TO SLICE THE SUSHI INTO PIECES WITH A VERY SHARP, DAMP KNIFE.

4. UNMOLD THE SUSHI BY PRESSING DOWN ON THE LID AS YOU LIFT UP THE SIDES. FINISH SLICING THE SUSHI.

← TOPPINGS
← SUSHI RICE
← FILLINGS
← SUSHI RICE

Figure 6-9: Pressing sushi.

6. Spread any seasonings on the rice called for in your recipe, top with filling ingredients, and press down with the lid again.

7. Repeat Steps 3 through 6, pressing down on the final layer or toppings.

8. Remove the lid and, using the knife guides on the mold, partially slice the sushi into pieces, wiping your knife on a damp cloth before each slice to prevent tearing the slices apart.

9. Unmold the sushi by pressing on the lid as you lift up on the sides of the mold and finish slicing the sushi pieces apart, again wiping your knife on a damp cloth before each slice.

10. Serve immediately, or if nothing perishable is in the pressed sushi, you can cover it with plastic wrap and keep it in a cool place for a few hours.

Breezing into Scattered Sushi

Scattered sushi *(chirashi-zushi)* is like a sushi salad — the ingredients are scattered or mixed in the sushi rice, giving you the taste of the sushi with no shaping or rolling involved. Just put prepared sushi rice in a bowl, mix in or top it with everyday or special ingredients, and you're all set. Make it in individual portions, or serve it in a big bowl so people can help themselves.

Techniques are not part of making these two types of scattered sushi, but do remember to treat your rice gently to keep it looking and tasting fresh. Don't get carried away tossing it around.

Tokyo-style scattered sushi

Tokyo-style sushi is the scattered sushi you're most likely to see in sushi bars, where glistening slices of pristinely beautiful raw fish top a generous bowl of fragrant, cool sushi rice. You can use ingredients other than raw fish, such as daikon radish (see Chapter 3), but most ingredients are placed on top of the sushi rice, not in it. An example is our recipe for Marinated Tuna Tokyo-Style Scattered Sushi in Chapter 9. The tuna rests on top of the rice, not in it.

The sushi name game

We don't want to venture too deeply into the linguistic world in this book, but sushi lovers are often curious as to why a popular sushi dish can have so many different names. Translating Japanese to English can lead to different names for the same type of sushi, just as the season, the region, and a sushi chef's personal preference may cause a name change here or abroad. For example, *chirashi-zushi* translates most closely to "scattered sushi," but its second most common English name is "sushi rice salad," because this is very descriptive of what it is.

Osaka-style scattered sushi

In Osaka-style sushi, ingredients are mixed into the sushi rice, and some ingredients are also scattered on top for decoration. It's the most popular home-style sushi in Japan. This style of sushi uses cured or cooked ingredients rather than raw fish, making it the perfect do-ahead dish. Mixing the cooked ingredients and vegetables into just-made sushi rice while it's still a little warm helps it all combine beautifully.

Osaka-style scattered sushi sometimes contains sweeter ingredients than Tokyo-style sushi, as in our Ground Turkey and Vegetable Osaka-Style Scattered Sushi in Chapter 10, in which the turkey is cooked in sweetened soy sauce and sake (rice wine). Osaka-style scattered sushi, garnished with pretty cut-out vegetables (see Chapter 7), is frequently served at celebrations in Japan.

Stuffing Tofu Pouches with Sushi

Tofu pouch sushi *(inari-zushi)* is named after the Japanese god of grains, whose messenger is the fox. Myth has it that foxes love to eat the deep-fried tofu *(abura-age)* that's used as the pouch. (Find out more about deep-fried tofu in Chapter 3.) Coincidentally, our favorite shape of pouch sushi actually resembles a little fox ear (see Figure 6-10). Tofu pouch sushi is the perfect sushi to make at home and take to a friend's house because the tofu pouch protects and holds in the sushi filling so nicely.

Thin slices of deep-fried tofu split open much as pita bread does, allowing you to stuff them with sushi rice alone (see Chapter 5) or with sushi rice mixed with the flavorful ingredients you like. Before stuffing, the deep-fried tofu is usually boiled in water to remove excess oil and then slowly simmered in a mixture of sugar, water, soy sauce, and sake, giving the fried tofu a tantalizing sweet-salty taste. Neither raw fish nor cooked fish or meats are generally used, making tofu pouch sushi perfect for vegetarian sushi recipes. Two recipes in Chapter 10 offer instructions for preparing tofu pouches before stuffing them.

Deep-fried tofu is sold in packages of square or rectangular slices. You don't need any special technique to prepare tofu pouch sushi, but for variety, you can cut the tofu slices into different shapes and stuff them a number of different ways. Here are two of our favorite ways to prepare them:

- **Cut each square of deep-fried tofu on the diagonal, forming two triangles.** After the cut pouches have been seasoned as described earlier, you stuff each one with an oval ball of sushi rice, creating a plump little triangle (see Figure 6-10) that resembles a little fox ear, as in our Sweet Tofu Pouch Sushi in Chapter 10.

- **Cut each square of deep-fried tofu in half, forming two rectangles.** After you season the pouches, you fill them with a sushi rice filling, much as you would fill a little paper bag, so you can see the colorful fillings through the open top of the little pouches. For an example, see our Carrots, String Beans, and Lemon Zest Tofu Pouch Sushi in Chapter 10.

STUFFING TOFU POUCH SUSHI

1. OPEN THE TOFU POUCH AND STUFF IT WITH A SUSHI RICE BALL.

2. SERVE TOFU POUCH SUSHI (INARI-ZUSHI) WITH PICKLED GINGER.

Figure 6-10: Stuffing tofu pouch sushi.

Venturing On to Creative Sushi

Creative sushi *(sosaku-zushi)* is all about abandoning most of sushi's conventions and doing your own thing. It's a hot phenomenon internationally, and it's not going to cool off anytime soon because it includes the fresh, flavorful heart and soul of all sushi recipes — the vinegared rice — yet allows the cook to take it from there on a personal, free-form culinary adventure.

A creative sushi recipe can start with a traditional sushi technique but then use ingredients that are new to sushi, such as the ones used in these recipes:

✔ **Mexican Hand Rolls:** The hand roll is traditional, but the tropical ingredients in this recipe (in Chapter 9), spiced up with chili powder and fresh lime juice, are new to sushi.

✔ **Birthday Cake Pressed Sushi:** Pressed sushi is traditional, but filling it with egg salad (see Chapter 11) is not.

Creative sushi can also be a freestyle technical presentation of sushi, using recognized Japanese ingredients, or not, like the following wild, wonderful-looking and -tasting recipes in Chapter 12:

✔ **Oysters on the Half Shell with Tempura Sushi Rice Balls**

✔ **Grilled Yellowtail Sushi Tamales with Spicy Mango Salsa**

Each creative sushi recipe in this cookbook is unique and comes with its own set of instructions. Use our examples of new sushi as a springboard for your own recipes.

Chapter 7

Slicing and Dicing the Sushi Way

In This Chapter
▶ Mastering the use of Japanese knives
▶ Slicing fish five different ways
▶ Cutting fresh vegetables six different ways
▶ Using a Japanese mandoline, a vegetable peeler, and decorative cutters

*P*recisely cut ingredients are an important part of sushi. The Japanese have known for centuries that how you cut, slice, or dice ingredients affects not only their visual appeal but also how they taste and feel in your mouth. The taste and texture of a paper-thin slice of avocado in your mouth are quite different than the taste and texture of a thick slice of avocado. Both are welcome and delicious, but different. This perception and appreciation of precise cutting are especially true for the sashimi-grade fish (meaning high-quality fish that can be eaten raw) used in sushi.

Japanese knives, like Samurai swords of old, are extremely sharp, and if you care for them properly, you can pass them down to the next generation of sushi chefs in your house. We discuss purveyors, selection, and care of these knives at length in Chapter 2. In this chapter, we go over the techniques to use when cutting blocks and fillets of fish, as well as when cutting vegetables for *Sushi For Dummies* recipes.

Getting a Grip on Sushi Knives

Two single-edged Japanese knives are important to making clean, smooth, even cuts for sushi: the sashimi knife and the vegetable knife. (Sushi chefs also use a cleaver, or *deba-bocho,* to cut and fillet fish, but it's likely you'll buy sashimi-grade fish already cut in blocks and fillets. At least that's what our fish recipes call for, so you don't need to purchase this cleaver.)

Japanese knives are effective and fun to use. If you're thinking about adding a Japanese knife to your selection but your cooking utensils fund is running low, buy the sashimi knife if raw fish is a favorite of yours, or the vegetable knife if vegetables are your favorite thing to eat. See Chapter 2 for information about where to buy Japanese knives. If you don't want to invest in a new knife, you can use your thinnest, sharpest, nonserrated knives to cut fish and vegetables for sushi.

Slicing with a sashimi knife

A finely honed, single-edged Japanese sashimi knife *(sashimi-bocho)* makes light work of cutting raw fish into beautiful, smooth pieces and slices.

There's an accepted way to hold a sashimi knife, but you may hold it however you're comfortable, provided that you can produce smooth, even cuts. These steps explain the accepted way to hold a sashimi knife:

1. **Grasp the handle comfortably with your index finger stretched out on the top of the handle up toward the blade (refer to Figure 2-3 in Chapter 2 for a visual).**

2. **Extend your index finger a little way out onto the cutting portion of the blade for better control.**

3. **Make a cut with one smooth motion, starting at the base of the blade for the initial cut and slicing through the item, finishing the cut near the tip of the knife.**

   The knife is so sharp that one gentle cutting motion, backed up by the weight of the blade, is all you need to make beautifully smooth cuts.

Cutting with a vegetable knife

The Japanese vegetable knife cuts very thin, precise pieces of food, much thinner than most other knives can.

There's an accepted way to hold a Japanese vegetable knife, but you may hold it however you're comfortable, provided that you can make smooth, even cuts. These steps describe the accepted way to hold a Japanese vegetable knife:

1. **Grasp the handle up toward the blade end of the handle. The knuckle of your index finger should be almost on top of the handle, edging out onto the knife (refer to Figure 2-3 in Chapter 2).**

2. **Establish a good grip by gently pressing your thumb into the side of the handle and curling your other fingers around the handle.**

    You now have a good working grip on the knife. Because this knife is so sharp, one gentle cutting motion, backed up by the weight of the blade, is all you need to make beautifully smooth cuts.

Working with Fresh Fish

Your goal when slicing precious, sashimi-grade raw fish is precise, smooth, even slices. How thick or thin you slice the fish depends on the fish and your recipe. Pieces of raw fish for sushi are small and easy to eat in one or two bites.

We describe five different ways of cutting fish in this section. (Note: We assume that you're right-handed. Left-handed single-edged Japanese knives, which are honed on the left side of the blade, can be special ordered. See Chapter 2.)

Before you begin slicing your fish by using any of the techniques in this chapter, keep the following tips in mind:

- ✔ A charming Japanese sushi expression says, "If the fish is too thin, the rice wins. If the fish is too thick, the fish wins." A balance is what you're looking for when slicing raw fish for sushi.

- ✔ Absolutely fresh raw fish has a bright, translucent sheen to the flesh; the flesh is firm and moist and has no scent at all, except cool and fresh. Smelly fish is old fish, unfit for sushi or anything else.

- ✔ Cleanliness counts when cutting foods, especially raw seafood. Clean hands, knives, and cutting boards are very important, as we explain in Chapter 4. Guard against cross-contamination by working with raw seafood separately from cooked seafood and other ingredients. Use paper towels, not cloth towels, to clean up work surfaces.

- ✔ To preserve the integrity of the fish, be sure, when handling fresh fish, that your hands are cool. Dip your hands in ice water and then dry them, if necessary.

If you don't want to cut your own sashimi-grade raw fish for sushi recipes, ask your local sushi bar or fine fish market if it'll sell you fish sliced the way you want it, ready to go. Pick up the fish just before your meal, taking it home on ice in a cooler. Refrigerate the fish in the coldest part of the refrigerator until you need it. Or, if you choose to buy frozen sashimi-grade raw fish (we often do), be sure to defrost it in the refrigerator, not on the counter. You'll find that it's easiest to slice just before it's completely defrosted.

See Chapter 4 for detailed information on how to select and handle fresh fish; where to buy sashimi-grade fish that can be shipped to you; and food safety information and warnings regarding raw fish.

Slicing straight down

Straight cuts *(hira giri),* shown in Figure 7-1, are used in finger sushi, sushi rice balls, scattered sushi, or pressed sushi, such as our Tuna, Cucumber, and Black Sesame Seed Pressed Sushi with Soy-Mirin Dipping Sauce in Chapter 9. This is also a favorite cut for sashimi. Straight cuts can be as thick or thin as your recipe calls for, from ½ inch thick for sashimi to paper-thin for pressed sushi and sushi rice balls. Here's how you make the cut:

1. **Place a block of raw fish (roughly 2½ to 3 inches wide, 1 to 1½ inches thick, and the length you need for the number of slices of raw fish you need) on a cutting board in front of you horizontally.**

   If you're using a fillet, have the skinned side up and the thicker side away from you.

2. **Check the fish for any small bones, removing them with tweezers.**

3. **Moisten your knife with a damp paper towel before each slice to prevent the fish from sticking to the knife and tearing.**

4. **Begin your first slice on the right side of the fish. Lightly place the knife's blade, up toward its base, on the fish. As smoothly as possible, pull the knife toward you through the fish in one stroke, using the entire length of the blade, until you complete the cut.**

   Don't saw the fish apart. One slow, smooth, light cut, using the weight of the knife and the full length of the blade to help you, is best.

5. **Gently move the slice a few inches away and tip it over.**

Continue cutting the number of slices you need, following Steps 3 through 5.

Shaking hands sushi-bar style

Japanese sushi chefs shout *"Irashai,"* meaning "welcome," when patrons enter the sushi bar. If the chef knows you, he may reach across the bar and rap knuckles with you, much like boxers rap gloves together before a fight. Where and when this sushi-bar handshake started we can't determine, but it makes a lot of sense hygienically. A traditional, or open-handed, handshake is out of the question for working sushi chefs because they're handling raw fish and must keep their hands clean. Now, when you go to a sushi bar and the sushi chef reaches forward over the bar and presents his fist, you know what to do!

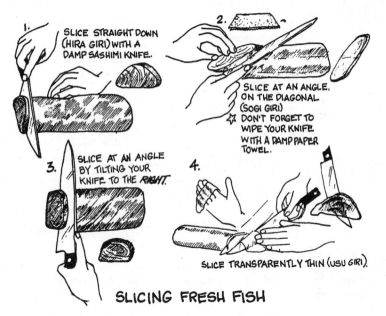

Figure 7-1: Slicing fresh fish.

Slicing at an angle

 Angle cuts *(sogi giri)* are versatile cuts (refer to Figure 7-1) used in finger sushi, sushi rice balls, pressed sushi, and inside-out rolls, such as the Rainbow Inside-Out Rolls in Chapter 8. You can make angle cuts in two ways: In the first technique, you cut diagonally across the piece of fish, creating a more graceful, slightly longer rectangular piece of fish than a straight cut. If you tilt the knife to the right for the cut, you get even wider slices. In the second technique, you slice straight across the piece of fish, but you slant your knife to the right, creating a wider rectangle (almost square-shaped) slice. This second cutting technique creates angle-cut slices that aren't as long as the first technique's angle cuts. Slices up to ¼ inch thick are appropriate for the sushi just mentioned. Here's how you create angle cuts:

1. **Place a block of raw fish (roughly 2½ to 3 inches wide, 1 to 1½ inches thick, and the length you need for the number of slices of raw fish you need) on a cutting board in front of you horizontally.**

   If you're using a fillet, have the tapered tail portion on your left and the thicker side of the fillet away from you.

2. **Check the fish for any small bones, removing them with tweezers.**

3. **Moisten your knife with a damp paper towel before each slice to prevent the fish from sticking to the knife and tearing.**

4. **To establish an angle for all the angle slices, begin by placing the base of the blade on the diagonal on the left side of the fish, tilting the knife a little to the right.**

5. **As smoothly as possible, pull the knife toward you through the fish in one stroke, using the entire length of the blade, until you complete the cut.**

   Then you can *butterfly* this first triangular piece by cutting it almost in half and opening it up as you would a book, so that it becomes one flat piece.

6. **Begin your second cut by following the diagonal established in your first cut, cutting slices in whatever thickness you need**.

   Remember to moisten your knife with a damp paper towel before each slice.

7. **Gently move the slice a few inches away and tip it over.**

8. **Continue cutting the number of slices you need, following Steps 2 through 7.**

Here's the second way to make angle cuts:

1. **Follow Steps 1 through 3 in the preceding set of steps.**

2. **Place the base of the knife blade on the left side of the fish, straight across the fillet or block of fish, tilt the knife**

to the right, and slice as smoothly as possible until you complete the cut.

Don't saw the fish apart.

3. **Continue with Step 2 until you have the number of slices you need.**

Slicing transparently thin

Slicing raw fish so sensuously thin that you can see through it *(usu giri),* similar to seeing through thin frosted glass, is a bit tricky to master but doable after a little practice (refer to Figure 7-1). This decorative cut is used mainly on fillets of firm white-fleshed fish such as flounder, sea bream, or red snapper. The slices are fanned out on colorful plates, sashimi-style, or placed on top of sushi, allowing the colors beneath the fish to shimmer through. Here's how you slice transparently thin:

1. **Follow Steps 1 through 3 of "Slicing at an angle," earlier in this chapter.**

2. **Begin your first slice on the left side of the fish by tipping the knife severely to the right, almost horizontal with the fish.**

3. **Lightly place the knife's blade, up toward its base, on the fish and, as smoothly as possible, pull the knife toward you through the fish in one motion, using the entire length of the blade, until you complete the cut.**

4. **Carefully lift and then delicately lay the slice on a pretty plate, sashimi style, or on top of sushi.**

5. **Repeat Steps 1 through 4 until you have all you need.**

Cutting sticks

Think French fries, not deep-fried fish sticks, and you have the size about right for sticks use in sliced rolls and hand rolls, such as the Tuna Sliced Rolls in Chapter 9.

1. **Follow Steps 1 through 4 of the section "Slicing straight down," earlier in this section, making the slices ⅓ to ½ inch thick.**

2. **Cut each slice into ⅓-inch to ½-inch sticks.**

3. **Repeat Steps 1 and 2 until you have all you need.**

Dicing

Diced raw fish *(kaku giri)* is intentionally very small, (⅓ inch or less) for a few reasons: taste, texture, and to fit in sushi, such as hand rolls, or on sushi, such as battleship sushi. You can make the dices larger if you like, as long as they work for the sushi you have in mind. Deep red cubes of blue fin tuna sparkle like rubies piled high in a hand roll, like our Spicy Tuna Hand Rolls in Chapter 8.

1. **Follow Steps 1 through 2 of the section "Cutting sticks," earlier in this chapter, cutting the sticks ⅓ inch wide or less.**

2. **Gently hold a few of these sticks together and then cut across them into dices of ⅓ inch or less.**

3. **Repeat Steps 1 and 2 until you have all you need.**

Working with Fresh Vegetables

Cool, firm, fresh fish is delicious by itself, but a complement of perfectly cut vegetables is always welcome to heighten the experience. A Japanese vegetable knife comes into play (refer to Figure 2-3 in Chapter 2) when you need to cut vegetables different ways for sushi. After you master these techniques, you'll be using these cuts not only in sushi but in all your veggie dishes! With any of the cuts, your goal is precise, smooth, even slices.

Note: We assume that you're right-handed in our directions and illustrations. We use a cucumber to demonstrate all the cuts. Take a moment to practice your cuts on a cucumber or carrot.

Cutting ribbons

Ribbons are long, wide strips of vegetables often used in finger sushi and pressed sushi, such as the Tuna, Cucumber, and Black Sesame Seed Pressed Sushi in Chapter 9. Thin ribbon cuts are the beginning cuts in making slivers and minced vegetables. Thick ribbon cuts are the beginning cuts in matchsticks and cubes.

1. **Start with a 3-inch to 4-inch piece of unpeeled cucumber.**

2. **Depending on your recipe, cut thin (⅛ inch or less) or thicker ribbons, using the front edge of the blade. Push the knife away from you through the cucumber.**

3. **Repeat Steps 1 and 2 until you have all the slices you need.**

CUTTING VEGETABLES: RIBBONS, SLIVERS, MATCHSTICKS

CUT RIBBONS WITH A JAPANESE VEGETABLE KNIFE.

CUT SKINNY, THIN SLIVERS.

CUT THICK RIBBONS (ABOUT ¼ INCH TO ⅓ INCH) INTO MATCH STICKS.

Figure 7-2: Cutting vegetable ribbons, slivers, and matchsticks.

Cutting slivers

Vegetable slivers (refer to Figure 7-2) are used in scattered sushi, hand rolls, sliced rolls, and inside-out rolls, such as the Grilled Shrimp and Thai Basil Inside-Out Roll with Spicy Lime Dipping Sauce in Chapter 11.

1. **Follow Steps 1 and 2 in the preceding section, "Cutting ribbons," making the thinnest possible ribbon cuts (⅛ inch or less).**

2. **Stack the ribbons one on top of the other. Push them out with the palm of one hand, like you'd push out a deck of cards.**

3. **Using the front edge of the blade and pushing the knife away from you, slice the ribbons lengthwise into the thinnest slivers possible until you have all you need.**

Cutting matchsticks

Matchstick cuts (which look like skinny French fries) are used in sliced rolls and hand rolls, such as the daikon radish and cucumber matchsticks we describe in Chapter 14.

1. **Follow Steps 1 and 2 in the "Cutting ribbons" section, earlier in this chapter, making thick (about ¼-inch to ⅓-inch) ribbon cuts.**

2. **Stack the ribbons one on top of the other. Pushing the knife away from you, slice the ribbons lengthwise into ¼-inch to ⅓-inch square sticks (refer to Figure 7-2) until you have all you need.**

Cutting paper-thin slices

When we say "thinly sliced" in a recipe, we mean much thinner than the Western cook is used to seeing. "Paper-thin" in the sushi kitchen means so thin that you could almost blow the paper-thin sliced items, such as scallions, out of their dish with one small puff of breath. Red Snapper Finger Sushi with Spicy Daikon Relish in Chapter 9 makes use of this cut to create paper-thin slices of jalapeño pepper. There's no technique, per se, so just try to achieve the thinnest slices possible. Go slowly at first, to have better control over the thinness of the cut and to protect your fingers.

Dicing

Our sushi recipes use diced vegetables, about ¼ to ⅓ inch thick, suitable for small bites. Diced vegetables are used in battleship sushi, sliced sushi, and hand rolls. Our recipe for Ground Turkey and Vegetable Osaka-Style Scattered Sushi in Chapter 10 uses diced bamboo shoots.

1. **Follow Steps 1 and 2 in the "Cutting matchsticks" section earlier in this chapter.**

2. **Cut across a stack of matchsticks, pushing the knife away from you, forming ¼-inch to ⅓-inch dice until you have all you need.**

Mincing

Mincing means to cut, or chop, vegetables into the smallest pieces possible. Minced vegetables show up everywhere in sushi, from tofu pouches to sliced rolls, hand rolls, and battleship sushi. Guacamole Battleship Sushi in Chapter 9 uses minced onions, cilantro, and serrano chili.

1. **Follow Steps 1 through 3 in the section "Cutting slivers," earlier in this chapter.**

2. **Cut across a small handful of slivers until you have as much as you need.**

Taking advantage of a few shortcut tools

Cutting and slicing by hand is fast and efficient, but sometimes taking shortcuts by using helpful tools besides knives is the way to go. Flip to Chapter 2 for information about where to buy these tools.

Using a Japanese mandoline

Japanese mandoline (see Figure 7-3) is a fancy name for this tabletop vegetable slicer. It creates perfectly uniform cuts, whether ribbons, rounds, or slivers. We use it frequently in our sushi kitchens, such as when we're making the Cucumber and Wakame Salad in Chapter 13. Use according to your mandoline manufacturer's instructions.

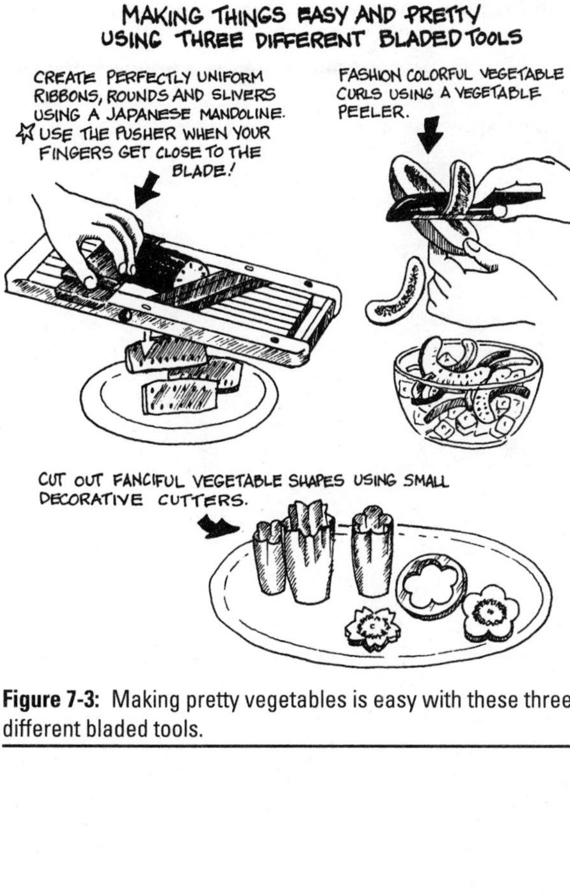

MAKING THINGS EASY AND PRETTY USING THREE DIFFERENT BLADED TOOLS

CREATE PERFECTLY UNIFORM RIBBONS, ROUNDS AND SLIVERS USING A JAPANESE MANDOLINE. ☆ USE THE PUSHER WHEN YOUR FINGERS GET CLOSE TO THE BLADE!

FASHION COLORFUL VEGETABLE CURLS USING A VEGETABLE PEELER.

CUT OUT FANCIFUL VEGETABLE SHAPES USING SMALL DECORATIVE CUTTERS.

Figure 7-3: Making pretty vegetables is easy with these three different bladed tools.

Using a vegetable peeler

A good vegetable peeler (refer to Figure 7-3) can do more to dress up a dish than you might imagine. Use one to create narrow ribbons or slices of vegetables for our tricolor vegetable curls recipe (see Chapter 14), which uses carrots, white daikon radish, and dark-green-edged cucumber. This colorful trio of veggies, when soaked in ice water to crisp and curl them up, makes an attractive addition to a sushi party buffet.

Using decorative cutters

Using decorative cutters is an easy way to add seasonal or playful touches to sushi (refer to Figure 7-3). They give you precise shapes that an untrained hand can't carve. Even sushi chefs use these sharp little molds because they're so convenient and accurate. Small cookie cutters usually aren't sharp or strong enough to cut through firmer vegetables such as carrots or radishes.

Decoratively shaped cut-out vegetables are used in scattered sushi, such as the Ground Turkey and Vegetable Osaka-Style Scattered Sushi in Chapter 10, or whenever you want a decorative look.

Part III

Rock-and-Rollin' Sushi Recipes

"Sticky rice is good to go."

In this part . . .

*C*hances are, the sushi recipe that you'd love to whip up at home is in this part of *Sushi For Dummies*. First up is Chapter 8, devoted to sushi bar favorites that keep sushi bar patrons from coast to coast coming back for more. I (Mineko) have been teaching sushi for years and happily share with you my tried-and-true recipes for these favorites. Each recipe is chock-full of helpful hints for beginners and more-experienced sushi cooks alike.

Chapters 9 through 12 offer up other time-tested sushi recipes that are as fun to prepare as they are delicious. In Chapter 9, we launch into quick-and-easy sushi, knowing that at times you want satisfaction fast. In Chapter 10, we offer do-ahead sushi for those time-crunched moments in life when you want to sidestep the last-minute rush. Chapter 11 focuses on chi-chi sushi, when fancy occasions require a little something extra in elegance and imagination. Finally, in Chapter 12, we cook up some extreme sushi that blows away any thoughts that sushi is limited in taste, texture, or presentation.

Chapter 8

Creating Sushi Bar Favorites at Home

In This Chapter

▶ Focusing on raw seafood

▶ Savoring cooked seafood sushi

▶ Staying cool with crisp cucumber sushi

*I*f you haven't eaten sushi in a sushi bar and are dying to know what all the excitement's about, look no further. The nine sushi bar recipes in this chapter hold the answer, shouting loud and clear that it's all about taste, texture, adventure, and visual appeal. Eight of the nine recipes focus on seafood, some of it raw, such as the classic sushi bar favorite Tuna Finger Sushi, and some of it cooked, such as the crunchy and wonderful Shrimp Tempura Inside-Out Rolls. The ninth recipe, Cucumber Sliced Rolls, is exquisite for its simple, clean, refreshing flavor, a perfect counterpoint to seafood sushi items.

If you're new to the sushi scene, we encourage you to read Chapters 4 through 7 before attempting the recipes in this chapter. Or at least be prepared to flip between chapters the first few times you whip up your favorite recipes. But once you have the hang of it, you won't be flipping around again. Mastering sushi quickly becomes second nature, just like assembling and tossing a salad.

Sushi bars vary these recipes to suit their customers' tastes, just as you can vary them to suit yours.

Adventuring into Raw Seafood

Ask sushi bar patrons what their favorite thing to eat at a sushi bar is, and most of them will say raw fish. Good sushi bars excel at procuring the very best and freshest seafood that the fishmongers have to offer. You must show the same care when selecting, transporting, and handling raw seafood (see Chapter 4) that the sushi chef does. If you do, enjoying the adventure of making raw seafood favorites at home will make you happy, too!

Tuna Finger Sushi

There's something startlingly wonderful about the cold, velvety smoothness and rich taste of raw tuna against the chewiness and clean flavor of sushi rice, which is why Tuna Finger Sushi *(maguro no nigiri-zushi)* is such a big hit in sushi bars. If you're new to sushi, finger sushi is oblong, bite-size rice balls topped with raw or cooked seafood or whatever strikes the sushi chef's or patron's fancy. See Chapter 4 for other kinds of fresh seafood, besides tuna, that's suitable for eating raw on top of finger sushi.

Special sushi tools: *Sashimi knife (see Chapter 2)*

Preparation time: *8 minutes, plus 1½ hours to prepare the sushi rice*

Yield: *8 finger sushi*

1 cup prepared sushi rice (see Chapter 5)	*⅓ pound block sashimi-grade raw tuna*
½ teaspoon wasabi paste, or to taste (see Chapter 3)	*Soy sauce*
	Pickled ginger

1 Prepare 8 finger sushi (see Chapter 6), using the sushi rice. Lightly dab as little or as much wasabi paste as you like across the top of each finger sushi.

2 Slice the tuna at an angle (see Chapter 7) into 8 slender slices, each one approximately ⅛ inch thick and ½ to ¾ ounce. Wipe your knife with a damp paper towel before each slice.

3 Drape a slice of tuna lengthwise over the top of each finger sushi.

4 To give the tuna finger sushi a finished look, lay a damp paper towel over the tuna and gently press the fish and rice ball together, not squishing them. Serve immediately with soy sauce and pickled ginger.

Vary it! *Garnish each finger sushi with a touch of salmon roe for a very pretty finish (as shown in the color insert).*

Per finger sushi: *Calories 77 (From Fat 2); Fat 0g (Saturated 0g); Cholesterol 8mg; Sodium 1,297mg; Carbohydrate 10g (Dietary Fiber 1g); Protein 7g.*

Spicy Tuna Hand Rolls

Hand rolls are in the winner's circle for sushi lovers because they're so crisp, tasty, and easy to make and eat. Here, the tastes are kept simple by using fresh tuna and just enough spicy mayonnaise sauce to lift the tuna's flavor. When making hand rolls, buy the highest-quality nori you can afford because the nori is such a dominant part of a hand roll's taste and texture. Although nori is sold roasted, we always reroast the nori just before using it to crisp it up and refresh its flavors.

Preparation time: *10 minutes, plus 1½ hours to prepare the sushi rice*

Yield: *4 hand rolls*

1½ teaspoons mayonnaise

1½ teaspoons thick, hot chili sauce, or to taste

⅛ teaspoon hot sesame oil (rayu), or to taste

¼ pound block sashimi-grade raw tuna, diced

2 sheets nori, reroasted (see Chapter 3)

1 cup prepared sushi rice (see Chapter 5)

Soy sauce

Pickled ginger

1 Prepare the spicy mayonnaise by stirring together the mayonnaise, hot chili sauce, and hot sesame oil in a bowl.

2 Add the diced tuna (see Chapter 7) to the bowl, turning it over to coat it well. Refrigerate the tuna if you're not using it right away.

3 Cut the nori sheets in half, forming 4-x-7-inch half sheets.

4 Place a half sheet of nori in the palm of your left hand, shiny side down. Dip your right hand in a bowl of vinegared water and then tap your fingers on a damp towel to remove excess water. Place about ¼ cup of the sushi rice on the nori, toward the top portion of the nori, patting the rice out in a diagonal, from the top area of the nori toward the heel of your palm (refer to Figure 6-8 in Chapter 6).

5 Spoon one-fourth of the spicy tuna onto the rice. Fold the bottom left corner of the nori over the fillings and then continue rolling to the right until you have a cone-shaped roll (refer to Figure 6-8 in Chapter 6). Make 3 more hand rolls, following these instructions. Serve immediately with soy sauce as a dipping sauce, and pickled ginger to cleanse the palate.

Per hand roll: *Calories 133 (From Fat 17); Fat 2g (Saturated 0g); Cholesterol 14mg; Sodium 1,409mg; Carbohydrate 17g (Dietary Fiber 1g); Protein 10g.*

Spicy Scallop Hand Rolls

It's a toss-up for us as to which hand roll we like better, this one or the Spicy Tuna Hand Rolls offered earlier in the chapter. Both are spicy, but in different ways because the heat comes from different sources, chili sauce in the tuna recipe, and wasabi here. Both feature raw seafood, but the meaty flavor of raw tuna is quite different from the sweetness of scallops. Be careful not to overpower the delicate sweetness of the scallops with too much wasabi.

Preparation time: *10 minutes, plus 1½ hours to prepare the sushi rice*

Yield: *4 hand rolls*

¼ pound sashimi-grade sea scallops

1 tablespoon mayonnaise

¼ teaspoon wasabi paste, or to taste (see Chapter 3)

4 teaspoons smelt roe (masago)

2 sheets nori, reroasted (see Chapter 3)

1 cup prepared sushi rice (see Chapter 5)

1 ounce daikon radish sprouts (kaiware) or other radish sprouts, rinsed, patted dry, and trimmed of their roots

Soy sauce

Pickled ginger

1 Take the raw scallops out of the refrigerator just when needed. Rinse, drain, and pat them dry with paper towels. Dice the scallops (see Chapter 7) into one-third ⅓-inch pieces.

2 Stir the mayonnaise and wasabi paste together in a medium-size bowl until smooth. Gently fold the smelt roe and diced sea scallops into the wasabi mayonnaise. Refrigerate if not using immediately.

3 Cut the nori sheets in half, forming 4-x-7-inch half sheets.

4 Place a half sheet of nori in the palm of your left hand, shiny side down. Dip your right hand in a bowl of vinegared water then tap your fingers on a damp towel to remove excess water. Place about ¼ cup of the sushi rice on the nori, toward the top portion of the nori, patting the rice out in a diagonal, from the top area of the nori toward the heel of your palm (refer to Figure 6-8 in Chapter 6).

5 Lay one-fourth of the sprouts on top of the rice, letting some of their little leaves stick out of the nori for looks. Spoon one-fourth of the spicy scallop mixture onto the sprouts.

6 Fold the bottom left corner of the nori over the fillings and then continue rolling to the right until you have a cone-shaped roll (refer to Figure 6-8 in Chapter 6). Serve immediately with soy sauce as a dipping sauce, and pickled ginger to cleanse the palate. Make 3 more hand rolls, following these instructions.

Vary It! *Substitute watercress for the daikon sprouts. Both possess a refreshing, peppery taste.*

Tip: *Host a hand-rolls-only party (see Chapter 14) and serve these scallop hand rolls along with three other, very different tasting hand rolls: Spicy Tuna Hand Rolls in this chapter and the Mexican Hand Rolls and the Roast Beef and Watercress Hand Rolls, both in Chapter 9.*

Per hand roll: *Calories 155 (From Fat 38); Fat 4g (Saturated 1g); Cholesterol 43mg; Sodium 1,461mg; Carbohydrate 18g (Dietary Fiber 1g); Protein 10g.*

Rainbow Inside-Out Rolls

As pretty as they are scrumptious, the Rainbow Inside-Out Rolls are ambitious to make at home. But the effort is worth it if you love raw seafood like millions of other people do. Inside is *kani kama* (imitation crab) and crisp cucumber. Covering the outside of our version of this roll are slices of ruby red tuna, creamy white red snapper, and coral-colored salmon, alternated with slices of green avocado for a change in taste, texture, and color. Making this type of roll for the first time can be fun but challenging, so be sure to read the insider details leading to success when making inside-out rolls in Chapter 6.

The selection of fish is entirely up to you, but remember to select different colors for looks and taste. (See Chapter 4 for information on sashimi-grade fish.) What's important is that you wind up with 16 slices of raw fish (4 slices per roll), each slice about ½ ounce and measuring 1 inch x 2 inches x ⅛-inch thick. To get this amount, you need to buy a little more of each fish than is actually used in the recipe.

Special sushi tools: *Bamboo mat covered in plastic wrap, sashimi knife (see Chapter 2)*

Preparation time: *45 minutes, plus 1½ hours to prepare the sushi rice*

Yield: *4 inside-out rolls (24 pieces)*

4 ounces sashimi-grade tuna	8 teaspoons reroasted white sesame seeds (see Chapter 3)
2 ounces sashimi-grade salmon	
2 ounces sashimi-grade red snapper	2 teaspoons wasabi paste, or to taste (see Chapter 3)
4 ounces kani kama (imitation crab), preferably leg-style	1 avocado, peeled and sliced lengthwise into thin (⅛-inch) slices
1 Japanese cucumber, salt-scrubbed (see Chapter 3)	Soy sauce
2 sheets nori	Pickled ginger
4 cups prepared sushi rice (see Chapter 5)	

(continued)

(continued)

1 Slice the tuna at an angle (see Chapter 7) into eight ⅛-inch-thick slices. Slice both the salmon and red snapper at an angle into four ⅛-inch-thick slices each. Cover and refrigerate the slices until needed.

2 Split the *kani kama* into strips. Trim the cucumber's ends, making it 7 inches in length. Cut it into quarters, lengthwise (see Figure 8-1). Refrigerate the *kani kama* and cucumber quarters until needed.

3 Cut each sheet of nori in half, making each sheet 4 inches x 7 inches. Place a plastic-wrapped bamboo mat in front of you, with its slats parallel to the edge of the table or countertop. Place a trimmed sheet of nori lengthwise, shiny side down, on the edge of the bamboo mat closest to you (refer to Figure 6-7 in Chapter 6). Dip your hands in a bowl of vinegared water and then tap your fingertips on a damp towel to remove the excess water. Press 1 cup of the sushi rice evenly over the nori. Sprinkle 2 teaspoons of sesame seeds over the rice.

4 Pick up the nori, turn it over, and place it rice side down, lengthwise, on the edge of the bamboo mat closest to you.

5 Fill the roll in this order: Spread ½ teaspoon of the wasabi paste across the length of the nori, not in the exact center, but a little closer to you. Cover the wasabi with a slice of cucumber. Bunch one-fourth of the *kani kama* next to the cucumber. (Bunching makes it easier to roll up the sushi roll.)

6 Lift the edge of the mat closest to you with both hands, keeping your fingers over the fillings, and roll the mat and its contents until the edge of the mat touches straight down onto the nori, enclosing the fillings completely. Lift up the edge of the mat you're holding, and continue rolling the inside-out roll away from you until it's sealed (refer to Figure 6-7 in Chapter 6). Tug on the mat to tighten the seal. Place the roll on a damp, clean, smooth surface.

7 Gently place 2 slices of tuna, 1 slice of salmon, 1 slice of red snapper, and up to one-fourth of the avocado in an alternating, diagonal pattern, overlapping each other, across the length of the roll. Lay the bamboo mat over the completed roll. Squeeze gently to give it shape (see Figure 8-2).

8 Lay a sheet of plastic wrap over the roll. Slice the roll into 6 equal, bite-size pieces, wiping your knife with a damp paper towel between each slice. Discard the plastic wrap. Make 3 more rolls, following these steps. Serve immediately, accompanied by soy sauce as a dipping sauce, and pickled ginger to cleanse the palate.

Per piece: Calories 105 (From Fat 18); Fat 2g (Saturated 0g); Cholesterol 9mg; Sodium 1,349mg; Carbohydrate 14g (Dietary Fiber 2g); Protein 7g.

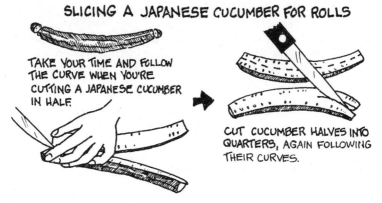

Figure 8-1: Slicing a Japanese cucumber for rolls.

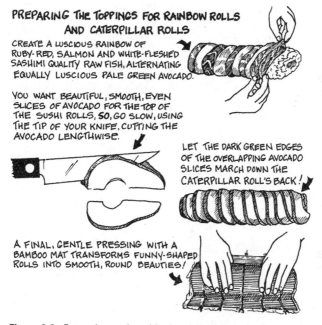

Figure 8-2: Preparing and positioning the toppings for the Rainbow Inside-Out Rolls and Caterpillar Inside-Out Rolls.

Savoring Cooked Seafood

Applying heat to fish and shellfish changes their taste, texture, and appearance dramatically, enticing everyone who loves seafood into the kitchen to cook. We've chosen four of the most popular cooked seafood sushi bar recipes for you to whip up in your kitchen. The Caterpillar Inside-Out Rolls are a vision in green, completely topped with avocado slices. The Shrimp Tempura Inside-Out Rolls are speckled beauties highlighting white sesame seeds coating the rolls' rice exterior. The ever popular California Inside-Out Rolls showcase cooked crab on the inside and, for those who don't mind a touch of raw seafood, flavorful smelt roe, too. Finally, the Shrimp Finger Sushi is simplicity itself in looks: one plump, rosy-colored shrimp on each sushi rice ball.

Caterpillar Inside-Out Rolls

Lovely to look at in its pleated green robe of avocado, this Caterpillar Inside-Out Roll contains a secret ingredient — barbecued freshwater eel. It is sold in packages of one freshwater eel *(unagi)* that's been butterflied, grilled, and covered in a sweet barbecue sauce. Barbecued *unagi* looks something like a slender, brown butterflied trout. It tastes deliciously rich, a little like pork. Squeamish? Just go for it, join the sushi adventure, and you'll taste why Caterpillar Rolls rule!

Although glazing sauce comes packaged with the eel, making your own is easy and gives better results. The homemade sauce is used as an additional glaze for the eel and to drizzle over the completed roll when it's served. If you make the Glazed Barbecued Eel and the sushi rice in advance, these 4 rolls take about 30 minutes to make. Be sure to read the details leading to success when making inside-out rolls in Chapter 6.

Special sushi tools: *Bamboo mat wrapped in plastic wrap, sashimi knife (see Chapter 2)*

Preparation time: *1 hour, plus 1½ hours to prepare the sushi rice*

Cooking time: *3 minutes (broiling the eel)*

Yield: *4 inside-out rolls (24 pieces)*

1 Japanese cucumber, salt-scrubbed (see Chapter 3)	*1 Glazed Barbecued Eel (see the following recipe)*
2 sheets nori	*Japanese pepper (sansho)*
4 cups prepared sushi rice (see Chapter 5)	*2 large avocados*
	Pickled ginger

1 Trim the ends of the cucumber, making it 7 inches in length. Cut it lengthwise into quarters (refer to Figure 8-1). If the cucumber is over 1 inch wide, slice it into sixths (by cutting each half into thirds).

2 Cut each sheet of nori in half, making each one 4 inches x 7 inches. Place a plastic-wrapped bamboo mat in front of you, with its slats parallel to the edge of the table or countertop. Lay a 4-x-7-inch sheet of nori lengthwise, shiny side down, on the edge of the wrapped bamboo mat closest to you (refer to Figure 6-7 in Chapter 6). Dip your hands in a bowl of vinegared water and then tap your fingertips on a damp towel to remove excess water. Press 1 cup of the sushi rice evenly over the nori. Pick up the rice-covered nori, turn it over, and place it rice side down, lengthwise, on the edge of the bamboo mat closest to you.

3 Fill the roll in this order: Lay 1 piece of eel across the length of the nori, not in the exact center, but a little closer to you, folding the tail piece in if it hangs way over the edge of the nori. Bunch a cucumber stick next to the eel. Season with *sansho* to taste.

4 Lift the edge of the mat closest to you with both hands, keeping your fingertips over the fillings, and roll the mat and its contents until the edge of the mat touches straight down on the nori, enclosing the fillings completely. Lift up the edge of the mat you're holding, and continue rolling the inside-out roll away from you until it's sealed. Tug on the mat to tighten the seal (refer to Figure 6-7 in Chapter 6). Place the roll on a damp, clean, smooth surface. You're now ready to peel and slice one of the avocados, lengthwise, and decorate the top of the roll.

5 Cover the whole top of the roll with overlapping slices of avocado (refer to Figure 8-2), slicing the avocado slowly to achieve smooth, even, slender, ⅛-inch-thick slices. Lay the plastic-wrapped bamboo mat over the avocado-covered roll. Squeeze very gently to shape the roll. Don't press too hard or the mat will make indentations in the avocado slices.

6 Lay a sheet of plastic wrap over the roll. Slice the roll into 6 equal, bite-size pieces, wiping your knife with a damp towel before each slice. Discard the plastic wrap. Make 3 more rolls, following these instructions. Serve with the remainder of the homemade eel glazing sauce and pickled ginger.

Glazed Barbecued Eel

3 tablespoons soy sauce

3 tablespoons mirin (sweet sake)

1 tablespoon sugar

1 tablespoon sake (rice wine)

Japanese pepper (sansho)

1 package (6 to 7 ounces) freshwater eel (unagi), barbecued

1 Make a glazing sauce by combining the soy sauce, mirin, sugar, and sake in a small pot. Simmer over medium heat for 10 to 12 minutes, until the sauce achieves a syrupy consistency. Watch carefully not to burn this sauce or it becomes bitter. Remove the sauce from the heat and add the *sansho* to taste. Set aside.

(continued)

(continued)

2 Slice the barbecued eel into 4 lengthwise pieces and lay them out on a baking sheet covered with aluminum foil. Broil the eel, meaty side up, until the packaged glaze on the eel begins to bubble, a minute or two at most. Remove the eel from the broiler. Brush the top of the hot eel with a little of the homemade glazing sauce, saving most of the sauce to serve with the Caterpillar Rolls.

Vary It! *If eel's not your thing, substitute ½ pound sliced teriyaki chicken (see Chapter 10). In either case, be playful and stick two sprouts of daikon radish sprouts into the top of this very green roll to resemble caterpillar antennas.*

Per piece: *Calories 112 (From Fat 35); Fat 4g (Saturated 1g); Cholesterol 14mg; Sodium 495mg; Carbohydrate 14g (Dietary Fiber 2g); Protein 3g.*

Shrimp Tempura Inside-Out Rolls

Crunchy is good, shrimp is good, and these two things together are great! This inside-out roll takes a bit of time, but boy, is it worth it. Break up the work by preparing the sushi rice, frying the shrimp, and slicing the cucumber ahead of time. That way, the last-minute push to assemble the 4 rolls takes only 30 minutes. It's my (Judi's) favorite roll. Chapter 6 explains all about making inside-out rolls.

Special sushi tools: *Bamboo mat wrapped with plastic wrap, deep-fat thermometer, sashimi knife (see Chapter 2)*

Preparation time: *45 minutes, plus 1½ hours to prepare the sushi rice*

Cooking time: *15 minutes*

Yield: *4 inside-out rolls (24 pieces)*

8 Shrimp Tempura (see the following recipe)	*4 cups prepared sushi rice (see Chapter 5)*
1 ounce (one-third package) daikon radish sprouts (kaiware) or other radish sprouts	*8 teaspoons reroasted white sesame seeds (see Chapter 3)*
	2 teaspoons wasabi paste, or to taste (see Chapter 3)
½ Japanese cucumber	*Soy sauce*
½ avocado	*Pickled ginger*
4 sheets nori	

1 Prepare the Shrimp Tempura. Rinse, dry, and trim the daikon radish sprouts. Sliver the cucumber (see Chapter 7) and, when you're ready to make the rolls, peel and slice the avocado.

2 Cut a 3-inch-wide strip off each sheet of nori, making each one 5 inches x 7 inches. Lay a plastic-wrapped bamboo mat in front of you, with its slats parallel to the edge of the table or countertop. Place a trimmed sheet of nori lengthwise, shiny side down, on the edge of the bamboo mat closest to you (refer to Figure 6-7 in Chapter 6). Dip your fingers in a bowl of vinegared water and then tap your fingertips on a damp towel to remove excess water. Press 1 cup of prepared sushi rice evenly over the nori. Sprinkle 2 teaspoons of sesame seeds over the rice.

3 Pick up the rice-covered nori, turn it over, and place it, rice side down and lengthwise, on the edge of the bamboo mat closest to you.

4 Fill the roll in this order: Spread one-fourth of the wasabi paste across the length of the nori, not in the exact center, but a little closer to you. Cover the wasabi with one-fourth of the daikon sprouts, letting some of the leaves extend out of the ends of the nori. Place one-fourth of the cucumber slivers on top of the sprouts. Bunch 2 Shrimp Tempura, laid out so that their tails stick out of the opposite ends of the nori, next to the cucumber. Lay one-fourth of the avocado slices against the shrimp, as close together as possible.

5 Lift the edge of the mat closest to you with both hands, keeping your fingertips over the fillings, and roll the mat and its contents until the edge of the mat touches straight down on the nori, enclosing the fillings completely. Lift up the edge of the mat you're holding, and continue rolling the inside-out roll away from you until it's sealed. Tug on the mat to tighten the seal (refer to Figure 6-7 in Chapter 6). Place the roll on a damp, clean, smooth surface.

6 Lay a sheet of plastic wrap over the roll. Slice the roll into 6 bite-size pieces, wiping your knife with a damp towel before each slice. Discard the plastic wrap. Make 3 more rolls, following these instructions. Serve with soy sauce as a dipping sauce, and pickled ginger to cleanse the palate.

Shrimp Tempura

8 large shrimp (about ½ ounce each), peeled and tails left on

¼ cup plus 2 tablespoons commercial tempura mix

¼ cup cold water or cold beer

1 quart rice bran oil or corn or canola oil

1 Using a sharp paring knife, remove any visible vein running down the shrimp's back. Rinse the shrimp well under cold running water and then pat them dry with a paper towel. Make 3 to 4 shallow slits on the underside of each shrimp to keep them from curling when deep-fried, and cut off the tips of the tail shells (they can hold water that spatters when frying), as shown in Figure 8-3.

(continued)

(continued)

2 Sift ¼ cup of the tempura mix onto the cold water or beer. Using chopsticks or a fork, stir the tempura mix into the water or beer, but just briefly, only enough to combine the ingredients; the mixture should be lumpy. Put the remaining 2 tablespoons of dry tempura mix on a plate.

3 Using a deep fryer or a 2-quart or larger heavy pan set over medium heat, heat the oil to 350 degrees, as indicated on a deep-fat thermometer, and hold it there throughout deep-frying the shrimp.

4 Pick up a shrimp by the tail, dredge it through the dry tempura mix, and dip it into the tempura batter, lightly coating it. Slide in 3 or 4 shrimp and fry until the tempura batter is crisp and golden, about 1 minute. Drain them on paper towels. Cook the rest of the shrimp in the same manner.

Per piece: Calories 96 (From Fat 17); Fat 2g (Saturated 0g); Cholesterol 4mg; Sodium 1,322mg; Carbohydrate 15g (Dietary Fiber 2g); Protein 4g.

CUTTING SLITS IN THE SHRIMP—
TRIMMING THE TAILS FOR SHRIMP TEMPURA ROLLS

BE SURE TO CUT OFF THE TIPS OF THE SHRIMP'S TAIL, RELEASING ANY TRAPPED WATER THAT MIGHT SPLATTER IN THE HOT OIL!

CUT SHALLOW SLITS IN THE BELLY OF THE SHRIMP SO IT STAYS STRAIGHT WHEN DEEP FRIED, MAKING IT EASY TO ROLL UP INSIDE THE ROLL.

Figure 8-3: Preparing the shrimp for Shrimp Tempura Rolls.

California Inside-Out Rolls

Some people say that this inside-out roll was invented in Los Angeles during the early 1960s to counter the reservations that some people new to sushi bars might have about raw fish. Reservations have given way to raves of acceptance today, but this hasn't slowed down this cooked crab roll's popularity. In our recipe, we use imitation crabmeat, *kani kama* (made of cooked pollock), because it's tasty, available year-round, and affordable and splits into convenient, straight strips, making it easy to roll up. Smelt roe, although raw, is so popular as an optional ingredient in this cooked seafood roll that we've added it. But you can eliminate it, if you like, and still have a great tasting roll. If you've not done so, please read the helpful information on making inside-out rolls in Chapter 6.

Special sushi tools: *Bamboo mat wrapped with plastic wrap, sashimi knife (see Chapter 2)*

Preparation time: *45 minutes, plus 1½ hours to prepare the sushi rice*

Yield: *4 inside-out rolls (24 pieces)*

1 ounce (¼ cup) smelt roe (masago)	1 avocado
2 tablespoons mayonnaise	4 sheets nori
2 tablespoons thinly sliced scallions	4 cups prepared sushi rice (see Chapter 5)
½ Japanese cucumber, salt-scrubbed (see Chapter 3)	8 teaspoons reroasted white sesame seeds (see Chapter 3)
1 ounce daikon sprouts (kaiware) or other radish sprouts	Soy sauce
4 ounces kani kama (imitation crabmeat), preferably leg-style	Pickled ginger

1 Make a smelt roe mayonnaise for the inside of the rolls by gently stirring the smelt roe, mayonnaise, and sliced scallions together in a small bowl. Refrigerate if not used right away.

2 Sliver the cucumber (see Chapter 7). Rinse, dry, and trim the roots off the daikon sprouts. Split 4 leg-style pieces (each 3-inch to 4-inch-long piece weighs about 1 ounce) of *kani kama* in half lengthwise. Peel and slice the avocado just before making the rolls, not ahead of time, to avoid discoloration.

3 Cut a 3-inch-wide strip off each sheet of nori, making them 5 inches x 7 inches. Lay a plastic-wrapped bamboo mat in front of you, with its slats parallel to the edge of the table or countertop. Place a trimmed sheet of nori lengthwise, shiny side down, on the edge of the bamboo mat closest to you (refer to Figure 6-7 in Chapter 6). Dip your hands in a bowl of vinegared water and then tap your fingertips on a damp towel next to you to remove excess water. Press 1 cup of prepared sushi rice evenly over the nori. Sprinkle 2 teaspoons of reroasted sesame seeds over the rice.

4 Pick up the nori, turn it over, and place it rice side down, lengthwise, on the edge of the bamboo mat closest to you.

(continued)

(continued)

5 Fill the roll in this order: Spread one-fourth of the smelt roe mayonnaise sauce across the length of the nori, not in the exact center, but a little closer to you. Cover the sauce with one-fourth of the radish sprouts, letting some of their little leaves extend out of the ends of the nori. Lay one-fourth of the *kani kama* on top of the sprouts. Bunch one-fourth of the slivered cucumber as close to the *kani kama* as possible. Lay one-fourth of the avocado slices as close to the other fillings as possible.

6 Lift the edge of the mat closest to you with both hands, keeping your fingertips over the fillings, and roll the mat and its contents until the edge of the mat touches straight down on the nori, enclosing the fillings completely. Lift up the edge of the mat you're holding, and continue rolling the inside-out roll away from you until it is sealed. Tug on the mat to tighten the seal (refer to Figure 6-7 in Chapter 6). Place the roll on a damp, clean, smooth surface. Lay a sheet of plastic wrap over the roll. Slice the roll into 6 equal bite-size pieces, wiping your knife with a damp towel before each slice. Discard the plastic wrap.

7 Make 3 more rolls, following Steps 3 through 6. Serve slices as an appetizer, or serve one whole sliced roll per person as a light meal. Accompany it with soy sauce as a dipping sauce, and pickled ginger to cleanse the palate.

Vary It! *If cooked crabmeat is available, by all means use it. Or, fill the roll with just luscious avocado for a vegetarian treat (as shown in the color insert).*

Tip: *Cover and refrigerate leftover slices overnight and then pop them into a toaster oven and toast them for a hot, crispy sushi snack.*

Per piece: *Calories 100 (From Fat 25); Fat 3g (Saturated 1g); Cholesterol 9mg; Sodium 1,357mg; Carbohydrate 14g (Dietary Fiber 2g); Protein 4g.*

Shrimp Finger Sushi

Shrimp Finger Sushi *(ebi no nigiri-zushi)* is a beloved sushi bar staple. The trick to pleasantly chewy, but not tough, boiled shrimp is boiling them just long enough to cook through, no more. Threading a skewer into the shrimp ensures that they cook straight.

Special sushi tools: *6- to 8-inch bamboo skewers*

Preparation time: *15 minutes, plus 1½ hours to prepare the sushi rice*

Cooking time: *3 minutes*

Yield: *8 finger sushi*

1 cup prepared sushi rice (Chapter 5)   *Soy sauce*

8 jumbo shrimp (¾ ounce each), in their   *Pickled ginger*
shells

½ teaspoon wasabi paste, or to taste
(see Chapter 3)

1 Prepare 8 finger sushi (see Chapter 6), using the sushi rice. Set aside, covered, in a cool place. Bring a pot of salted water to a boil (for cooking the shrimp).

2 Run a bamboo skewer through each shrimp from the head to the tail end, coming in just under the bottom shell (see Figure 8-4). Cook them in the boiling salted water for about 3 minutes, just until cooked through. Immediately plunge them into ice water to stop the cooking.

3 Drain and dry the shrimp. Twist the skewers out of the shrimp and peel off the shells. Butterfly each shrimp, starting from the tail toward the head.

4 Dab wasabi paste on the top of the rice balls. Drape a butterflied shrimp over the top of each sushi rice ball. Give them a finished look by laying a damp paper towel over the shrimp, gently pressing the shrimp and rice ball together. Serve with soy sauce and pickled ginger.

Per finger sushi: *Calories 78 (From Fat 3); Fat 0g (Saturated 0g); Cholesterol 42mg; Sodium 1,338mg; Carbohydrate 10g (Dietary Fiber 1g); Protein 7g.*

SKEWERING AND BUTTERFLYING SHRIMP
FOR SHRIMP FINGER SUSHI

1. SLIDE A SHARP BAMBOO SKEWER INTO THE SHRIMP FROM THE HEAD-END TO THE TAIL-END, JUST UNDER THE SHELL, SO THE SHRIMP BOILS UP NICE AND STRAIGHT.

2. BUTTERFLY THE BELLY SIDE OF THE BOILED SHRIMP FROM THE TAIL-END TO THE HEAD-END SO IT LIES FLAT ON THE RICE BALL. BE <u>CAREFUL</u> NOT TO CUT ALL THE WAY THROUGH!

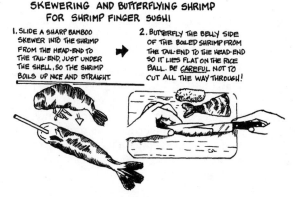

Figure 8-4: Skewering and butterflying shrimp for Shrimp Finger Sushi.

Refreshing Your Sushi Palate with Japanese Cucumbers

Flavorful, Japanese cucumbers (see Chapter 3) aren't watery, making them the perfect cucumber for sushi. You don't want wet cucumbers, or any wet ingredients for that matter, coming in contact with sushi rice or the rice gets unpleasantly soggy.

 ## Cucumber Sliced Rolls

Cucumber Sliced Rolls *(kappa-maki)* are a time-honored favorite on sushi bar menus around the world. They're thin sliced rolls, consisting of a half sheet of nori and only one filling ingredient, making the quality of that ingredient paramount. We explain all you need to know about sliced rolls in Chapter 6.

Special sushi tools: *Bamboo mat, sashimi knife (see Chapter 2)*

Preparation time: *25 minutes, plus 1½ hours to prepare the sushi rice*

Yield: *4 thin rolls (24 pieces)*

1 Japanese cucumber, salt-scrubbed (see Chapter 3)	*2 teaspoons reroasted white sesame seeds (see Chapter 3)*
2 sheets nori	*Soy sauce*
2 cups prepared sushi rice (see Chapter 5)	*Pickled ginger*
2 teaspoons wasabi paste, or to taste (see Chapter 3)	

1 Trim the cucumber to 7 inches long. Cut it into quarters, lengthwise (refer to Figure 8-1), or cut lengthwise into six slices if the cucumber is more than 1 inch wide.

2 Cut each sheet of nori in half, making each one 4 inches x 7 inches. Lay a bamboo mat in front of you, with the bamboo slats parallel to the edge of the table or countertop. Place a half sheet of nori lengthwise, shiny side down, on the edge of the mat closest to you. Dip your hands in a bowl of vinegared water and then tap your fingertips on a damp towel to remove excess water. Spread ½ cup of rice evenly on the nori, leaving a ½-inch strip of nori not covered with rice on the edge farthest away from you (refer to Figure 6-5 in Chapter 6).

3 Season the rice with one-fourth of the wasabi, sprinkle on one-fourth of the sesame seeds, and then lay a stick of cucumber in the center of the rice. Lift up the edge of the mat closest to you, keeping your fingertips on the cucumber, and roll the mat and its contents away from you until the edge of the mat touches straight down on the far edge of the rice (refer to Figure 6-6 in Chapter 6). Tug on the mat to tighten the roll. Lay the mat down on the counter and move the partially done roll back to the edge of the mat closest to you. Lift the mat again and finish rolling up the cucumber roll. Tug on the mat to tighten the seal.

4 Cut the roll into 6 equal pieces, wiping your knife with a damp towel before each slice. Make 3 more rolls, following Steps 2 through 4. Serve with soy sauce as a dipping sauce, and pickled ginger to cleanse your palate.

Vary It! *Sliver the cucumber for a different look and texture. Or, fill the roll with a slender assortment of colorful slivered vegetables such as carrot, cucumber, and red bell pepper (as shown in the color insert).*

Per piece: *Calories 49 (From Fat 2); Fat 0g (Saturated 0g); Cholesterol 0mg; Sodium 1,285mg; Carbohydrate 8g (Dietary Fiber 1g); Protein 3g.*

Left: Cucumber Sliced Roll (Chapter 8) made with slivered red pepper, carrot, and cucumber
Center: Tuna Sliced Roll (Chapter 9) made with salt-grilled salmon (Chapter 14)
Right: California Inside-Out Roll (Chapter 8)
© *FoodPix*

Salmon Roe Battleship Sushi (Chapter 9)
©Kazu/Alamy

Shrimp Finger Sushi (Chapter 8)
©Kazu/Alamy

Tuna Finger Sushi (Chapter 8) made with salmon roe garnish
©StockFood/FoodCollection

Assortment of hand rolls from a
hand roll sushi party (Chapter 14)
© Getty Images

This splendid sushi buffet includes Avocado
and Tapenade Finger Sushi (Chapter 11)
made without tapenade, Shrimp Finger
Sushi (Chapter 8), and Salmon Roe
Battleship Sushi (Chapter 9).
©Steve Hamblin/Alamy

Chapter 9

Quick-and-Easy Sushi: Finger-Snapping Fast Recipes

In This Chapter

▶ Digging into veggies at the sushi table

▶ Satisfying seafood cravings

▶ Giving in to meat and poultry cravings

*L*et us guess — your life is hectic with work, school, social obligations, and maybe kids, and you're looking for quick-and-easy sushi recipes to save you time and energy. Well, look no further! The recipes in this chapter are a snap: They employ easy sushi techniques, tend to take less time than more complex sushi recipes, use fewer ingredients than many sushi recipes, and use ingredients that, with a few exceptions, are available in your local grocery store.

But, we don't want to mislead you into thinking quick-and-easy recipes in the kingdom of sushi are as quick-and-easy as opening a can of soup (although we do open cans in Hawaiian-Style Spam and Pineapple Pressed Sushi). Every sushi recipe requires properly prepared sushi rice, which takes about 1½ hours to make, most of the time spent letting the rice soak or cook (see Chapter 5). But if you prepare it early in the day, or do a lot of other things — chop the ingredients and set the table — during the soaking (30 minutes) and cooking (20 to 25 minutes) phases, you'll speed things along considerably. Quicker yet, make use of sushi rice you've frozen, as explained in Chapter 5, and you'll have sushi on the table promptly.

If sushi is new to you, peruse Chapters 4 through 7 before you tackle the recipes in this chapter. If you start there, you're bound to be a sushi pro in no time at all.

Assembling Simple Veggie Sushi

Tofu (soybean curd) and tropical fruits are highlighted in our three vegetarian quick-and-easy sushi recipes. All the ingredients (except for nori) used in these three recipes are familiar and available at grocery stores. In one recipe, slices of tofu soak up a fragrant citrus sauce; sticks of mango, jicama, and cucumber make for a colorful and refreshing Mexican-style hot weather hand roll in another; and in the third recipe, guacamole, everybody's favorite avocado dip, comes out on top of battleship sushi.

 Tofu Finger Sushi with Ponzu Sauce

Tofu is a source of cholesterol-free protein for not only vegetarians but also for anyone who's captivated by its subtle taste, custardlike texture, and ability to absorb flavors. Ponzu sauce, a citrus-flavored soy sauce, is frequently served with milder fish and vegetable sushi along with freshly grated gingerroot. To save time, have the tofu draining in the fridge, the finger sushi and ponzu sauce prepared, the nori strips and scallions cut, and the ginger grated. Then assembling these sushi takes just a few minutes. To make the preparation quicker yet, buy bottled ponzu sauce. Chapter 6 thoroughly explains two quick-and-easy ways to make finger sushi.

Preparation time: 20 minutes, plus 1½ hours to prepare the sushi rice and 1 hour to drain the tofu

Yield: 8 finger sushi

1 cup prepared sushi rice (see Chapter 5)

14 ounces water-packed tofu, regular or firm (not soft)

1 sheet of nori

1 teaspoon peeled and grated gingerroot, squeezed to release excess juices

2 teaspoons thinly sliced scallions, rinsed and patted dry (see Chapter 3)

Ponzu Sauce (see the following recipe)

1 Open the tofu package, draining off the water, and carefully remove the delicate tofu block in one solid piece. Wrap the tofu block in an absorbent kitchen towel and set it on a large plate. Set another plate or small dish on top of the wrapped tofu, as shown in Figure 9-1. Refrigerate at least 1 hour, allowing the tofu to give up excess water.

2 Prepare 8 finger sushi (see Chapter 6), using the sushi rice.

3 Cut a sheet of 7-x-8-inch nori into 2 pieces, each 4 inches x 7 inches. Cut one of these pieces into 8 strips, each ½ inch x 4 inches. (Save the other half sheet for a hand roll.)

4 Slice the drained tofu crosswise into 8 slices, each ⅓ inch thick. (Save the leftover tofu for another use.) Secure a slice of tofu to each finger sushi by wrapping a ½-inch-x-4-inch strip of nori, crosswise, around the tofu and finger sushi (see Figure 9-1).

5 Place a tiny bit of grated gingerroot and sliced scallions on top of each nori strip. Serve immediately, with Ponzu Sauce as a dipping sauce.

Ponzu Sauce

Yield: *½ cup*

¼ cup soy sauce	*2 tablespoons fresh lime juice*
1 tablespoon fresh lemon juice	*1 tablespoon fresh grapefruit juice*

1 Mix all the ingredients together.

2 Refrigerate until needed. Serve the sauce cold or at room temperature.

Go-With: *Serve with Guacamole Battleship Sushi (see the recipe later in this chapter).*

Per finger sushi: Calories 71 (From Fat 13); Fat 1g (Saturated 0g); Cholesterol 0mg; Sodium 650mg; Carbohydrate 9g (Dietary Fiber 0g); Protein 5g.

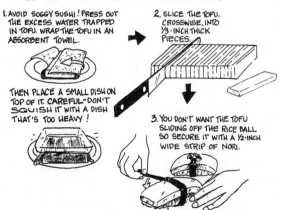

EASY STEPS TO MAKING TOFU FINGER SUSHI

1. AVOID SOGGY SUSHI! PRESS OUT THE EXCESS WATER TRAPPED IN TOFU. WRAP THE TOFU IN AN ABSORBENT TOWEL.

THEN PLACE A SMALL DISH ON TOP OF IT. CAREFUL—DON'T SQUISH IT WITH A DISH THAT'S TOO HEAVY!

2. SLICE THE TOFU, CROSSWISE, INTO ⅓-INCH THICK PIECES.

3. YOU DON'T WANT THE TOFU SLIDING OFF THE RICE BALL SO SECURE IT WITH A ½-INCH WIDE STRIP OF NORI.

Figure 9-1: Easy steps to making Tofu Finger Sushi.

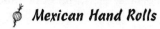

🌶 *Mexican Hand Rolls*

Sushi has a huge fan base in Mexico's bigger cities, right down to sushi carts on the streets. Hand rolls, by their very nature, are fast food. You just slap a little sushi rice on a half sheet of nori, top it with favorite ingredients, and quickly roll it up. No big deal. Our Mexican Hand Rolls are perfect hot weather snacks, combining cool, flavorful sticks of mango, jicama, and cucumber with a dash of chili powder and fresh lime juice for a kick. You want the sticks of fruit and cucumber about the thickness of French fries.

Preparation time: *10 minutes, plus 1½ hours to prepare the sushi rice*

Yield: *4 hand rolls*

1 tablespoon fresh lime juice

4 sticks mango, each about ⅓ inch thick x 3 inches long

4 sticks jicama, each about ⅓ inch thick x 3 inches long

4 sticks Japanese cucumber, salt-scrubbed (see Chapter 3), each about ⅓ inch thick x 3 inches long

Chili powder

2 sheets nori, reroasted (see Chapter 3)

1 cup prepared sushi rice (see Chapter 5)

1 Pour the fresh lime juice onto a small plate. Roll the sticks of mango, jicama, and cucumber in the lime juice. Sprinkle the sticks with chili powder to taste.

2 Cut the nori sheets in half, forming 4-x-7-inch half sheets. Place a half sheet of nori in the palm of your hand, shiny side down. Dip your hands into a bowl of vinegared water and then tap your fingertips on a damp towel to release excess water. Place about ¼ cup of the sushi rice on the nori, toward the top portion of the nori, patting the rice out in a diagonal from the top area of the nori toward the heel of your palm (refer to Figure 6-8 in Chapter 6).

3 Lay 1 stick each of the mango, jicama, and cucumber on top of the rice, letting their tips stick out over the top edge of the nori for looks.

4 Fold the bottom left corner of the nori over the fillings and then continue rolling to the right until you have a cone-shaped roll (refer to Figure 6-8 in Chapter 6). Serve immediately.

Vary It! *Add avocado to the fillings and this recipe's luscious quotient goes way up! Or, use any fruit you like in place of mango, such as pineapple, papaya, Asian pear, or even watermelon.*

Per hand roll: *Calories 75 (From Fat 2); Fat 0g (Saturated 0g); Cholesterol 0mg; Sodium 51mg; Carbohydrate 17g (Dietary Fiber 1g); Protein 1g.*

Guacamole Battleship Sushi

Guacamole is on everyone's favorite food list. It turns out that guacamole tastes sensational with vinegared rice, wasabi paste, and soy sauce. If you have a favorite store-bought guacamole, use that and cut your preparation time (not including the rice) by more than half. Battleship sushi starts by shaping finger sushi that you wrap with little nori strips, creating tiny battleship-looking sushi. You can find the techniques for making battleship sushi in Chapter 6.

Preparation time: *25 minutes, plus 1½ hours to prepare the sushi rice*

Yield: *8 pieces*

1 cup prepared sushi rice (see Chapter 5)

1 sheet nori

1 teaspoon wasabi paste (see Chapter 3), or to taste

⅔ cup Guacamole (see the following recipe)

1 Prepare 8 finger sushi (see Chapter 6), using the sushi rice.

2 Cut the nori into 8 strips, each 1 inch x 7 inches (refer to Figure 6-3 in Chapter 6).

3 Wrap a 1-inch-wide strip of nori around the sides of each finger sushi, shiny side out (sticking it closed with a grain of rice, if necessary), creating a tiny collar all around the rice (refer to Figure 6-3 in Chapter 6).

4 Dab a little wasabi paste on top of rice inside the nori collar. Delicately spoon one-eighth of the Guacamole into each nori collar. Serve immediately while the nori is crisp.

Guacamole

Yield: ⅔ cup

⅔ cup finely chopped ripe but still firm avocado

2 teaspoons minced onions

2 teaspoons minced cilantro

2 teaspoons minced serrano chile, or to taste

¼ teaspoon fresh lime juice

Salt to taste

Gently stir together all the ingredients. Use immediately, before it discolors, or press plastic wrap down onto the guacamole and refrigerate it up to several hours.

Per piece: Calories 54 (From Fat 18); Fat 2g (Saturated 0g); Cholesterol 0mg; Sodium 111mg; Carbohydrate 8g (Dietary Fiber 1g); Protein 1g.

Reeling in Easy Seafood Sushi

Sushi rice and seafood are practically synonymous in sushi lovers' minds. The pairing of vibrant, chewy sushi rice and fresh fish is a taste treat that rapidly becomes addictive, whether the seafood is cooked or raw. Try it both ways, using our recipes, and you'll see what we mean.

Using cooked fish

The Japanese have a history of making all kinds of delicious things out of fish, one of them cooked fish paste, or *surimi*. *Surimi* that's shaped and flavored like crabmeat is called *kani kama*. By all means, use fresh, cooked, shredded crabmeat for the recipe in this section, but don't hesitate to use *kani kama*, too. Sushi bars fill California Rolls (see our recipe in Chapter 8) with *kani kama* all the time.

Crabmeat and Avocado Pressed Sushi with Wasabi Mayonnaise

These dressy-looking little pieces of easy-to-do, four-ingredient pressed sushi are perfect appetizers for a cocktail party, wedding shower, or any other dressy occasion. We hear from beginners all the time how easy it is to make pressed sushi. You can't mess up the shape because the mold does that work for you.

Special sushi tools: *Sushi mold that makes 5 pieces (see Chapter 2)*

Preparation time: *45 minutes, plus 1½ hours to prepare the sushi rice*

Yield: *20 pieces*

4 cups prepared sushi rice (see Chapter 5)	*4 ounces cooked, shredded crabmeat, or 4 ounces shredded kani kama (imitation crabmeat)*
¼ cup Wasabi Mayonnaise (see the following recipe)	
1 large avocado or 2 smaller avocados, firm but ripe, thinly sliced lengthwise	*Garnishes: cilantro leaves, thin round slices of jalapeño pepper, lemon wedges*

1 Wipe all three parts of the sushi mold with a damp towel. Using damp fingertips, pick up and spread about ½ cup (about 3 ounces) of the sushi rice evenly across the bottom of the mold. Press down with the lid (refer to Figure 6-9 in Chapter 6).

2 Remove the lid and wipe it off with a damp towel. Dab one-eighth of the Wasabi Mayonnaise on the rice and then top the seasoned rice with an even layer of the avocado, dark green edges facing out. Spread another ½ cup of the sushi rice evenly over the avocados. Press down with the lid.

3 Dab another one-eighth of the Wasabi Mayonnaise on the rice. Finish the mold with one-fourth of the shredded crabmeat or *kani kama*. Press down with the lid a final time.

4 Remove the lid. Using the knife guides on the mold, partially slice the sushi into 5 pieces, wiping your knife on a damp cloth before each slice to prevent tearing the slices apart.

5 Unmold the sushi by pressing down with the lid while pulling up on its sides. Finish slicing the sushi pieces apart, again wiping your knife on a damp cloth before each slice. Top each piece of sushi with a cilantro leaf or a thin round slice of jalapeño pepper. Make 3 more pressed sushi the same way. Serve immediately with lemon wedges.

Vary It! *Alternate the fillings, making two of the pressed sushi with crabmeat on top and two with avocado on top.*

Tip: *Lining the mold with plastic wrap makes removing the pressed sushi easier for some people.*

Wasabi Mayonnaise

Yield: ¼ *cup*

4 tablespoons mayonnaise	*1 teaspoon wasabi paste, or to taste (see Chapter 3)*

Stir the mayonnaise and wasabi paste together until well blended. Use right away or refrigerate several hours until needed.

Per piece: *Calories 92 (From Fat 35); Fat 4g (Saturated 1g); Cholesterol 7mg; Sodium 76mg; Carbohydrate 12g (Dietary Fiber 1g); Protein 2g.*

Using raw fish

You need only a few simple, flavorful ingredients, combined with care, to create a fabulous taste explosion in your mouth. The raw seafood recipes in this section give you just that — "wow" moments you can't wait to repeat again, or should we say *eat* again. Tuna, known for its clean taste and meaty texture, is our number one fish, used in four recipes. *Hamachi* (Japanese yellow-tail), red snapper, smoked salmon, and salmon roe are also used here, enough choices to please raw seafood fanatics. We explain how to buy, transport, and store sashimi-grade (suitable for eating raw) seafood in Chapter 4.

Tuna Sushi Rice Balls

Sushi rice balls are so easy to make that you could call them child's play, especially when they have only three ingredients, such as in this recipe. You shape them by twisting a small amount of prepared sushi rice in plastic wrap until you form a perfect ball (see Chapter 6). Unlike finger sushi, which traditionally calls for serving two pieces at a time, rice balls have no serving tradition, so you can serve as many as you like. Slicing the fish thinly requires a little patience the first slice or two, but the task goes quickly thereafter.

Preparation time: *15 minutes, plus 1½ hours to prepare the sushi rice*

Yield: *8 sushi rice balls*

4 ounces sashimi-grade tuna	*Soy sauce*
2 cups prepared sushi rice (see Chapter 5)	*Pickled ginger*
1 teaspoon wasabi paste, or to taste (see Chapter 3)	

1 Slice the raw tuna at an angle into 8 pieces, each approximately ⅛-inch thick, 2 inches square and weighing about ½ ounce (see Chapter 7 for more on slicing fish). Wipe your knife with a damp paper towel before each slice. You'll have a little tuna left over, which you can use as described in the sidebar "Finding new uses for not-so-pretty fish slices," later in this chapter.

2 Prepare 8 sushi rice balls, each ¼ cup in size, by filling a damp ¼ cup measuring cup with the sushi rice.

3 Place a slice of tuna on a 10-inch piece of plastic wrap, cover with ¼ cup of the sushi rice, pick up the edges of the plastic wrap, and twist the rice package into a ball (refer to Figure 6-4 in Chapter 6). Don't twist so tightly that the fish looks squished, but just enough to form a firm ball.

4 Unwrap and place the rice ball, tuna side up, on a plate. Make 7 more rice balls the same way. Garnish the top of each rice ball with a small bead of wasabi paste. Serve immediately with soy sauce as a dipping sauce, and pickled ginger to refresh the palate.

Go-With: *Serve with the Cucumber and Wakame Salad in Chapter 13.*

Per rice ball: *Calories 105 (From Fat 3); Fat 0g (Saturated 0g); Cholesterol 6mg; Sodium 1,326mg; Carbohydrate 17g (Dietary Fiber 1g); Protein 6g.*

Spicy Hamachi Hand Rolls

Give people crispy hand rolls, and they go nuts over the taste. Teach them how to make this easy type of sushi, which takes only moments, and they go nuts over the fact that they can make them at home all the time. When sushi novices are ready for more exotic fillings, we steer them in this recipe's direction. Eating *hamachi* (Japanese yellowtail) raw is a sensuously rich experience, much sought after by raw fish lovers everywhere. Two other very Japanese ingredients that play up to hamachi's full-bloom flavor go into this roll: tangy, pickled plums *(umeboshi)* and shiso leaves *(ooba)*, a fragrant member of the mint family.

Preparation time: *20 minutes, plus 1½ hours to prepare the sushi rice*

Yield: *4 hand rolls*

8 shiso leaves

¼ pound sashimi-grade hamachi

3 tablespoons reroasted white sesame seeds (see Chapter 3)

1 tablespoon (¾ ounce) minced pickled plums (umeboshi)

1½ teaspoons thinly sliced jalapeño peppers, or to taste

2 teaspoons soy sauce

2 sheets nori, reroasted (see Chapter 3)

1 cup prepared sushi rice (see Chapter 5)

1 Stack 4 of the shiso leaves on top of each other and then roll them up in a tight bundle. Slice them paper thin (see Chapter 7).

2 Cut the *hamachi* into ⅓-inch-thick sticks (think French fries in thickness).

3 Stir the reroasted sesame seeds, pickled plums, jalapeños, and soy sauce together in a medium-sized bowl until well combined. Gently fold in the sliced shiso leaves and sticks of *hamachi*.

4 Cut the nori sheets in half, forming 4 half sheets, each 4 inches x 7 inches. Lay a half sheet of nori in the palm of your hand, shiny side down. Dip your right hand in a bowl of vinegared water and then tap your fingers on a damp towel to remove excess water. Place about ¼ cup of the sushi rice on the nori, toward the top portion of the nori, patting the rice out in a diagonal from the top area of the nori toward the heel of your palm (refer to Figure 6-8 in Chapter 6).

5 Top the rice with 1 whole shiso leaf, letting the leaf's edge stick out of the nori for looks. Spoon one-fourth of the spicy *hamachi* mixture onto the leaf.

6 Fold the bottom left corner of the nori over the fillings and then roll the right side over until you have a cone-shaped roll (refer to Figure 6-8 in Chapter 6). Serve immediately while the nori is crisp. Make 3 more hand rolls, following these instructions.

Per hand roll: *Calories 142 (From Fat 41); Fat 5g (Saturated 1g); Cholesterol 16mg; Sodium 646mg; Carbohydrate 16g (Dietary Fiber 1g); Protein 9g.*

Red Snapper Finger Sushi with Spicy Daikon Relish

We've found that beginners want a recipe now and then that has more complex, exotic tastes. This recipe sounds difficult and time consuming, but it's not. If your rice is made or if you use leftover frozen sushi rice (see Chapter 5), and you have your fishmonger or a sushi bar slice the fish for you, you can have this sushi ready in less than 30 minutes. Here, the mild, almost sweet taste of red snapper *(tai)* cries out for a fiery complementary condiment. The answer comes back in Spicy Daikon Relish *(Momijioroshi,* see the following recipe), a classic Japanese condiment frequently served with red snapper and other white-fleshed fish. If you'd welcome an additional burst of heat, slip a slice of jalapeño pepper under the red snapper.

Daikon, a long, giant white radish, is a mainstay in the sushi kitchen, loved for its pure white flesh that possesses a spicy-sweet appeal. Some creative cook thought to stick dried red chiles into the radish, coming up with a rosy-colored condiment loaded with heat. Save yourself some time, if you like, and take a *Momijioroshi* shortcut — add thick, hot chili sauce or chili flakes to grated daikon.

Special sushi tools: *Sashimi knife (see Chapter 2)*

Preparation time: *30 minutes, plus 1½ hours to prepare the sushi rice*

Yield: *8 finger sushi*

1 cup prepared sushi rice (see Chapter 5)

⅓ pound thick fillet of sashimi-grade red snapper

8 paper-thin, round slices of jalapeño pepper (optional)

2 teaspoons Spicy Daikon Relish (see the following recipe)

1 tablespoon thinly sliced scallions, rinsed and patted dry (see Chapter 3)

Ponzu Sauce (see the recipe earlier in this chapter or use a store-bought variety)

1 Prepare 8 finger sushi (see Chapter 6), using the sushi rice.

2 Slice the red snapper at an angle into 8 slices, each about ⅕-inch thick (see Chapter 7 for tips on slicing). Wipe your knife with a damp paper towel before each slice.

3 If you want, lay a slice of jalapeño pepper on top of each finger sushi. Drape a slice of red snapper lengthwise over the top of each finger sushi.

4 To give the finger sushi a finished look, lay a damp paper towel over the red snapper and press the fish and rice ball together gently, not squishing them.

5 Put a tiny pinch (¼ teaspoon) of Spicy Daikon Relish and one-eighth of the sliced scallions on top of each finger sushi. Serve immediately, with Ponzu Sauce as a dipping sauce.

Vary It! *Substitute halibut for the red snapper.*

Spicy Daikon Relish (Momijioroshi)

Yield: *2 teaspoons*

4 to 6 small dried red chiles, seeded   *1 piece (8 ounces) peeled daikon radish*

1 Poke holes for the dried chiles into one end of the daikon, using a sturdy chopstick. Wiggle the chopstick around to open each hole a bit. Force the dried chiles into the holes, using the chopstick to push them in.

2 Grate the chile-studded daikon in a circular motion over a fine grater until you have about 3 teaspoons. Pieces of dried chile will flake off, which is no problem. Just stuff the big ones back in or discard them. You want little flecks of chile in the finished Spicy Daikon Relish. Refrigerate, well covered, if not used right away. Grated daikon radish begins to smell to high heaven within 30 minutes or so but tastes great nevertheless.

3 Squeeze the excess liquid out of the Spicy Daikon Relish before putting pinches of it on the sushi. Use within a few hours, before the flavors begin to change.

Per finger sushi: Calories 59 (From Fat 6); Fat 0g (Saturated 0g); Cholesterol 7mg; Sodium 644mg; Carbohydrate 8g (Dietary Fiber 0g); Protein 6g.

Smoked Salmon Sushi Rice Balls

In the course of a meal in a Japanese home, you may see sushi rice balls served, but not finger sushi, which is more of a sushi bar item. These quick-as-a-wink-to-make, four-ingredient Smoked Salmon Sushi Rice Balls, like their kissing cousin, Tuna Sushi Rice Balls, are 2- or 3-bite sushi.

Preparation time: *15 minutes, plus 1½ hours to prepare the sushi rice*

Yield: *8 sushi rice balls*

1 tablespoon capers, rinsed and minced	8 whole capers
2 cups prepared sushi rice (see Chapter 5)	8 lemon wedges
3 ounces sliced, smoked salmon, cut into 8 pieces, each 2 inches square	

1 Gently mix the minced capers into the sushi rice until well combined.

2 Prepare a sushi rice ball by filling a damp ¼ cup measuring cup with the rice mixture.

3 Place a 2-inch piece of smoked salmon on a 10-inch piece of plastic wrap and then cover the salmon with ¼ cup of the sushi rice mixture. Pick up the edges of the plastic wrap and twist the rice package into a ball (refer to Figure 6-4 in Chapter 6).

4 Unwrap and place the rice ball, salmon side up, on a plate. Make 7 more Smoked Salmon Rice Balls the same way. Garnish the top of each rice ball with a whole caper. Serve immediately with lemon wedges.

Per rice ball: *Calories 77 (From Fat 3); Fat 0g (Saturated 0g); Cholesterol 2mg; Sodium 306mg; Carbohydrate 14g (Dietary Fiber 0g); Protein 3g.*

Tuna, Cucumber, and Black Sesame Seed Pressed Sushi

Great taste is a prerequisite to any sushi, but so is great appearance. Pressed sushi captures both looks and taste in colorful layers of rice and fillings, plus pressed sushi is easy for everyone to do. Laying the sliced tuna on top of each of the four pressed sushi is like putting together a puzzle. Any size slice is fine, as long as all slices are the same thickness and cover the top of the rice completely. Chapter 6 has a complete description of what goes into pressing sushi.

Special sushi tools: *Sushi mold that makes 5 pieces; sashimi knife, vegetable knife, or Japanese mandoline (see Chapter 2)*

Preparation time: *45 minutes, plus 1½ hours to prepare the sushi rice*

Yield: *20 pieces*

¾ pound thick fillet or block of sashimi-grade tuna

1 Japanese cucumber, salt-scrubbed (see Chapter 3)

4 cups prepared sushi rice (see Chapter 5)

4 teaspoons wasabi paste (see Chapter 3)

2 teaspoons reroasted black sesame seeds (see Chapter 3)

Soy-Mirin Marinade, used as a dipping sauce (see the recipe later in this chapter)

1 Using a sashimi knife, slice the tuna about ¼ inch thick, in pieces that will snuggle together to cover the top of each pressed sushi. Refrigerate the tuna until needed.

2 Cut off the ends of the cucumber, making it 7 inches long, the length of the mold. Cut this 7-inch piece into thin ribbons (with the skin on), using a vegetable knife or Japanese mandoline (refer to Figures 7-2 and 7-3 in Chapter 7). Set aside briefly.

3 Wipe all three parts of the sushi mold with a damp towel. Using damp fingertips, pick up and spread about ½ cup (about 3 ounces) of the sushi rice evenly across the bottom of the mold. Press down with the lid (refer to Figure 6-9 in Chapter 6).

4 Remove the lid and wipe it off with a damp towel. Dab ½ teaspoon of the wasabi paste on the rice and then top with an even layer of cucumber ribbons. Spread another ½ cup sushi rice evenly over the cucumbers. Press down with the lid again.

5 Dab ½ teaspoon wasabi paste on the sushi rice. Lay tuna slices across the top of the sushi rice, completely covering it. Press down with the lid a final time.

6 Remove the lid. Using the knife guides on the mold, partially slice the sushi into 5 pieces, wiping your knife on a damp cloth before each slice to prevent tearing the slices apart.

7 Unmold the sushi by pressing down on the lid as you lift up on the sides. Complete slicing the sushi pieces apart, again wiping your knife on a damp cloth before each slice. Sprinkle the pieces of sushi with ½ teaspoon reroasted black sesame seeds.

8 Make 3 more pressed sushi the same way. Serve this pressed sushi immediately, accompanied by Soy-Mirin Marinade as a dipping sauce (you find the recipe later in this chapter).

Vary It! Alternate the fillings, making two of the pressed sushi with tuna on top and two with cucumbers.

Per piece: Calories 82 (From Fat 4); Fat 1g (Saturated 0g); Cholesterol 8mg; Sodium 341mg; Carbohydrate 12g (Dietary Fiber 0g); Protein 6g.

Tuna Sliced Rolls

The story goes that this roll was created as a quick snack for gamblers who didn't want to leave the table, thus its name *"tekka-maki,"* or gamblers' roll. Medium-sized sliced rolls with just one filling, such as ours, are the easiest sliced rolls to make. Chapter 6 offers helpful details about sliced rolls.

Special sushi tools: *Bamboo mat, sashimi knife (see Chapter 2)*

Preparation time: *20 minutes, plus 1½ hours to prepare the sushi rice*

Yield: *4 medium rolls (32 pieces)*

½ pound block of sashimi-grade tuna, roughly 1 inch thick

4 sheets nori

4 cups prepared sushi rice (see Chapter 5)

2 teaspoons wasabi paste, or to taste (see Chapter 3)

¼ cup thinly sliced scallions, rinsed and patted dry (see Chapter 3)

Soy sauce

Pickled ginger

1 Slice the fish straight down, into pieces about ½ inch thick (see Chapter 7). Then slice these pieces in half horizontally, creating sticks of fish about ½ inch in size.

2 Place a bamboo mat in front of you, its slats parallel to the edge of the countertop or table. Lay a sheet of nori lengthwise, shiny side down, on the edge of the bamboo mat closest to you. Dip your hands in a bowl of vinegared water and then tap your fingertips on a damp towel to remove excess water. Spread 1 cup of the sushi rice evenly on the nori, leaving a 2½-inch-wide strip of nori, not covered with rice, on the edge farthest away from you (refer to Figure 6-5 in Chapter 6). Spread one-fourth of the wasabi paste across the center of the rice and then sprinkle one-fourth of the scallions on the wasabi paste. Lay 2 or 3 sticks of tuna, end to end, across the center of the rice, spanning the length of the nori.

3 Lift up the edge of the mat closest to you, keeping your fingertips on the fillings, and roll the mat and its contents away from you until the edge of the mat touches straight down on the far edge of the rice (refer to Figure 6-6 in Chapter 6). Tug on the mat to tighten the roll. Lay the mat down on the counter and move the partially done roll back to the edge of the mat closest to you. Lift the mat again and finish rolling up the roll. Tug on the mat to tighten the seal.

4 Cut the roll into 8 equal pieces, wiping your knife with a damp towel before each slice. Make 3 more rolls, following these instructions. Serve with soy sauce as a dipping sauce, and pickled ginger to cleanse your palate.

Go-With: *Cucumber Rolls (see Chapter 8) taste great with Sliced Tuna Rolls!*

Vary it! *You can also prepare the rolls with salt-grilled salmon (see Chapter 14) instead of raw tuna for a tasty treat (as shown in the color insert).*

Per piece: *Calories 43 (From Fat 1); Fat 0g (Saturated 0g); Cholesterol 3mg; Sodium 191mg; Carbohydrate 8g (Dietary Fiber 0g); Protein 3g.*

Salmon Roe Battleship Sushi

Salmon roe *(ikura)* is a big hit around the world for its rich flavor; show-stopping large, shiny orange-red roe; and velvety texture. You don't want to bury its looks or taste, so this easy sushi only has four ingredients. Salmon roe is available at Asian markets, or you can order it by phone or online (see the resources in Chapters 3 and 4). It's usually about $20 a pound, much less than other roe like true caviar. Battleship sushi starts with finger sushi that you wrap with little nori strips, creating tiny sushi that look like — yes, you guessed it — battleships.

Preparation time: *15 minutes, plus 1½ hours to prepare the sushi rice*

Yield: *8 pieces*

1 cup prepared sushi rice (see Chapter 5)

1 sheet nori

¾ teaspoon wasabi paste, or to taste (see Chapter 3)

4 ounces salmon roe (ikura)

1 Prepare 8 finger sushi (see Chapter 6), using the sushi rice.

2 Cut the nori into 8 strips, each 1 inch x 7 inches (refer to Figure 6-3 in Chapter 6).

3 Wrap a 1-inch-wide strip of nori around the sides of each finger sushi, shiny side out (sticking it closed with a grain of rice, if necessary), creating a tiny collar all around the rice (refer to Figure 6-3 in Chapter 6).

4 Dab a little wasabi paste on top of the rice inside of the nori collar. Delicately spoon about one-eighth, or 1 tablespoon, of the salmon roe into each nori collar. Serve immediately while the nori is crisp.

Vary It! *Vary the roe that fills this sushi for looks as well as flavor. Use wasabi tobikko (pale green), smelt roe (orange), or flying fish roe (reddish-orange).*

Per piece: *Calories 64 (From Fat 13); Fat 1g (Saturated 1g); Cholesterol 49mg; Sodium 34mg; Carbohydrate 7g (Dietary Fiber 0g); Protein 3g.*

Marinated Tuna Tokyo-Style Scattered Sushi

Anybody can put together a rice bowl, which is what scattered sushi is. Tokyo-style scattered sushi is a generous bowl of prepared sushi rice topped with any number of ingredients, in this case marinated tuna. Scattered sushi is one of the two easiest sushi to make (sushi rice balls are the other). It takes only 40 minutes for the full flavor of the Soy-Mirin Marinade to penetrate and tinge the surface of the raw tuna an attractive ruddy brown — well worth the wait. If you marinate the fish, slice the scallions, and reroast the sesame seeds while the rice cooks, the last-minute assembly takes only a few minutes.

Special sushi tools: *Sashimi knife (see Chapter 2)*

Preparation time: *15 minutes, plus 1½ hours to prepare the sushi rice and 40 minutes to let the tuna marinate*

Yield: *4 servings*

¾ pound block of sashimi-grade tuna

⅓ cup Soy-Mirin Marinade (see the following recipe)

6 cups prepared sushi rice (see Chapter 5)

4 teaspoons reroasted white sesame seeds (see Chapter 3)

¼ cup thinly sliced scallions, rinsed and patted dry (see Chapter 3)

8 shiso leaves

4 teaspoons wasabi paste, or to taste (see Chapter 3)

Pickled ginger

1 Place the block of raw tuna in a small dish. Pour the cold Soy-Mirin Marinade over the tuna. Refrigerate the fish for 40 minutes, turning it once, after 20 minutes. (You can leave the fish in the marinade a little longer, but know that it will get darker and soak up more flavor, overpowering the tuna after an hour or so.)

2 Slice the tuna straight down into pieces (see Chapter 7), each about ⅓ inch thick (about ½ ounce). Wipe your knife with a damp paper towel before each slice.

3 Scoop 1½ cups of the sushi rice into each of 4 bowls. Sprinkle 1 teaspoon of the sesame seeds and one-fourth of the sliced scallions over each rice bowl.

4 Lay one-fourth of the tuna slices over the rice in each bowl, in whatever pattern you choose. Drizzle a little of the marinade over the fish slices. Garnish each bowl with 2 shiso leaves, 1 teaspoon wasabi paste, and pickled ginger. Serve immediately.

Soy-Mirin Marinade (Zuke)

Not only is this marinade a good flavor enhancer for fish, but it also makes a good dipping sauce for sushi and sashimi (raw fish).

Yield: ⅓ cup

6 tablespoons soy sauce

2 tablespoons mirin

2 tablespoons sake

> Combine all the ingredients in a small pan. Bring to a boil over medium heat. Boil for 1 minute. Cool completely before using or refrigerate until needed.

Vary It! *Use this marinade on a piece of beef and see how wonderful it is! Grill the beef medium rare and serve it, thinly sliced, on top of the rice as you do the tuna.*

Per serving: *Calories 556 (From Fat 30); Fat 3g (Saturated 1g); Cholesterol 38mg; Sodium 2,144mg; Carbohydrate 93g (Dietary Fiber 3g); Protein 30g.*

Finding new uses for not-so-pretty fish slices

If your raw fish slicing techniques are a little rough at first and you think your slices aren't pretty enough for finger sushi, but you still want to eat such incredibly good sashimi-grade fish, don't despair. Try one of these suggestions:

✔ Mince ragged slices and use them as toppings for battleship sushi (see instructions on making battleship sushi in Chapter 6).

✔ Overlap ragged slices of yellowtail, tuna, or other boldly-flavored fish

with slices of avocado, hiding your problems. Rich-tasting fish like these not only look beautiful paired with avocado but also taste better. Serve with lemon wedges or soy sauce.

✔ Stack bits of ragged slices in a martini glass, sprinkle on a little soy sauce and a scattering of minced chives, and you've created a pretty, fresh dish.

Stepping Up the Pace with Beef, Poultry, and Pork Sushi

Knowing that sushi rice functions much like bread in a sandwich allows for lots of creative culinary freedom, especially in the quick-and-easy sushi category. After some very tasty experimenting, we came up with three winners in this category for meat, poultry, and pork lovers, each one using familiar ingredients that you can pick up in any good grocery store. Make your rice in the morning, and when you get home from work, you'll have sushi on the table in no time at all.

Hawaiian-Style Spam and Pineapple Pressed Sushi

Take a tropical vacation with this Hawaiian-style pressed sushi that capitalizes on Spam's sweet ability to marry well with pineapple. Pressed sushi is a cinch to make because the mold does all the shaping for you. This particular pressed sushi is doubly easy because it uses few ingredients and features slices of Spam, which easily fit in the 2-x-7-inch mold.

Special sushi tools: *Sushi mold that makes 5 pieces (see Chapter 2)*

Preparation time: *30 minutes, plus 1½ hours to prepare the sushi rice*

Yield: *20 pieces*

2 cans (8 ounces each) pineapple slices in unsweetened juice, juice reserved

¼ cup soy sauce

1 tablespoon mirin

12-ounce can of Spam, the meat cut into 8 slices, each ¼ inch thick

4 cups prepared sushi rice (see Chapter 5)

2 teaspoons wasabi paste, or to taste (see Chapter 3)

2 teaspoons reroasted sesame seeds (see Chapter 3)

20 parsley leaves

Pickled ginger

1 Pour the reserved pineapple juice, the soy sauce, and the mirin into a large frying pan. Bring this mixture to a boil over medium-high heat. Boil the mixture for 5 or 6 minutes, or until slightly thickened.

2 Add the Spam slices to the pan and cook them about 1 minute per side, just long enough to take on a little color and flavor. Lift the Spam out of the frying pan, drain on paper towels, and cool completely. After the seasoned Spam is at room temperature, it's ready to use in this sushi.

3 Wipe all 3 parts of the sushi mold with a damp towel. Using damp fingertips, pick up and spread about ½ cup (about 3 ounces) of the sushi rice evenly across the bottom of the mold. Press down with the lid (refer to Figure 6-9 in Chapter 6).

4 Remove the lid and wipe it off with a damp towel. Dab ½ teaspoon of the wasabi paste across the rice and top the seasoned rice with 2 slices of the seasoned Spam, end to end. Spread another ½ cup of sushi rice evenly over the Spam. Sprinkle with 1 teaspoon of the sesame seeds. Press down with the lid a final time (refer to Figure 6-9 in Chapter 6).

5 Remove the lid. Using the knife guides on the mold, partially slice the sushi into 5 pieces, wiping your knife on a damp cloth before each slice to prevent tearing the slices apart.

6 Unmold the sushi by pressing down on the lid as you lift up the sides of the mold. Finish slicing the sushi pieces apart, again wiping your knife on a damp cloth before each slice. Top the sushi pieces with broken-up sections of pineapple, arranged in any pattern you find attractive. Garnish each one with a parsley leaf and a bit of pickled ginger. Make 3 more pressed sushi the same way. Serve immediately.

Per piece: *Calories 136 (From Fat 44); Fat 5g (Saturated 2g); Cholesterol 12mg; Sodium 808mg; Carbohydrate 18g (Dietary Fiber 1g); Protein 4g.*

Spicy Chicken Salad Sliced Rolls

Who knew that everyday chicken salad could be so extraordinarily good when bumped up in taste by red onions, wasabi paste, and sushi rice? You can make chicken salad from scratch following this recipe, or you can pick up your favorite chicken salad from the deli and use leftover frozen sushi rice (see Chapter 5), which cuts the prep time down to 20 minutes to make and serve. (If you buy chicken salad instead of making your own, be sure that the chunks of chicken aren't so big that you can't roll up the roll. Stir in a little wasabi paste and minced red onions when you get the deli salad home.) Chapter 6 explains the tricks of the sushi trade when making sliced rolls.

Special sushi tools: *Bamboo mat (see Chapter 2)*

Preparation time: *40 minutes, plus 1½ hours to prepare the sushi rice*

Yield: *4 medium rolls (32 pieces)*

¼ cup mayonnaise	Salt and pepper
2 teaspoons wasabi paste, or to taste (see Chapter 3)	4 sheets nori
1½ cups cooked, shredded chicken meat	4 cups prepared sushi rice (see Chapter 5)
½ cup minced celery	8 slender, tender inner celery stalks
⅓ cup minced red onion	Soy sauce
¼ cup minced parsley	Pickled ginger
1 or more teaspoons fresh lemon juice	

1 Make the chicken salad by first stirring the mayonnaise and wasabi paste together until well combined. Stir in the chicken, celery, red onion, and parsley. Season the chicken salad to taste with lemon juice, salt, and pepper.

2 Place a bamboo mat in front of you, its slats parallel to the edge of the table or countertop. Lay a sheet of nori lengthwise, shiny side down, on the edge of the bamboo mat closest to you. Dip your hands in vinegared water and then tap your fingertips on a damp towel to remove excess water. Spread 1 cup of the rice evenly on the nori, leaving a 2½-inch-wide strip of nori not covered with rice on the edge farthest away from you (refer to Figure 6-5 in Chapter 6).

3 Spread one-fourth of the chicken salad across the center of the rice, left to right, in as straight a line as possible, keeping the chicken salad in as tight a line as possible. Lay two celery stalks down lengthwise, end to end, over the top of the chicken salad, allowing a bit of their ruffled leaves to stick out the end for looks.

4 Lift up the edge of the mat closest to you, keeping your fingertips on the fillings, and roll the mat and its contents away from you until the edge of the mat touches straight down on the far edge of the rice (refer to Figure 6-6 in Chapter 6). Tug on the mat to tighten the roll. Lay the mat down on the counter and move the partially done roll back to the edge of the mat closest to you. Lift the mat again and finish rolling up the roll. Tug on the mat again to tighten the seal.

5 Cut the roll into 8 equal pieces, wiping your knife with a damp towel before each slice. Make 3 more rolls, following these instructions. Serve with soy sauce as a dipping sauce, and pickled ginger to cleanse your palate.

Vary It! *Fill the roll with your favorite tuna salad recipe.*

Per serving: *Calories 63 (From Fat 18); Fat 2g (Saturated 0g); Cholesterol 7mg; Sodium 236mg; Carbohydrate 8g (Dietary Fiber 1g); Protein 3g.*

Roast Beef and Watercress Hand Rolls

Pick up some sliced roast beef at your local deli for this hand roll, come home, and if the rice is done ahead or you're using leftover frozen sushi rice (see Chapter 5), you'll have dinner ready in minutes.

Preparation time: *8 minutes, plus 1½ hours to prepare the sushi rice*

Yield: *4 hand rolls*

2 sheets nori, reroasted (see Chapter 3)

1 cup prepared sushi rice (see Chapter 5)

2 or more tablespoons Wasabi Mayonnaise (see the recipe earlier in this chapter)

4 lettuce leaves, preferably red leaf

4 thin slices (¼ pound) roast beef, each rolled up in a bundle

4 sprigs watercress

Soy sauce

1 Cut the nori sheets in half, forming 4 half sheets, each 4 inches x 7 inches. Place a half sheet of nori in the palm of your hand, shiny side down. Dip your hands into a bowl of vinegared water and then tap your fingertips on a damp towel to release excess water. Place about ¼ cup of the sushi rice on the nori, toward the top portion of the nori, patting the rice out in a diagonal from the top area of the nori toward the heel of your palm (refer to Figure 6-8 in Chapter 6). Spread Wasabi Mayonnaise to taste on the rice.

2 Lay 1 piece of lettuce on top of the rice, letting the leaf's edge extend off the edge of the nori for looks. Place a rolled piece of roast beef on top of the lettuce and then add a sprig of watercress.

3 Fold the bottom left corner of the nori over the fillings up toward the right. Continue rolling to the right until you have a cone-shaped roll (refer to Figure 6-8 in Chapter 6). Serve immediately while the nori is crisp, with soy sauce as a dipping sauce. Make 3 more rolls, following these instructions.

Vary It! *Try slivers of daikon and daikon sprouts in place of watercress and lettuce.*

Per hand roll: *Calories 149 (From Fat 59); Fat 7g (Saturated 1g); Cholesterol 18mg; Sodium 390mg; Carbohydrate 15g (Dietary Fiber 0g); Protein 7g.*

Chapter 10

Do-Ahead Sushi: Sidestepping the Last-Minute Rush

*W*hipping up sensational sushi at home, even on a very busy day, can be part of your dinner game plan. All you have to do is remember to do the last word of the previous sentence — plan.

Planning is the key to saving time when making sushi. We say it throughout the book, but it bears repeating: Read your chosen recipe all the way through before you get started. That way, you can spot what the time clogs might be before they happen (missing ingredients that require a trip to the store, for example), and know in advance where the timesavers are (chopping and cooking some of the ingredients the night before or making the sushi rice hours before your guests arrive). And remember that you're biggest do-ahead timesaver will be to prepare and freeze sushi rice to have on hand whenever the urge to make sushi arises (see Chapter 5).

You can make every one of the recipes in this chapter ahead of time, some way ahead. For example, in the Ground Turkey and Vegetable Osaka-Style Scattered Sushi, a party dish if ever there was one, you can chop and cook certain ingredients over the course of two days. If you choose the Grilled Peppers and Eggplant Inside-Out Rolls, you can roll them up, slice them, put them on a pretty platter, and kept them in a cool corner for hours before you serve them. Whichever recipe you prefer, you'll choose to make it again — not only because the recipes are delightfully do-ahead but also because they're delightfully delicious!

We want you sushi-proof from the get-go, so please, if you've not already done so, read Chapters 4 through 7 before you start making these do-ahead recipes.

Veggie Sushi

Vegetables and sushi rice *(su-meshi)* were meant to find each other and lock arms at the dinner table. Vegetables and sushi complement each other so harmoniously that we wonder why some sushi lovers overfocus on raw fish and sushi combinations, not giving vegetable sushi enough consideration, especially when looking for do-ahead recipes. Because prepared sushi rice must stay at room temperature and raw or cooked vegetables don't spoil at room temperature, you can completely assemble veggie sushi hours ahead. Add the fact that sashimi-grade fish is not always available, and vegetables become the home sushi chef's best friend. Try the recipes in this chapter, and you'll be sold on the taste of vegetable sushi, making them a solid part of your sushi repertoire from here on out.

Puckeringly good do-ahead sushi

Pickles of any kind are do-ahead favorite ingredients, not only for their taste but because they're already prepared to eat. After you enjoy the salty-sweet-sour taste of Japan's favorite pickled vegetable, pickled daikon radish *(takuan),* a core flavor in our Avocado, Cucumber, and Pickled Daikon Radish Sliced Rolls, pickled daikon radishes will take their rightful place in your refrigerator next to the dill pickles.

Fatty tuna from the land: The avocado

When the avocado first came to Japan, it was called "fatty tuna *(o-toro)* from the land." This is because avocado possesses much the same buttery texture as fatty tuna. It's a staple in sushi bars, as it's bound to be in your sushi kitchen. Here's what you need to know about avocados and sushi:

- Avocados ripen off the tree. Plan ahead and buy unripe avocados, meaning firm to the touch. You can buy them soft to the touch, which indicates ripeness, but often they've been squeezed by other shoppers, which bruises the fruit. Avocado skin color varies with the season: black or dark green in the summer months and more of a leaf green in the winter. Unripened avocados ripen at room temperature over the course of several days. You can speed up this process by ripening them in a closed paper bag or aluminum foil.

- You want to use avocados that are buttery in texture, not watery. A watery avocado doesn't taste as good, plus it dissipates the taste of the sushi. Our two favorites are Hass and Fuerte. Hass is currently the only avocado available year-round. This is a blessing because its remarkable nutty and fruity-in-its-own-way flavor makes it our number one choice. Hass's bumpy peel turns from deep green to almost black as it ripens. Fuerte is available mainly from late fall through early spring. Its smooth peel remains green even when ripe. But both have thick, buttery flesh, so you can use either one.

- To cut and peel an avocado, cut it in half lengthwise and then twist the halves in opposite directions. The pit will stick in one half. Spike the pit with the back portion of the knife's blade (careful!) and then gently turn the knife, twisting the seed free of the fruit. To preserve the lovely, faintly nubby-looking texture of the avocado flesh next to the peel, don't scoop it out with a spoon. Cut the avocado halves into quarters. Then peel the skin away from each quarter.

- Sushi recipes calling for thinly sliced avocados require avocados that are ripe but still firm. This means the avocado will give a little, not a lot, when pressed. You don't want to slice a squishy avocado for finger sushi or any rolled sushi that features the avocado slices on top, such as the Caterpillar Inside-Out Rolls in Chapter 8. It's not going to be a pretty sight. Save the slightly squishy ones for recipes calling for diced avocados, such as Guacamole Battleship Sushi in Chapter 9.

Avocado, Cucumber, and Pickled Daikon Radish Sliced Rolls

Daikon radishes look like long, white parsnips, but they possess a mildly sweet-hot taste. Because daikon radish is a root, it grows in different thicknesses and lengths, so it's pickled and packaged in different sizes. Frequently it's pickled a bright yellow color, which we prefer for this recipe.

Cut the pickled daikon radish, cucumber, and red onion the day before, and then the only vegetable to cut when you're ready to make the rolls is the avocado, which discolors if cut too far ahead. You can roll up these rolls 5 or 6 hours ahead, keeping them covered in a cool corner of the kitchen. These thick rolls are chock-full of flavorful ingredients, so slice each ingredient no thicker than explained, or rolling up the rolls can be difficult. Chapter 6 explains how to make picture-perfect sliced rolls.

Special sushi tools: *Bamboo mat, vegetable knife (see Chapter 2)*

Preparation time: *35 minutes, plus 1½ hours to prepare the sushi rice*

Yield: *4 thick rolls (32 pieces)*

5 ounces yellow pickled daikon radish	*½ cup peeled and thinly sliced red onion*
1 Japanese cucumber, salt-scrubbed (see Chapter 3)	*2 ounces alfalfa sprouts*
	4 sheets nori
1 avocado	*6 cups prepared sushi rice (see Chapter 5)*

1 Cut the pickled daikon radish into 8-inch-long matchsticks that are ¼ inch thick (see Chapter 7 for information on cutting vegetables). Trim the cucumber's ends, making it 8 inches in length, and then cut the cucumber into quarters lengthwise (refer to Figure 8-1 in Chapter 8). If the cucumber is over 1 inch wide, slice it into sixths (by cutting each half into thirds), or the pieces will be too thick for the roll. Cut the avocado in half and then in quarters, and then peel the quarters (see the sidebar "Fatty tuna from the land: The avocado," later in this chapter). Slice each avocado quarter into 3 thick slices.

2 Place a bamboo mat in front of you with its slats parallel to the edge of the countertop or table. Lay a sheet of nori lengthwise, shiny side down, on the edge of the bamboo mat closest to you. Dip your fingers in a bowl of vinegared water and then tap your fingertips on a damp towel to remove excess water. Spread 1½ cups of the sushi rice evenly on the nori, leaving a 1-inch-wide strip of nori not covered with rice (refer to Figure 6-5 in Chapter 6) on the edge farthest away from you.

3 Bunch a slice of pickled daikon radish, cucumber, and 3 slices of avocado together, in the center of the rice, spanning the 8-inch length of the nori. Top these vegetables with one-fourth of the sliced red onion and one-fourth of the alfalfa sprouts.

4 Lift up the edge of the mat closest to you, keeping your fingertips on the fillings, and roll the mat and its contents away from you until the edge of the mat touches straight down on the far edge of the rice (refer to Figure 6-6 in Chapter 6). Tug on the mat to tighten the roll. Lay the mat down on the counter and move the partially done roll back to the edge of the mat closest to you. Lift the mat again and finish rolling up the roll. Tug on the mat to seal it well.

5 Cut the roll into 8 equal pieces by cutting halves into halves and then into quarters, wiping your knife with a damp towel before each slice. Make 3 more rolls, following these instructions.

Tip: *You don't have to go to a Japanese market to buy pickled daikon radish. You can use your favorite pickles, sweet or sour.*

Per piece: *Calories 59 (From Fat 10); Fat 1g (Saturated 0g); Cholesterol 0mg; Sodium 47mg; Carbohydrate 11g (Dietary Fiber 1g); Protein 1g.*

Stuffing tofu pouches ahead

Tofu pouch sushi *(inari-zushi)* is one of the easiest and most transportable of all the sushi types to prepare. Slices of deep-fried tofu *(abura-age)* are used to hold the sushi rice. They split open much like pita bread does and can be cut into triangles or rectangles to be stuffed. Cook the tofu pouches a day ahead if you like, and stuff them hours ahead. In this section, we offer two versions of tofu pouch sushi: The Sweet Tofu Pouch Sushi, stuffed with only sushi rice, is the most well known, and the Carrots, String Beans, and Lemon Zest Tofu Pouch Sushi contains a mixture of sushi rice and brightly colored vegetables.

Sweet Tofu Pouch Sushi

Take these plump little 3-inch triangular pouches of sushi to the office, to a friend's house, or anywhere you want to take do-ahead sushi. People are pleasantly surprised when they first eat a Sweet Tofu Pouch Sushi because they expect it to be savory, not sweet.

Preparation time: *25 minutes, plus 1½ hours to prepare the sushi rice*

Cooking time: *15 minutes*

Yield: *24 pieces*

Preparing the tofu pouches

12 squares (3 packages) deep-fried tofu	⅓ cup sake
½ cup water	⅓ cup soy sauce
⅓ cup sugar	

1 Cut each 3-inch square or rectangular piece of deep-fried tofu diagonally into 2 triangles. Bring 3 to 4 quarts of water to a boil in a large pot. Add the cut tofu pieces and bring back to a boil over medium-high heat. After the water comes to a boil, lower the heat and simmer the tofu pieces for 2 minutes to release excess oil, pushing them down with a spoon occasionally. Remove from the heat and drain the tofu pieces.

2 Place the tofu pieces in a smaller pot, approximately a 3-quart size, and pour the ½ cup water, sugar, sake, and soy sauce over them. Cover the tofu with a plate almost as wide as the pot to keep it submerged. Bring the contents of the pot to a boil over medium-high heat. After the liquid comes to a boil, lower the heat and simmer the tofu pieces for 12 to 15 minutes, allowing this sweet-salty sauce to reduce and the tofu to take on the flavor of the sauce. Press down on the plate several times while the tofu pieces are simmering. Remove from the heat and let the tofu pieces cool down in the sauce at least 20 minutes before stuffing. (Or refrigerate the tofu pieces in their sauce until the next day.)

Stuffing the tofu pouches

6 cups prepared sushi rice (see Chapter 5)   Pickled ginger

1 Pick a piece of tofu out of the sauce and gently squeeze it over an empty bowl (so you don't get sticky rice in the sauce in the tofu pot as you go along stuffing them all). Gently pull open the cut side of the pouch. With the damp hand that squeezed the tofu piece, shape a golf-ball-size amount (about ¼ cup) of sushi rice into an oval shape.

2 Carefully and gently stuff the rice ball down into the tofu pouch (refer to Figure 6-10 in Chapter 6) and then gently fold the two edges of the pouch over the rice ball, enclosing it. Tofu pouches are delicate and will rip if you're too rough with them, so take care. Set the filled tofu pouch sushi, enclosed side down, in a flat, shallow container, one that will allow you to snuggle the other 23 pieces into it. (Keeping the tofu pouch sushi close together until you serve them helps them stay moist and retain their shape.)

3 Make the other 23 pieces as Steps 1 and 2 explain. Pour out and refrigerate the remaining sauce from the tofu pot to glaze the sushi when you serve it. Until then, cover the sushi with plastic wrap. Keep in a cool place up to 12 hours. When ready to serve, put the tofu pouches on a plate, brushing each one with a little of the reserved room temperature sauce. Offer pickled ginger on the side to cleanse the palate. A dipping sauce isn't served with this sushi.

Tip: *Plan on 2 or 3 tofu pouches per person as a snack, or 5 pieces with a simple soup, like our Miso Soup in Chapter 13.*

Tip: *Don't skip the first step, boiling the tofu pouches to release excess oil, or your tofu pouch sushi will be greasy.*

Per piece: Calories 112 (From Fat 13); Fat 1g (Saturated 0g); Cholesterol 0mg; Sodium 594mg; Carbohydrate 20g (Dietary Fiber 1g); Protein 3g.

🌶 Carrots, String Beans, and Lemon Zest Tofu Pouch Sushi

Deep fried tofu *(abura-age)* can be cut on the diagonal to form 2 triangles suitable for stuffing (see the Sweet Tofu Pouch Sushi recipe earlier in this chapter), or you can cut it in half to stuff like little paper bags. In this recipe, you cut them like paper bags. They're served sitting on their bottom seam, left open on top to show off the colorful, zingy-tasting filling. Carrots, String Bean, and Lemon Zest Tofu Pouch Sushi taste best after they sit for several hours. Perfect do-ahead sushi! This is one of the few recipes we offer in which you can't add the other ingredients to room temperature sushi rice. You must mix the ingredients into the warm sushi rice while it's easy to do so. Of course, you can always use frozen, reheated prepared sushi rice if you're in a do-ahead mood (see Chapter 5), and you can cook the tofu pouches a day ahead if you like. Stuff them hours ahead.

Preparation time: 35 minutes, plus 1½ hours to prepare the sushi rice

Cooking time: 15 minutes

Yield: 24 pieces

Preparing the tofu pouches

12 squares (3 packages) deep-fried tofu	⅓ cup sake
½ cup water	⅓ cup soy sauce
⅓ cup sugar	

Cut each tofu square in half, into 2 little rectangles. Then cook the tofu pouches according to the "Preparing the tofu pouches" instructions in Steps 1 and 2 of the preceding recipe, Sweet Tofu Pouch Sushi.

Stuffing the tofu pouches

1 cup shredded carrots	2 tablespoons lemon zest (the grated yellow part of the peel)
¾ cup (about 2 ounces) slivered string beans	2 tablespoons reroasted white sesame seeds (see Chapter 3)
1 tablespoon mirin	Pickled ginger
5 cups warm, prepared sushi rice (see Chapter 5)	

1 Bring a small pot of salted water to a rapid boil. Plunge the carrots and string beans into the water, boil them for 1 minute, drain them, and then dump them into a small bowl, tossing them with the mirin.

2 After the rice is cooked, seasoned, and cooled but still warm, mix in the boiled carrots and string beans and the lemon zest and sesame seeds. Let this rice mixture cool to room temperature.

3 Pick a piece of tofu out of the sauce and gently squeeze it over an empty bowl (so you don't get sticky rice in the sauce in the tofu pot as you go along stuffing them all). Gently pull open the cut side of the pouch. With the damp hand that squeezed the tofu piece, pick up about ¼ cup of the sushi rice mixture.

4 Carefully and gently stuff the rice mixture into the tofu pouch. Tofu pouches are delicate and will rip if you're too rough with them, so take care. Set the completed tofu pouch sushi, bottom side down, into a flat, shallow container, one that will allow you to snuggle the other 23 pieces into it. (Keeping the tofu pouch sushi close together until you serve them helps them stay moist and retain their shape.)

5 Make the other 23 pieces, as described in Steps 3 and 4. Cover the sushi with plastic wrap. Keep in a cool place up to 12 hours. When ready to serve, put the Carrot, String Bean, and Lemon Zest Tofu Pouch Sushi on a pretty plate, with pickled ginger on the side to cleanse the palate. No dipping sauce is served with this sushi.

Vary It! *Slivered snow peas work well in the place of string beans, but boil them for just 15 seconds, not 1 minute.*

Per piece: *Calories 110 (From Fat 16); Fat 2g (Saturated 0g); Cholesterol 0mg; Sodium 586mg; Carbohydrate 19g (Dietary Fiber 2g); Protein 3g.*

Grilling colorful veggies for do-ahead sushi

It's love at first sight when someone sees this roll, exploding with colorful fillings that include deep purple eggplant, bright red and yellow peppers, and ruffled green lettuce — all ingredients that you can slice and grill ahead of time! Top it all off with a playful coating of black and white sesame seeds, add a seriously good do-a-day-ahead Miso Dipping Sauce to bring out the grilled flavors of the vegetables, and you get all sophisticated appetites engaged.

🍶 Grilled Peppers and Eggplant Inside-Out Rolls with Miso Dipping Sauce

Once in a great while, when creating a recipe, you hit on a combination of and treatment of ingredients that positively ignite with flavor and color. This is one of those recipes. You can make the rolls ahead and keep them in a cool corner of the kitchen for several hours. If this is your first attempt at inside-out rolls, please read all about making them in Chapter 6.

Special sushi tools: Bamboo mat wrapped with plastic wrap, vegetable knife (see Chapter 2)

Preparation time: 45 minutes, plus 1½ hours to prepare the sushi rice

Cooking time: 20 minutes

Yield: 4 inside-out rolls (24 pieces)

Preparing the fillings

2 Japanese eggplants (about 3 to 4 ounces each), quartered lengthwise

1 sweet red bell pepper (about 6 ounces), seeded and quartered

1 sweet yellow bell pepper (about 6 ounces), seeded and quartered

4 scallions, trimmed to 9 inches in length

2 tablespoons extra-virgin olive oil

1 Put the eggplants, sweet red and yellow peppers, and the scallions in a bowl. Drizzle the olive oil over them and then, using your hands, smear the olive oil all over the vegetables. This olive oil coating flavors the vegetables and keeps them from sticking to the grill.

2 Preheat the grill or broiler to medium-high. Grill (or broil) the eggplants for 6 to 8 minutes, or until they take on some color. Grill the scallions for 4 to 6 minutes, being sure that they don't burn. Set aside these grilled vegetables.

3 Grill the peppers under medium-high heat, the skin side exposed to the heat, for 8 to 10 minutes, or until the skins begin to blister. Remove them from the heat and put the hot peppers in aluminum foil for 5 minutes to sweat and loosen their skin. Peel the peppers and then cut each quarter into ½-x-3-inch pieces. Set aside.

Rolling up the rolls

4 sheets nori

4 cups tightly packed prepared sushi rice (see Chapter 5)

1 tablespoon reroasted white sesame seeds (see Chapter 3)

1 tablespoon black reroasted sesame seeds

8 small romaine lettuce leaves, or 4 large ones

Miso Dipping Sauce (see the following recipe)

1 Cut a 3-inch-wide strip off each sheet of nori, making each one 5 inches x 7 inches. Lay a plastic-wrapped bamboo mat in front of you with its slats parallel to the edge of the table or countertop. Place a sheet of trimmed nori lengthwise, shiny side down, on the edge of the wrapped bamboo mat closest to you (refer to Figure 6-7 in Chapter 6). Dip your hands into a bowl of vinegared water and then tap your fingertips on a damp towel to remove excess water. Press 1 tightly packed cup of prepared sushi rice evenly over the nori. Sprinkle ¼ tablespoon of white sesame seeds and ¼ tablespoon of black sesame seeds over the rice.

2 Pick up the rice-covered nori, turn it over, and place it, rice side down and nori side up, lengthwise on the edge of the bamboo mat closest to you.

3 Fill the roll in this order: Lay 2 small lettuce leaves (or 1 large leaf split in half lengthwise) out lengthwise on the nori, not in the exact center, but a little closer to you, with their ruffled tips extending over the edges for looks. Bunch one-fourth of the red peppers, one-fourth of the yellow peppers, 2 pieces of eggplant, and 1 scallion on top of the lettuce.

4 Lift the edge of the mat closest to you with both hands, keeping your fingers over the fillings, and roll the mat and its contents until the edge of the mat touches straight down on to the nori, enclosing the fillings completely (refer to Figure 6-7 in Chapter 6). Lift up the edge of the mat you're holding and continue rolling the inside-out roll away from you until it's sealed. Tug on the mat to tighten the roll.

5 Lay a sheet of plastic wrap over the completed roll. Slice the roll into 6 equal pieces, wiping your knife with a damp cloth before each slice.

6 Make 3 more rolls, following Steps 1 through 5. Serve slices as an appetizer or serve 1 sliced roll per person as a light meal, accompanied by Miso Dipping Sauce.

Tip: Roast the vegetables the day you're making the rolls to take advantage of their freshly grilled flavor. If you substitute a larger eggplant than the slender Japanese variety, be sure the slices are no wider than ½ inch.

Miso Dipping Sauce

Yield: *5 tablespoons*

2 tablespoons mirin

2 tablespoons rice vinegar

1 tablespoon dark miso

¼ teaspoon hot chili sauce, or to taste

Mix the ingredients together until smooth. Refrigerate until needed.

Per piece: *Calories 25 (From Fat 14); Fat 2g (Saturated 0g); Cholesterol 0mg; Sodium 34mg; Carbohydrate 2g (Dietary Fiber 1g); Protein 1g.*

Sweet Tuna and Sushi Rice

When I (Mineko) first came to this country, not much was available in the way of Japanese ingredients where I lived, so I made do with what I could find. One great, tasty do-ahead ingredient I found in the grocery store was canned tuna. Because I always have prepared sushi rice in the freezer (see Chapter 5), I can make this pressed sushi whenever I want, several hours before I serve it.

Sweet Tuna and Snow Peas Pressed Sushi

The contrast of the crunchy snow peas, the soft, slightly sweet tuna, and the chewy vinegared sushi rice is very appealing in this pressed sushi. Make this sushi an hour or two ahead and keep it covered in a cool corner of the kitchen. Read all about pressed sushi in Chapter 6.

Special sushi tools: Sushi mold that makes 5 pieces (see Chapter 2)

Preparation time: 30 minutes, plus 1½ hours to prepare the sushi rice

Cooking time: 5 minutes

Yield: 20 pieces

1 teaspoon vegetable oil	¼ pound snow peas, strings removed, slivered
1 can (6 ounces) albacore tuna, packed in water, well drained	2 teaspoons mirin
4 teaspoons sugar	4 cups prepared sushi rice (see Chapter 5)
4 teaspoons soy sauce	1 tablespoon reroasted white sesame seeds (see Chapter 3)
2 tablespoons sake	

1 Pour the oil into a nonstick frying pan and place it over medium heat. Once hot, add the tuna, sugar, and soy sauce. Cook for about 1 minute, breaking the tuna into smaller pieces. Add the sake and continue breaking the tuna into the smallest flakes possible, while cooking for another 4 to 5 minutes. Remove the tuna from the heat and let cool.

2 Bring a pan of lightly salted water to a boil and plunge the snow peas into the water for 15 seconds or so. Drain and then plunge them into a bowl of ice water to stop the cooking and set their color. Drain well, pat them dry, and season with the mirin.

3 Wipe all 3 parts of the sushi mold with a damp towel. Using damp fingertips, pick up and spread about ½ cup (about 3 ounces) of the sushi rice evenly across the bottom of the mold. Press down with the lid (refer to Figure 6-9 in Chapter 6).

4 Remove the lid and wipe it off with a damp towel. Spread one-fourth of the cooked and flaked tuna evenly over the rice. Layer another ½ cup of sushi rice evenly over the tuna by putting small portions of the rice on top of the tuna and then spreading it out. Press down with the lid.

5 Pat the snow peas dry. Top the rice with one-fourth of the dried snow peas and then sprinkle with one-fourth of the sesame seeds. Press down with the lid a final time.

6 Remove the lid. Using the knife guides on the mold, partially slice the sushi into 5 pieces, wiping your knife on a damp cloth before each slice.

7 Unmold the sushi by pressing down with the lid while pulling up on its sides. Finish slicing the sushi pieces apart, wiping your knife before each cut. Make 3 more pressed sushi, following these instructions.

Tip: *Don't use wet ingredients in sushi, or the rice gets soggy. So be sure that the tuna and snow peas are fairly dry before putting them on the rice.*

Per piece: *Calories 72 (From Fat 7); Fat 1g (Saturated 0g); Cholesterol 3mg; Sodium 129mg; Carbohydrate 12g (Dietary Fiber 0g); Protein 3g.*

Willow tree sushi

In Japan, saying someone is like a willow tree means that the person is flexible, and bends with the circumstances — like the willow bends with the wind. Willow tree sushi is our way of recommending that you bend with the circumstances in your kitchen, using what's on hand whenever you can.

Having all the necessary ingredients when you want to make sushi is great, but just as wonderful is being confident that you can substitute for things you don't have, even using leftovers to create new combinations. For example, sushi requires small quantities of ingredients because so much of sushi is eaten in small portions or bites. Sushi is your chance to make good use of small portions of leftovers that may not be enough of a meal by themselves. Get creative with the leftovers from your next barbecue by using strips of grilled steak, chicken, fish, or vegetables in sliced rolls, or chop these same ingredients up and mix them into Osaka-style scattered sushi, following the techniques used in our Ground Turkey and Vegetable Osaka-Style Scattered Sushi found in this chapter.

If you try, you'll find dozens of ways to make use of leftovers and favorite ingredients in your kitchen that we haven't thought of. All you need is a little bit of imagination and an interest in making more sushi more often because sushi is fun to make and eat.

Chicken and Turkey Sushi

The two sushi recipes in this section are wake-up calls in taste and texture. To create them, you simply combine a flavorful sauce, poultry, vinegared sushi rice, and vibrant vegetables. The teriyaki chicken in the Teriyaki Chicken Sliced Rolls tastes great cooked that day or a day ahead. The flavors in the Ground Turkey and Vegetables Osaka-Style Sushi taste the best when the dish is made one to two hours ahead.

In Japan, Osaka-style scattered sushi is famous as a dish to take to public parks in the spring when the cherry trees are bursting with cotton-candy pink blooms. It's served decorated with cut-out vegetables resembling flower blossoms. The Ground Turkey and Vegetable Osaka-Style Scattered Sushi recipe, with its decorative vegetable flowers on top, makes as colorful a splash in the park as the trees. The Teriyaki Chicken Sliced Rolls recipe may not be as appropriate for flower viewing, but they're perfect when you have friends by to watch a game on TV.

When you consider their do-ahead nature, chances are good that you can be rolling up the Teriyaki Chicken Sliced Rolls and tossing up the Ground Turkey and Vegetable Scattered Sushi soon, taking them to the park or your living room.

Teriyaki Chicken Sliced Rolls

Teriyaki Chicken Sliced Rolls provide hearty appetizers, or they can be a complete meal if you serve 1 roll per person. The filling is kept simple, so you can really taste the sweet goodness of the tender teriyaki chicken and the cool crunchiness of the cucumber. You can prepare these medium-sized rolls an hour or two ahead. Chapter 6 explains how to make sliced rolls.

Special sushi tools: *Bamboo mat, sashimi knife (see Chapter 2)*

Preparation time: *15 minutes, plus 1½ hours to prepare the sushi rice*

Cooking time: *15 minutes*

Yield: *4 medium rolls (32 pieces)*

¾ to 1 pound chicken thighs or breasts, skinned and boned

1 tablespoon vegetable oil

3 tablespoons mirin

3 tablespoons soy sauce

4 teaspoons sugar

1 Japanese cucumber, salt-scrubbed (see Chapter 3)

4 sheets nori

4 cups prepared sushi rice (see Chapter 5)

1 Prick the chicken meat all over with a fork. Pour the oil into a large, heavy frying pan set over medium-high heat. After the oil is hot, add the chicken, cooking it for 6 to 8 minutes, turning it several times, until golden brown outside, but not necessarily cooked through. Turn off the heat. Using a paper towel, dab up any oil or fat in the pan before you add the ingredients for the teriyaki sauce in Step 2.

2 Blend the mirin, soy sauce, and sugar together and pour on top of the hot chicken in the pan. Turn the heat on to low, cover, and cook for 5 or more minutes, turning several times, until the chicken is just cooked through. Remove the lid and turn the heat up to high for 1 to 2 minutes, cooking until the sauce becomes thick and shiny. Remove from the heat. (At this point you can cool, cover, and refrigerate the chicken in its sauce up to a day ahead.) Slice the cooked and cooled chicken into ⅓-inch-thick strips.

3 While the chicken cools down, trim the cucumber to 8 inches in length. Cut the cucumber into quarters lengthwise (refer to Figure 8-1 in Chapter 8). If the cucumber is over 1 inch wide, slice it into sixths (by cutting each half into thirds), or the pieces will be too thick for the size of the nori. Set aside.

4 Lay a bamboo mat down with its slats parallel to the edge of the countertop or table. Place a sheet of nori lengthwise, shiny side down, on the edge of the bamboo mat closest to you. Spread 1 cup of rice evenly on the nori, leaving a 2½-inch-wide strip of nori (refer to Figure 6-5 in Chapter 6) not covered with rice on the edge farthest away from you. Lay 2 or more pieces of glazed chicken, end to end, across the center of the rice, spanning the length of the nori. Snuggle a piece of cucumber up next to the chicken.

5 Lift up the edge of the mat closest to you, keeping your fingertips on the fillings, and roll the mat and its contents away from you until the edge of the mat touches straight down on the far edge of the rice (refer to Figure 6-6 in Chapter 6). Tug on the mat to tighten the roll. Lay the mat down on the counter and move the partially done roll back to the edge of the mat closest to you. Lift the mat again and finish rolling up the roll. Tug on the mat to tighten the roll.

6 Cut the roll into 8 equal pieces, wiping your knife with a damp towel before each slice. Make 3 more rolls, following these instructions. No dipping sauce is served with this sushi.

Vary It! *Substitute fresh salmon for the chicken, adding 2 or 3 thin slices of fresh gingerroot to the teriyaki sauce ingredients.*

Tip: *Using chicken thighs makes for a more flavorful and moist roll than do chicken breasts.*

Per piece: *Calories 76 (From Fat 15); Fat 2g (Saturated 0g); Cholesterol 9mg; Sodium 156mg; Carbohydrate 11g (Dietary Fiber 0g); Protein 4g.*

Ground Turkey and Vegetable Osaka-Style Scattered Sushi

Osaka-style scattered sushi (see Chapter 6), or sushi rice salad, is a breeze to make. It's nothing more than a big bowl of rice tossed with flavorful ingredients. Taking care as you prepare each of the ingredients is the reason that it's so pretty and incredibly delicious.

You can prepare the ingredients while the rice soaks and cooks, or make the recipe in stages. Because it's easy but time consuming, we make it for a crowd of 10 to 12. Present it in a big, beautiful bowl or in a wooden sushi tub (see Chapter 2). This scattered sushi tastes best an hour or two after it's made, allowing the flavors to blend together nicely.

Preparation time: *1½ hours, plus 1½ hours to prepare the sushi rice*

Cooking time: *35 minutes*

Yield: *Makes 12 servings (18 cups, 1½ cups per person)*

Preparing the mushrooms and bamboo shoots

¾ ounce (about 8) dried shiitake mushrooms

2 cups water

8.5-ounce can bamboo shoots, rinsed and diced

⅓ cup soy sauce

¼ cup sugar

2 tablespoons mirin

1 Rinse off the shiitake mushrooms and soak them in the 2 cups water for 30 to 45 minutes, or until soft. Strain the soaking water and set aside. Chop the mushrooms into small pieces, discarding the stems.

2 Add the mushrooms, bamboo shoots, soy sauce, sugar, and mirin to a medium-sized pot. Pour in the reserved strained mushroom water. Bring the mixture to a boil over medium-high heat, and then lower the heat and simmer the mixture for 20 minutes. Remove from the heat and set aside. (You can do this step 2 to 3 days in advance and refrigerate the mixture until needed.)

Preparing the ground turkey

2 teaspoons vegetable oil

1 pound ground turkey (or chicken)

5 tablespoons soy sauce

¼ cup sugar

5 tablespoons sake

1 Pour the oil into a nonstick frying pan placed over a medium-high heat. After the oil is hot, add the ground turkey, breaking it into small, pebble-sized pieces.

2 Sprinkle the soy sauce, sugar, and sake over the turkey. Fry, stirring constantly, for 2 or 3 minutes until the turkey is done and the liquids absorbed. Remove from the heat and set aside. (You can do this step a day in advance and refrigerate the mixture until needed.)

Preparing the peas and carrots

1 pound (4 cups) frozen diced carrots and peas	*2 tablespoons mirin*

Cook the vegetables according to the manufacturer's instructions, taking care not to overcook them. Drain, season with mirin, and set aside.

Preparing the toppings

1 carrot	*12 large eggs*
1 pound (¼ small) jicama	*2 tablespoons mirin*
2 tablespoons rice vinegar	*2 teaspoons vegetable oil*
2 teaspoons sugar	

1 Peel and slice the carrot into ⅛-inch-thick pieces. Slice the jicama into ⅛-inch-thick pieces. Using small, ½-inch- to ¾-inch-wide decorative vegetable cutters (refer to Figure 7-3 in Chapter 7), cut out 2 dozen or so flowers or other pretty shapes and place them in a small bowl filled with the vinegar and sugar, which flavors them and gives them a fresh appearance hours after they've been cut. (You can do this step hours ahead.)

2 Whisk the eggs and mirin together well. Pour the oil into a nonstick frying pan set over medium heat. When hot, add the eggs and begin stirring slowly but constantly, cooking the eggs 10 to 12 minutes, breaking up scrambled egg lumps into smaller and smaller pieces, until they're the texture of coarse sand. Set aside briefly, or cover and refrigerate.

(continued)

(continued)

Assembling the scattered sushi

10 cups warm prepared sushi rice
(see Chapter 5)

4 sheets nori, finely crumbled

¼ cup reroasted white sesame seeds
(see Chapter 3)

1 Be sure all the ingredients to be mixed into the warm sushi rice are prepared and sitting out next to you before you turn out and season the
cooked rice with vinegar dressing.

2 After the rice is seasoned but still quite warm, gently fold in (in this order)
the prepared mushrooms and bamboo shoots, ground turkey, peas and
carrots, crumbled nori, and sesame seeds. Fan the rice as you fold in the
ingredients. Keep turning the rice mixture over and fanning it until cool.

3 Turn the sushi rice mixture out into a big serving bowl, or if you're using a
wooden sushi tub, leave it in the tub for service. Scatter the finely scrambled eggs over the rice as evenly as possible. Decorate the top of the
sushi rice with the vegetable flowers. Set the finished sushi aside in a cool
corner of the kitchen, covered, up to 2 hours.

Vary It! *As you've probably figured out, you can make this an all-veggie scattered sushi if that's your preference.*

Per serving: *Calories 487 (From Fat 108); Fat 12g (Saturated 3g); Cholesterol 240mg; Sodium
1,079mg; Carbohydrate 69g (Dietary Fiber 5g); Protein 22g.*

Ginger-Beef Roll

Not everyone likes the taste of nori, but that doesn't stop them
from enjoying rolled sushi. All that's required is to choose a different wrapping for the sushi, and lettuce is a great replacement. In
fact, we think that lettuce is sometimes a better flavor companion
than nori, as in the following Ginger Beef and Lettuce-Wrapped
Sliced Rolls. The tangy-salty flavor of the pickled mountain burdock *(yamagobo)* and the pleasantly sharp ginger taste of the beef
actually go better with the cool taste of lettuce than nori.

Marinate and cook the beef a day ahead. Roll up the lettuce rolls
hours ahead and then all you have left to do is slice them at the last
minute. Lettuce is more difficult to work with than nori because lettuce isn't as stiff nor does it lie as flat, but you'll get the hang of it
quickly.

Ginger Beef and Lettuce-Wrapped Sliced Rolls

When making the fresh ginger marinade for the beef in this recipe (or anything that's going to be grilled), use just the grated ginger juice, not the ginger fiber. The fiber burns quickly, giving the beef a scorched taste, which you don't want.

Pickled mountain burdock (*yamagobo*) looks like skinny carrots and tastes like pickled parsnips. It's an extraordinary flavor to couple with ginger-flavored beef. The only tricky part of the recipe is not tearing the tender lettuce as you work with it. That's why it's wisest to blanch extra pieces of lettuce so that you have plenty to work with.

Special sushi tools: *Bamboo mat wrapped with plastic wrap, sashimi knife (see Chapter 2)*

Preparation time: *35 minutes, plus 1½ hours to prepare the sushi rice*

Cooking time: *10 minutes*

Yield: *4 medium rolls (32 pieces)*

Preparing the ginger beef

2 ounces fresh gingerroot	½ pound rib eye or top sirloin, trimmed of fat
2 tablespoons soy sauce	
2 tablespoons mirin	1 teaspoon vegetable oil

1 Peel and grate the gingerroot in a circular motion until you have about 3 tablespoons of ginger. Squeeze the grated gingerroot to release all the juices. You should have about 2 tablespoons ginger juice for the marinade. Discard the ginger fiber.

2 Stir the ginger juice, soy sauce, and mirin together in the bottom of a small dish. Put the meat in the dish, turning to coat both sides with ginger marinade. Refrigerate the meat for 30 minutes, turning it once or twice.

3 Pour the vegetable oil into a heavy frying pan and place it over high heat. Once hot, fry the marinated meat, turning it over once or twice, for 4 to 5 minutes. Reduce the heat to low and pour in the ginger marinade. Cook the meat 4 to 5 minutes more, turning 2 or 3 times, until well done. Take the meat out of the pan and let it cool for 5 to 10 minutes before slicing it, allowing time for the juices to settle down. Slice the meat into ¼-inch-thick strips. Set aside briefly or refrigerate overnight.

(continued)

(continued)

Assembling the roll

12 large romaine lettuces leaves

8 pickled mountain burdock

4 cups prepared sushi rice (see Chapter 5)

1 Bring a large pot of water to a boil. Drop in 1 or 2 lettuce leaves at a time, blanching them for 3 to 5 seconds at most. Using tongs, remove them from the water and then plunge them into a bowl of ice water to stop the cooking and set their color. Drain them on paper towels. Repeat until all the leaves are blanched. Slice off, without slicing through the lettuce, the raised back of the lettuce ribs.

2 Place the plastic-wrapped bamboo mat in front of you with its slats parallel to the edge of the table or countertop. Lay 2 blanched lettuce leaves down, ribbed side up, on the edge of the wrapped bamboo mat closest to you. The stalk ends should be slightly overlapping in the middle. Carefully open them up until they're completely flat. Their combined shape should be roughly 7 inches wide x 8 inches long. Fold in the tips of the lettuce if they extend off the bamboo mat. If a leaf tears, replace it or patch it with pieces of an extra leaf.

3 Spread 1 cup of rice evenly on the lettuce, leaving a 2½-inch-wide strip of lettuce not covered with rice on the edge farthest away from you.

4 Lay 2 pieces of pickled mountain burdock, end to end, across the center of the rice, spanning the length of the lettuce. Bunch one-fourth of the ginger beef up next to the pickled burdock, spanning the length of the lettuce. Roll up this lettuce-wrapped roll as you would a nori-wrapped sliced roll (see Chapter 6): Lift the edge of the mat closest to you, keeping your fingers over the fillings. Roll the mat and its contents away from you until the edge of the mat touches straight down onto the far edge of the rice, enclosing the fillings completely. Tug on the mat to tighten the roll. Lift the edge of the mat up and finish rolling it up. Tug on the mat again to tighten the roll.

5 Lay a piece of plastic wrap over the roll. Cut the roll into 8 equal pieces, wiping your knife with a damp towel before each slice. Make 3 more rolls, following these instructions. Serve immediately or set aside in a cool place, covered, up to 2 hours.

Per slice: *Calories 54 (From Fat 12); Fat 1g (Saturated 1g); Cholesterol 4mg; Sodium 90mg; Carbohydrate 8g (Dietary Fiber 0g); Protein 2g.*

Chapter 11

Chi-Chi Sushi: Stepping Up to Glamorous Sushi

In This Chapter

▶ Filling elegant sushi with seafood

▶ Creating stylish veggie sushi

C hi-chi sushi is all about sophistica-tion, elegance, and style on a plate. To be chi-chi in our book, a recipe must meet the following criteria:

✔ It must not only capture beautiful colors, like our intricate Grilled Shrimp and Thai Basil Inside-Out Rolls, in which the wonderful russet tones of grilled shrimp are amplified by other strong colors in the fillings, but must also have an unexpected ingredient, like Thai basil.

✔ It must resonate like a harmonious piece of music, all of its ingredients playing off each other, like our Avocado and Tapenade Finger Sushi, where rich, creamy avocado slices round out the bright, acidic flavors of the olive-flavored tape-nade garnish. But the recipe must also be a new-to-sushi com-bination of flavors, such as the tapenade and avocado.

✔ It must possess an appealing shape, but this shape must be sophisticated or fancy, such as our Smoked Salmon Sushi Packages. Here, generous slices of smoked salmon are draped over plump sushi rice balls filled with minced egg, onions, and capers and then closed with a strip of nori, resembling a pretty package.

> ✔ It must not only touch on beauty, harmony, and shape but also should take into consideration a chic playfulness. An example is our Birthday Cake Pressed Sushi, in which sushi rice is presented in cake form, complete with candles, and topped with a layer of bright green and spicy wasabi tobiko (seasoned flying fish roe).

Your sushi will be not only chi-chi but so, so perfect if you take the time to read Chapters 4 through 7. Those chapters give you advice on the best ways to work with fish and vegetables the sushi way; discuss how to make fragrant, tasty sushi rice; describe the sushi techniques needed for these recipes; and explain how to cut, slice, and dice the sushi way.

Sampling Stylish Gifts from the Sea

Sushi's trademark ingredient is fresh seafood in all its glorious manifestations. The sophisticated recipes here put into play smoked salmon, grilled shrimp, flying fish roe, and, in one recipe, just a touch of anchovies.

Avocado and Tapenade Finger Sushi

Fresh lemon zest and tapenade, a tangy spread containing black olives, anchovies, and capers, packs the flavor punch in this simple — like a little black dress is simple — dressy sushi. Tapenade is sold in gourmet food stores and better grocery stores, usually in the olive section. Chapter 6 explains the two different techniques you can use when making finger sushi.

Preparation time: 30 minutes, plus 1½ hours to prepare the sushi rice

Yield: 8 finger sushi

1 sheet of nori

1 cup prepared sushi rice (see Chapter 5)

1 ripe but still firm avocado

2 teaspoons tapenade

2 teaspoons lemon zest (the grated yellow part of the peel)

1 Cut a sheet of 7-x-8-inch nori into 2 pieces, each one 4 inches x 7 inches. Cut one of these pieces into 8 strips, each one ½ inch x 4 inches. (Save the other half sheet for a hand roll.)

2 Prepare 8 finger sushi (see Chapter 6), using the sushi rice.

3 Peel and slice the avocado lengthwise into 16 slender slices, each one ⅛ inch thick (refer to Figure 8-2 in Chapter 8). You may have some avocado left over for another use. Top each finger sushi with 2 slender, lengthwise slices of avocado. Secure the slices to the finger sushi by wrapping a ½-inch-x-4-inch strip of nori, crosswise, around each one.

4 Drop ¼ teaspoon tapenade onto the center of each nori strip. Garnish with just a touch (about ¼ teaspoon) of the lemon zest.

Tip: *As you make more and more sushi, you'll have leftover prepared sushi rice in the freezer (see Chapter 5). Use it to make this sushi for a last-minute party.*

Vary It! *Make this recipe vegetarian by substituting a few minced kalamata olives for the tapenade, or simply use rich, buttery, avocado (as shown in the color insert).*

Per finger sushi: *Calories 76 (From Fat 39); Fat 4g (Saturated 1g); Cholesterol 0mg; Sodium 48mg; Carbohydrate 9g (Dietary Fiber 1g); Protein 1g.*

Perking up the looks of sushi garnishes

Giving a finished or artistic look to a plate is very important in the presentation of chi-chi sushi, or any sushi for that matter. Think seasonal, meaning that if it's fall, perhaps use one beautiful leaf (not for consumption, and not poisonous, of course) that's changing colors. Think reasonable, meaning use what you have on hand, such as a little parsley or other fresh herbs. Whatever you choose, give it a lively look by submerging it in cold water and leaving it there for 10 minutes or so. Parsley perks right up, and carrot ribbons curl up. Leaves from your garden take on a fresher appearance, but be sure to tell guests not to eat them. Shake the water off the garnish; don't dry it. You want the look of morning dew to add life to the garnish and plate.

Smoked Salmon Sushi Packages

Smoked salmon served with chopped eggs, onions, and just a touch of capers has always been a huge hit, but its popularity soars — and its sophistication quotient goes way up — when you wrap it all up in a fancy package. Serve 1 package per person as a first course at a formal dinner or 2 packages per person as the main course at a luncheon.

Preparation time: *45 minutes, plus 1½ hours to prepare the sushi rice*

Yield: *4 packages*

1⅓ cups sushi rice (see Chapter 5)

Tarragon Vinegar Dressing (see the following recipe)

1 hard-boiled egg, minced

1 tablespoon minced onion

1 tablespoon capers, rinsed

4 to 8 slices (about 3 to 4 ounces) smoked salmon

4 sprigs parsley or watercress

4 strips of nori, each ½ inch wide x 7 inches long

Lemon wedges

1 Cook, season, fan, and cool rice for this sushi as explained in Chapter 5, substituting the Tarragon Vinegar Dressing that's part of this recipe for the traditional rice vinegar dressing. While the rice is still warm, gently mix in the minced egg, onion, and capers.

2 Make a flat, round sushi rice patty (like a tiny hamburger patty) by filling the center of a 10-inch piece of plastic wrap with one-fourth of the sushi rice mixture (be sure to use damp hands). Lift and twist the plastic wrap and the rice ball in opposite directions until you form a flat, round rice patty (refer to Figure 6-4 in Chapter 6 for the twisting technique).

3 Unwrap and put the rice patty on a plate. Wrap it with a slice or two of smoked salmon, completely enclosing the rice patty. Top the salmon with a sprig of parsley. To secure the package, place a ½-inch-wide strip of nori over the rice patty, tucking it under to resemble ribbon.

4 Make 3 more packages the same way. Serve immediately with lemon wedges.

Tarragon Vinegar Dressing

1 tablespoon tarragon vinegar

½ teaspoon sugar

⅓ teaspoon salt

Stir all the ingredients together until dissolved.

Go-With: *Make a cucumber salad to serve on the side by cutting ribbons of cucumber (see Chapter 7), drizzling them with a little olive oil and lemon juice, and sprinkling them with lemon zest, sea salt, and cracked black pepper. Divine!*

Per package: Calories 129 (From Fat 22); Fat 2g (Saturated 1g); Cholesterol 60mg; Sodium 570mg; Carbohydrate 19g (Dietary Fiber 0g); Protein 7g.

Grilled Shrimp and Thai Basil Inside-Out Rolls with Spicy Lime Dipping Sauce

This showy roll gets a sophisticated and unexpected twist by changing the direction in which you lay the sheet of nori down in order to fill it. Normally, the nori is laid down lengthwise, but here we lay it down in a different way that exposes more of the colorful fillings than usual when the roll is complete. Making these stylish rolls is more complex and difficult than other rolls in this cookbook, but they're worth every minute. If this is your first inside-out roll experience, be sure to read about inside-out rolls in Chapter 6 before you begin.

Special sushi tools: *Bamboo mat wrapped with plastic wrap; 8 bamboo skewers, 6 to 8 inches long; sashimi knife (see Chapter 2)*

Preparation time: *1 hour, plus 1½ hours to prepare the sushi rice*

Cooking time: *15 minutes*

Yield: *4 inside-out rolls (24 pieces)*

Preparing the fillings

8 Grilled Shrimp (see the following recipe)

4 to 5 ounces jicama

1 medium carrot

4 large or 8 small red leaf lettuce leaves

8 sprigs Thai basil or other basil

1 Prepare the Grilled Shrimp as explained in the following recipe.

2 Peel and sliver the jicama and carrot. Rinse and dry the lettuce and basil. Split large lettuce leaves in half, or use 8 small leaves. You're ready to roll.

(continued)

(continued)

Rolling up the rolls

4 sheets nori

4 cups tightly packed prepared sushi rice
(see Chapter 5)

2 tablespoons reroasted black sesame
seeds (see Chapter 3)

1 Lay a plastic-wrapped bamboo mat in front of you with its slats parallel to
the edge of the countertop or table. Place a whole sheet of nori lengthwise, shiny side down, on the edge of the plastic-wrapped bamboo mat
closest to you (refer to Figure 6-7 in Chapter 6). Dip your hands in a bowl
of vinegared water and then tap your fingertips on a damp towel to
remove excess water. Press 1 tightly packed cup of the sushi rice evenly
over the nori. Sprinkle ½ tablespoon of reroasted sesame seeds over the
rice.

2 Pick up the rice-covered nori, turn it over, and place it, rice side down,
with a corner of the nori pointing toward you, like a diamond shape, on
the edge of the bamboo mat closest to you.

3 Fill the roll in this order: Place 2 small lettuce leaves (or 1 large one split
in half) lengthwise on the nori, not in the exact center, but a little closer to
you, with their ruffled tips extending over the edges for looks. Next, add 2
Grilled Shrimp, one-fourth of the carrots, one-fourth of the jicama, and 2
sprigs of basil. Bunch the fillings close together.

4 Lift the edge of the mat closest to you with both hands, keeping your fingers over the fillings, and roll the mat and its contents until the edge of
the mat touches straight down onto the nori, enclosing the fillings completely. Lift up the edge of the mat you're holding, and continue rolling the
inside-out roll away from you until it's sealed. Tug the mat to tighten the
roll. Place the roll on a damp, clean, smooth surface.

5 Lay a sheet of plastic wrap over the completed roll. Wipe a sharp knife
with a damp towel and cut both ends off the roll (they'll be large pieces).
Slice the middle section of the roll into 4 pieces, wiping your knife with a
damp towel before each slice.

6 Make 3 more rolls, following these instructions. Serve slices as an appetizer, or 1 sliced roll per person as a light meal, accompanied by Spicy
Lime Dipping Sauce (see the accompanying recipe).

Grilled Shrimp

8 jumbo shrimp (about ¾ ounce each), peeled, tail shells removed, and cleaned

8 bamboo skewers, soaked in water for 15 minutes

1 tablespoon dark sesame seed oil

¼ teaspoon salt

1 Insert a bamboo skewer through the middle of the shrimp from the head end to the tail end to straighten them out (refer to Figure 8-3 in Chapter 8). Roll the skewered shrimp in the sesame oil and then sprinkle with salt.

2 Grill (or pan-fry) the shrimp on both sides over medium heat until just cooked through, about 3 to 4 minutes. Be careful not to overcook the shrimp.

3 Twist to remove the bamboo skewer from each shrimp.

Spicy Lime Dipping Sauce

Yield: ½ cup

3 tablespoons rice vinegar

3 tablespoons fresh lime juice

1 tablespoon soy sauce

1 tablespoon sugar

2 teaspoons minced serrano chile, or to taste

1 tablespoon chopped Thai basil leaves or other basil leaves

Mix all the ingredients together in a small bowl. Refrigerate until needed.

Per piece: Calories 63 (From Fat 9); Fat 1g (Saturated 0g); Cholesterol 14mg; Sodium 115mg; Carbohydrate 11g (Dietary Fiber 1g); Protein 3g.

Birthday Cake Pressed Sushi

This is not your grandmother's birthday cake recipe, that's for sure. It's a big, fanciful-looking pressed sushi cake topped with wasabi tobiko, which is seasoned flying fish roe *(tobiko)*. It's playfully chi-chi and a good example of new, creative sushi. The recipe requires a springform pan, which you can purchase at kitchenware stores. Serve this Birthday Cake Pressed Sushi as a light luncheon or as a first course. Use a damp, clean, super-sharp, thin knife to cut this sushi cake, or it will mash down as you slice it. If you make the Egg Salad as much as a day head and the rice that morning, assembling the cake takes just 30 minutes.

Special sushi tools: *Sashimi knife (see Chapter 2)*

Preparation time: *50 minutes, plus 1½ hours to prepare the sushi rice*

Yield: *12 generous slices*

7½ cups prepared sushi rice (see Chapter 5)

2 cups Egg Salad (see the following recipe)

3 sheets nori, crumbled

4¾ to 5 ounces wasabi tobiko

1 teaspoon reroasted black sesame seeds (See Chapter 3)

Garnishes: lemon wedges, parsley sprigs

1 Place a sheet of plastic wrap down into and extending over the edge of a 9½-inch springform pan. Cut a cardboard round to fit just inside your pan (or use a 9-inch cake board if you have one). Cover it tightly with plastic wrap and set it aside.

2 Dip your hands in a bowl of vinegared water before working with the sushi rice. Tap your fingertips on a damp, wrung-out towel, set next to you, to remove any excess water.

3 Spread 2½ cups prepared sushi rice evenly across the bottom of pan, covering it completely. Press down with the plastic-wrapped cardboard lid, being sure to press down on the edges or sides of the rice, too, as shown in Figure 11-1.

4 Spoon on the Egg Salad and then smooth it out over the pressed rice, using the back of the spoon. Cover the Egg Salad with 2½ cups rice by placing the rice in small mounds around the top of the egg salad and then gently spreading the rice out evenly all over the egg salad. Press again with the cardboard lid, all around the mold. Sprinkle the crumbled nori evenly over the pressed rice. Add a final layer of 2½ cups rice. Press again all around the mold.

5 Finish this pressed cake by spooning on the wasabi tobiko, using the back of the spoon to smooth it out evenly over the rice. Sprinkle with the sesame seeds.

6 Release the clamp on the sides of the springform pan. Lift the sides off. Cut off the loose plastic wrap or tuck it under the bottom of the pan. Put the pressed cake on a cake stand, surround with lemon wedges and pars- ley sprigs, stick in your candles, and present the cake (see Figure 11-1)!

7 Cut the cake into 12 wedges, making sure that your knife is clean and damp (wipe it on the damp towel you should have by your side) to pre- vent tearing the pressed sushi cake apart. Take your time. Use the tip of the knife and cut in small motions. Don't try to cut the cake in half and then quarters. That technique won't work because of all the sticky rice that will stick to your knife. Cut it wedge by wedge, wiping the knife off frequently. Enjoy!

Egg Salad

Yield: *2 cups*

6 large eggs, boiled, peeled, and minced	*¼ cup minced celery*
¼ cup minced red or white onion (see Chapter 7)	*3 tablespoons mayonnaise*
	Salt to taste

Stir all the ingredients together until well combined. Refrigerate until needed.

Vary It! *If you have the bucks, substitute beluga or sevruga caviar for the wasabi tobiko!*

Go-With: *Champagne!*

Tip: *Use 2 cups egg salad from your favorite deli, as long as the eggs and other ingredients are minced. Big chunks of ingredients could make the pressed cake fall apart when cut.*

Per slice: *Calories 239 (From Fat 58); Fat 7g (Saturated 2g); Cholesterol 150mg; Sodium 233mg; Carbohydrate 36 (Dietary Fiber 1g); Protein 9g.*

PRESSING, UNMOLDING, AND SERVING THE BIRTHDAY CAKE PRESSED SUSHI

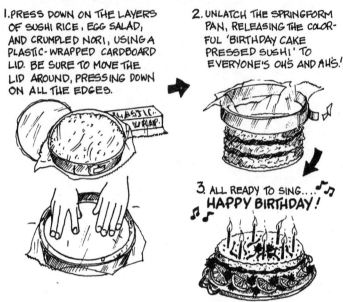

1. PRESS DOWN ON THE LAYERS OF SUSHI RICE, EGG SALAD, AND CRUMPLED NORI, USING A PLASTIC-WRAPPED CARDBOARD LID. BE SURE TO MOVE THE LID AROUND, PRESSING DOWN ON ALL THE EDGES.

2. UNLATCH THE SPRINGFORM PAN, RELEASING THE COLORFUL 'BIRTHDAY CAKE PRESSED SUSHI' TO EVERYONE'S OH'S AND AH'S!

3. ALL READY TO SING.... HAPPY BIRTHDAY!

Figure 11-1: Pressing, unmolding, and serving the Birthday Cake Pressed Sushi.

Appreciating Sophisticated Vegetable Sushi

It takes only one really chic sushi recipe to make an elegant statement. Gorgonzola Cheese and Spicy Sprouts Battleship Sushi is the one. Gorgonzola cheese is a stylish and new addition to sushi, especially when teamed up with spicy sprouts and a dash of rich, somewhat bitter walnut oil that links all the sushi's tastes together. Battleship sushi evolved as a way to capture loose fillings on top of finger sushi rice balls that would fall off the rice if it weren't for the little nori strips around the rice balls that serve as a reservoir.

⌀ Gorgonzola Cheese and Spicy Sprouts Battleship Sushi

Einstein's shock-wave hair looked like he'd stuck his finger in an electrical socket, part of his wild, creative look. This chic yet playful-looking finger sushi has the same comical look, topped with an explosion of sprouts. Full-bodied Gorgonzola blue cheese hides under a refreshing bite of sprouts, preferably an alfalfa and onion mix sometimes called Zesty Sprouts, but alfalfa alone is also fine.

Preparation time: *12 minutes, plus 1½ hours to prepare the sushi rice*

Yield: *8 finger sushi*

1 cup prepared sushi rice (see Chapter 5)

1 sheet nori, cut into 8 strips, each 1 inch x 7 inches

1½ ounces crumbled Gorgonzola cheese or other blue cheese

2 to 3 ounces Zesty Sprouts, or alfalfa sprouts

1½ to 2 teaspoons walnut oil

1 Prepare 8 finger sushi (see Chapter 6), using the sushi rice.

2 Wrap a 1-inch-wide strip of nori around the sides of each finger sushi, shiny side out, creating a tiny collar all around the rice (refer to Figure 6-3 in Chapter 6). Attach the nori with a grain of rice, if necessary. Delicately spoon one-eighth of the cheese (½ to ¾ teaspoon) into each collar.

3 Gently toss the sprouts with the walnut oil. Pick up and place as generous a bunch of sprouts as possible on top of each battleship sushi. Serve immediately while the nori is crisp.

Go-With: *Have friends by for drinks and serve these sushi with the Avocado and Tapenade Finger Sushi in this chapter and the Saketinis in Chapter 13.*

Per piece: Calories 60 (From Fat 22); Fat 3g (Saturated 1g); Cholesterol 5mg; Sodium 97mg; Carbohydrate 7g (Dietary Fiber 0g); Protein 2g.

Chapter 12

Extreme Sushi: Blowing Away the Boundaries

Creative sushi *(sosaku-zushi)* is taking the sushi world by storm (see Chapter 6). In the United States, Europe, Latin America, Asia, and even Japan — sushi's homeland — sushi bar chefs and home sushi cooks alike are raising the bar, crafting all kinds of exciting new tastes, textures, and international twists on sushi. Old-style sushi bars still flourish in Japan, offering traditional sushi that the populace has enjoyed for generations, dishes such as Tuna Finger Sushi and Cucumber Sliced Rolls (see Chapter 8), but creative sushi is what's hip and happening there, too.

Extreme sushi, as we call it, blasts creative sushi into the outer culinary stratosphere, that "Wow, I never knew sushi could be like this!" place that sushi lovers crave. We're daring enough to throw out old-style sushi conventions in favor of new sushi experiences, but not without a lot of careful thought and taste testing. Well-prepared sushi rice must stay the heart and soul of extreme sushi dishes. All other components must be chosen to marry well with the rice, such as our Oysters on the Half Shell with Tempura Sushi Rice Balls. We've nicknamed it our "honeymoon special recipe" because of its over-the-top sensual elegance and flair.

If you're launching your sushi-making efforts with a recipe from this chapter, give yourself a jump-start by reading Chapters 4 through 7 to find out about making perfect sushi rice; handling fresh seafood; cutting, slicing, and dicing the sushi way; and perfecting sushi-making techniques.

Loving Sushi on a Half Shell

Take cold, slippery-smooth raw oysters on the half-shell; serve with hot, crunchy tempura sushi rice balls; and you have a truly sensuous experience. First, slip a chilled, sweet oyster topped with a dollop of fiery Spicy Daikon Relish into your mouth. Then pop a crisp Tempura Sushi Rice Ball into your mouth, releasing a rush of bright tastes. Finally, swoon with delight!

Oysters on the Half Shell with Tempura Sushi Rice Balls

You can shuck the oysters just as you serve them, or do what we do on occasion: Call ahead and order shucked oysters on the half-shell from your local fishmonger. Be sure to bring them home on ice within an hour of serving them, or they lose their freshness. Tempura Sushi Rice Balls by themselves, topped with a dab of Spicy Daikon Relish, make great pick-up-and-eat one-bite appetizers.

To make this a do-ahead recipe, you can prepare the Ponzu Sauce, Spicy Daikon Relish, and Tempura Sushi Rice Balls several hours ahead. Reheat the rice balls in a 350-degree oven for several minutes until hot. Tempura Sushi Rice Balls are a perfect use of leftover sushi rice (see Chapter 5).

Preparation time: *35 minutes, plus 1½ hours to prepare the sushi rice*

Cooking time: *10 minutes*

Yield: *4 servings (2 oysters and 3 Tempura Sushi Rice Balls per person)*

8 oysters	½ cup Ponzu Sauce (see Chapter 9), or use store-bought sauce
12 Tempura Sushi Rice Balls (see the following recipe)	
2 teaspoons Spicy Daikon Relish (see Chapter 9)	1 tablespoon thinly sliced scallions (see Chapter 3), rinsed and patted dry

1 Scrub the live oysters under cold running water. Hold an oyster in your hand, cupped side down, on a thick towel (or use an oyster glove), push the tip of an oyster knife into the shell's hinge, twisting the knife side to side to pop the hinge open (refer to Figure 4-1 in Chapter 4). Scrape the meat off the flat top shell and then loosen the oyster from the rounded bottom shell. Open all the other oysters in the same manner.

2 Set 2 oysters in their bottom shells on each of 4 plates. Top each oyster with a dab of Spicy Daikon Relish and a pinch of scallions. Group 3 Tempura Sushi Rice Balls on each plate. Serve with the Ponzu Sauce (see Chapter 9) on the side.

Tempura Sushi Rice Balls

Yield: *12 rice balls*

¾ cup prepared sushi rice (see Chapter 5)

½ cup plus 2 tablespoons commercial tempura mix

½ cup ice-cold water or ice-cold beer

1 quart canola or vegetable oil

2 to 3 drops dark sesame oil (optional)

Sea salt

1 Dip your hands in a bowl of vinegared water and then tap your fingertips on a damp towel to remove excess water. Pick up about 1 tablespoon of the sushi rice and gently roll it into a small ball, using the palms of your hands. Make 11 more rice balls the same way, wetting your hands each time.

2 Sift ½ cup of the tempura mix onto the water or beer. Using chopsticks or a fork, mix the batter just briefly. You want the mixture to be lumpy. Put the remaining 2 tablespoons of the tempura mix on a plate.

3 Using a deep fryer or a 2-quart or larger heavy pan set over medium heat, bring the canola and sesame oil, if desired, up to 350 degrees, as indicated on a deep-fat thermometer. Keep the oil at that temperature throughout deep-frying the rice balls.

4 Roll 5 to 6 sushi rice balls in the dry tempura mix and then quickly dip them in the tempura batter. Slide them into the hot oil and deep-fry them until crisp, 4 to 5 minutes (this first batch may not turn golden as later batches will). Don't let them touch each other as they fry. Drain the rice balls on paper towels. Fry the remaining rice balls until crisp and lightly golden, draining them also. Sprinkle them with sea salt, to taste.

Go-With: *Oysters and Tempura Sushi Rice Balls are meant to be served with champagne!*

Tip: *A small sheet of absorbent tempura paper, folded slightly offset and placed underneath the Tempura Sushi Rice Balls, not only lends an authentic Japanese touch to the dish but also absorbs any excess oil. Tempura paper, looking like square sheets of white paper, is sold in different sizes in packages in Asian and Japanese markets (see resources in Chapters 3 and 14).*

Per serving: *Calories 284 (From Fat 135); Fat 15g (Saturated 1g); Cholesterol 7mg; Sodium 1,587mg; Carbohydrate 30g (Dietary Fiber 0g); Protein 7g.*

Tasting Tropical Seafood Sushi

As Latin cooks have known for centuries, corn husks make wonderful wrappings for cooking food. Here, they're more symbolic because they're not used as cooking vessels but as "dishes" in which to display the sushi ingredients, including fresh corn kernels. You can make this dish at any time of year, but it tastes best and most appropriate during summer months, when corn is in season and mangoes are plentiful.

Grilled Yellowtail Sushi Tamales with Spicy Mango Salsa

What better than a sweet-spicy tropical salsa to pick up the clean, refreshing taste of prepared sushi rice and the toasted flavor of grilled corn and yellowtail. Make the salsa and tie the corn husks ahead. We serve 2 tamales per person as a light meal, but 1 tamale makes a great first course for 8 people as well. Tamales are usually completely sealed in corn husks, but here we leave the husks open so that you can see these "extremely" pretty contents.

Preparation time: *1 hour, plus 1½ hours to prepare the sushi rice*

Cooking time: *10 minutes*

Yield: *8 tamales*

2 tablespoons sake

2 tablespoons plus 2 teaspoons soy sauce

½ pound yellowtail, or sea bass

2 ears fresh corn, in their husks

2 rounded tablespoons pickled ginger, chopped

4 cups firmly packed prepared sushi rice (see Chapter 5)

1½ cups Spicy Mango Salsa (see the following recipe)

16 cilantro sprigs

2 limes, cut into wedges

1 Pour the sake and 2 tablespoons of the soy sauce into a shallow dish. Place the fish in the dish, turning it to coat both sides with marinade. Cover and refrigerate about 15 minutes.

2 Strip the husks off the corn, choosing 8 attractive ones to hold the sushi. Tear 8 long strips of husk, each 1 inch wide off the other husks. Tie one end of each of the 8 corn husks shut with a husk strip, as illustrated in Figure 12-1. (If doing this step several hours ahead, keep the tied husks wrapped in damp paper towels covered with plastic wrap, in the refrigerator.) Set aside.

3 Place the husked corn and marinated fish on the grill over medium-high heat or under a broiler. Grill them about 5 minutes, turning the corn a few times. Baste the corn with the remaining 2 teaspoons soy sauce. Grill both the fish and corn about 5 minutes more, turning the corn a few times, until the fish is cooked through and some of the corn kernels have turned golden brown.

4 After the corn and fish are cool, flake the fish into small pieces. Cut the corn off the cob, using 1 cup in this recipe and reserving the rest for another use. Gently mix the 1 cup corn kernels, all the flaked fish, and the ginger into the sushi rice.

5 Divide the sushi rice mixture among the 8 tied corn husks. Damp fingers are the easiest way to do this. Spoon 1 to 2 tablespoons Spicy Mango Salsa into the open end of each corn husk for a pretty presentation. Garnish each with 2 cilantro sprigs and a lime wedge. Serve immediately, passing the remaining salsa. Tell your guests to eat a bite of salsa with each bite of rice and fish.

Spicy Mango Salsa

Yield: *2 cups (½ cup per person)*

1½ cups diced mango (about a 1-pound mango)

½ cup minced red onion

¼ cup chopped cilantro

1½ teaspoons minced serrano chile

¼ teaspoon salt, or to taste

Mix all the salsa ingredients together in a bowl, cover, and refrigerate up to 1 day.

Vary It! *This sushi tamale is excellent with grilled shrimp or squid in place of fish.*

Per tamale: *Calories 227 (From Fat 18); Fat 2g (Saturated 0g); Cholesterol 15mg; Sodium 576mg; Carbohydrate 41g (Dietary Fiber 2g); Protein 10g.*

CREATING CORN HUSKS FOR SUSHI TAMALES

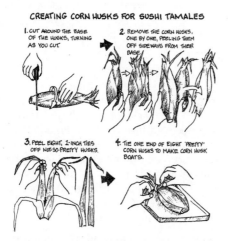

1. CUT AROUND THE BASE OF THE HUSKS, TURNING AS YOU CUT

2. REMOVE THE CORN HUSKS, ONE BY ONE, PEELING THEM OFF SIDEWAYS FROM THEIR BASE.

3. PEEL EIGHT, 1-INCH TIES OFF NOT-SO-PRETTY HUSKS.

4. TIE ONE END OF EIGHT 'PRETTY' CORN HUSKS TO MAKE CORN HUSK BOATS.

Figure 12-1: Tying corn husks for sushi tamales.

Unearthing Sushi from the Garden

Vegetarians love sushi for its rice-centric flavors. Add big, beautiful portobello mushrooms, and you're in veggie heaven.

Portobello Sushi Rice Cakes with Balsamic Sauce and Wasabi Oil

Take one large sushi rice ball, flatten it, pan-fry it until crispy, serve it with portobello mushrooms soaked through with a balsamic fusion sauce and wasabi oil drizzled on the plate, and you have a wild and crazy, but really good, extreme sushi recipe on your hands. This is a dressy-looking recipe, but it's too good to save for just dressy occasions. This is last-minute, knife-and-fork sushi.

Preparation time: *25 minutes, plus 1½ hours to prepare the sushi rice*

Cooking time: *25 minutes*

Yield: *4 servings*

3 tablespoons extra-virgin olive oil	*¼ cup mirin*
2 cups prepared sushi rice (see Chapter 5)	*1 tablespoon soy sauce*
4 small portobello mushrooms (each about 1½ ounces), cleaned and stems removed	*8 sprigs fresh thyme or oregano*
	8 whole roasted, unsalted almonds, coarsely chopped (about ½ ounce total)
Salt and pepper	*5 tablespoons Wasabi Oil (see the following recipe)*
½ cup water	
¼ cup balsamic vinegar	

1 Pour 2 tablespoons of the olive oil in a large, nonstick frying pan, tilting the pan to completely cover the bottom with oil, and then set it over medium heat. Pack a moist ½ cup measuring cup with the sushi rice to form a rice cake. Turn the rice cake out into the hot pan. Make 3 more rice cakes the same way, wiping out the measuring cup with a damp paper towel before making each one, and place them all in the frying pan, not touching each other. Fry them for 3 to 4 minutes, or until the cakes begin to crisp and turn light brown on the bottom. Turn and fry them 3 to 4 minutes more. Loosely cover the sushi rice cakes with aluminum foil and keep them warm in a 300 degree oven, up to 1 hour.

2 Wipe out the frying pan with paper towels, pour in the remaining 1 tablespoon olive oil, and set it back over medium heat. When hot, add the mushroom caps, sprinkling them with salt and pepper to taste. Cook them for 2 minutes or so on each side, until lightly browned.

3 Stir the water, balsamic vinegar, mirin, and soy sauce together. Pour the mixture into the frying pan (over the mushrooms), add 4 sprigs of the thyme, cover, and simmer the mushrooms for 5 minutes or so, until softened but still a little chewy. Set the mushrooms aside, covered, to keep them warm, leaving the sauce in the pan. Turn the heat up and rapidly boil the balsamic sauce until it coats the back of a spoon (it will measure about ½ cup), about 5 minutes.

4 To serve, place 1 warm sushi rice cake on each of 4 plates, tip a warm mushroom cap on to the rice cake's side, drizzle a little of the balsamic sauce around each rice cake and mushroom, sprinkle chopped almonds on top of the balsamic sauce, and finally drizzle around just a touch of the Wasabi Oil. Garnish the top of each rice cake with a sprig of fresh thyme. Serve immediately, passing the Wasabi Oil and any remaining balsamic sauce.

Wasabi Oil

Yield: *5 tablespoons*

3 tablespoons water

2 tablespoons wasabi powder

2 tablespoons extra-virgin olive oil

Stir 1 tablespoon of the water into the wasabi powder, making a paste. Stir in the remaining 2 tablespoons water and stir in the olive oil. If not using right away, cover with plastic wrap and refrigerate a day or so.

Tip: Use leftover prepared sushi rice (see Chapter 5) for the sushi rice cakes.

Per serving: *Calories 325 (From Fat 170); Fat 19g (Saturated 3g); Cholesterol 0mg; Sodium 488mg; Carbohydrate 34g (Dietary Fiber 2g); Protein 4g.*

Boomerang sushi

With more and more sushi bars opening in the United States, England, France, Mexico, and other points around the globe, it was bound to happen — sushi has boomeranged back to Japan in shapes and tastes that reflect other countries' takes on sushi as one of their own, new favorite foods. Sushi has moved out of Japanese sushi bars, the only food establishments that used to offer sushi, into trendy Japanese restaurants that give creative sushi *(sosaku-zushi)* a special place on their menu, using decidedly new-to-sushi ingredients, new-to-sushi shapes, and new-to-sushi presentations.

(continued)

(continued)

Restaurants in Japan now feature the likes of seared foie gras finger sushi with sweet soy glazing sauce, and smoked duck finger sushi with orange glazing sauce, both markedly French in attitude. Caprese finger sushi, made with mozzarella cheese, tomatoes, and fresh basil, as well as prosciutto and asparagus finger sushi both herald from — where else? — Italy. Chiles have long been a staple in the Japanese kitchen, but when the chiles are chipotle, and cream cheese is thrown into the mix, the recipe may well have originated in Mexico. To top it off, American-style sushi, such as the all-American California, caterpillar, and rainbow rolls, to name just three popular rolls, is being served in Japan today.

Saluting Independence Day

A major national holiday without sushi is unthinkable to us. So bring out the hot dogs, ketchup, and mustard, and don't forget the sushi rice — because we have just the Fourth of July Hot Dog Finger Sushi for you.

Fourth of July Hot Dog Finger Sushi

Two russet-colored hot dog slices rest on white finger sushi that's wrapped with a thin strip of black nori topped with a bright yellow dab of prepared mustard. Kids and adults alike get a kick out of this fun, Japanese-looking but all-American treat, and they love the taste!

Preparation time: *20 minutes, plus 1½ hours to prepare the sushi rice*

Cooking time: *3 minutes*

Yield: *8 finger sushi*

1 cup prepared sushi rice (see Chapter 5)

4 to 5 hot dogs (about ½ pound)

4 teaspoons ketchup

8 strips nori, each ½ inch wide x 4 inches long

2 teaspoons prepared mustard

1 Prepare 8 finger sushi (see Chapter 6), using the sushi rice.

2 Slice each hot dog into ¼-inch-thick pieces, cut on the diagonal, to achieve 4 center-cut pieces about 3 inches long. (Keep the ends and shorter pieces for another use.) You need a total of 16 pieces, 2 per finger sushi.

3 Fry the hot dog slices on both sides over medium-high heat until lightly browned. Drain on paper towels.

4 Dab a little ketchup on each finger sushi. Secure 2 hot dog slices to each rice ball by wrapping a strip of nori crosswise around the hot dogs, just like you do with the tofu finger sushi shown in Figure 9-1 in Chapter 9. Dab just a dollop of mustard on top of the strip of nori. Serve immediately.

Per finger sushi: Calories 108 (From Fat 61); Fat 7g (Saturated 3g); Cholesterol 12mg; Sodium 325mg; Carbohydrate 9g (Dietary Fiber 0g); Protein 3g.

Part IV
Enjoying Sushi Meals at Home and at the Sushi Bar

The 5th Wave   By Rich Tennant

"It's very good, but I wonder why they call it a 'Spouting Sea Dragon' roll."

In this part . . .

Sushi tastes great by itself, but it tastes even better when served with complementary dishes and drinks. Warming soups to build your appetite, cooling salads to refresh your palate, yummy little side dishes to add interest, drinks that complement the meal, and sweet finishes, whether perfectly ripe fruit or devilishly rich desserts — they're all in this part. So is a spectacular sushi hand roll party that's easy to carry off and won't break the bank.

When you're ready to step out of the kitchen into a sushi bar, we take you by the hand and lead you through the sushi bar's door, answering all your questions about what you'll see when you get there. We give you tips on how to order, what to order, how to eat all that beautiful sushi with your fingers (or with chopsticks), and what to expect when you pay the bill. Have a good time!

Chapter 13

Serving Sensational Sushi Sidekicks

In This Chapter

▶ Opening with appetizers

▶ Ladling out soups

▶ Sampling salads and side dishes

▶ Quenching your thirst

▶ Ending on a sweet note

*W*hen you're ready to make a full-scale sushi meal, starting with appetizers and finishing with dessert, you need a source of great-tasting recipes. That's where this chapter comes in handy.

The Japanese have a custom of eating small portions of many things. They judge a meal at its conclusion, not bite by bite, assessing whether the whole dining experience was pleasing. They expect a little something hot, something cold, something crunchy, something smooth, something light, something rich, something spicy, and something sweet. Plan your sushi meal to be served all at once, excluding dessert, or dish by dish, trying to achieve a personal balance of tastes and textures, or what seems right to you, when you're selecting recipes to serve around sushi.

We cover all the menu bases in this chapter, from tiny, one-bite appetizers such as Hard-Boiled Quail Eggs with Matcha Salt to sensational desserts such as Fire and Ice

Cream Sandwiches that get their sweet burn from wasabi. You can choose a side dish or two, such as Edamame (boiled soybeans) or Sake-Steamed Mussels and then decide what you'd like to drink with your sushi meal — green tea and Saketinis are both favorites.

Starting with an Appetizer

Some Japanese appetizers make good side dishes, and some side dishes make good appetizers. We like to serve Hard-boiled Quail Eggs with Matcha Salt as an appetizer, more than a side dish. Feel free to serve the side dishes offered later in this section as appetizers if they fit your bill of fare, especially the Edamame, or soybeans in their pod.

Hard-Boiled Quail Eggs with Matcha Salt

Most people eat their first hard-boiled quail egg out of curiosity. When they taste how much flavor these little ¼-ounce eggs have, especially when dipped in *matcha* (powdered green tea) salt, they go on to eat three or four more. Peeling quail eggs is like peeling chicken eggs in that sometimes the shells peel off smoothly and easily and sometimes they don't, so buy more than you need to allow for eggs that don't cooperate and break apart as you peel them.

Preparation time: *7 minutes*

Cooking time: *8 minutes*

Yield: *20 eggs (serves 4 people as appetizers)*

20 quail eggs (usually sold 10 to a package)	1 tablespoon vinegar
	Matcha Salt (see the following recipe)

1 Open the quail egg container carefully because the little eggs break easily. Submerge the eggs in a pot of cold water to which you've added the vinegar. Bring the water just to a boil and then reduce the heat, simmering the eggs 2 to 3 minutes, until cooked through.

2 Drain the eggs and put them in a bowl of ice water. When the eggs are cold (in just a few minutes), start peeling them.

3 Roll a wet egg on the counter, cracking the shell all over. Taking your time, peel the eggs from the rounded end first. After the eggs are peeled, rinse them off to remove any little bits of shell. Refrigerate the eggs, covered, up to 1 day.

4 Serve the eggs cold, stacked in a martini glass or pretty bowl, with Matcha Salt on the side as a dipping salt. The speckled shells are so attractive that we like to leave a few eggs in their shell for people to admire mixed in with the peeled eggs. Tell your guests to eat just a touch of Matcha Salt on the eggs, or they'll have bright green tongues!

Vary It! *If you can't find quail eggs, you can substitute chicken eggs in our recipe. One hard-boiled chicken egg, quartered, equals four quail eggs.*

Matcha Salt

Yield: *1 generous teaspoon*

1 teaspoon sea salt   ¼ teaspoon matcha

Stir the salt and *matcha* together. Cover the Matcha Salt tightly with plastic wrap until you're ready to use it (moisture in the air causes the powdered green tea to become damp).

Vary It! *Vary the salt mixture. Use paprika or black sesame seeds in place of the matcha. Serve all three colors with dozens of eggs at a big party.*

Go-With: *Serve these eggs with Saketinis (see the recipe later in this chapter). Serve the Matcha Salt with Tempura Sushi Rice Balls (see Chapter 12).*

Per serving: *Calories 71 (From Fat 45); Fat 5g (Saturated 2g); Cholesterol 380mg; Sodium 639mg; Carbohydrate 0g (Dietary Fiber 0g); Protein 6g.*

Serving Savory Soups

Soup is a traditional part of a Japanese meal. The soup isn't a big, fill-you-up bowl of soup, but one that captivates your taste buds, waking them to the possibilities to come.

Appreciating clear soup the Japanese way

To the Japanese, clear soup *(osumashi)*, such as the Clear Soup with Tofu, Wakame, and Shiitake Mushrooms in this chapter, when served in a covered Japanese lacquer soup bowl, is considered the perfect opportunity to experience using four of your five senses when enjoying fine food: seeing, touching, smelling, and tasting. Appreciating clear soup is amplified by appreciating the lacquer soup bowl in which it's served (see Chapter 14). This is a very Japanese concept, but if you give it a try, you'll see how much more you enjoy the soup if you appreciate the lacquer bowl in the process. Japanese lacquer soup bowls are traditionally either black or a

(continued)

(continued)

burnished orange-red color. You will come across a genuine lacquer bowl (not plastic) only in someone's home and some Japanese restaurants or sushi bars, but if you do, here's what you do:

✔ **See:** Admire the beauty of the soup bowl. Lift the rounded lid off the thin soup bowl, gently squeezing the thin sides of the bowl to release the lid if it sticks (sometimes hot soup causes the lid to stick). Set the lid down on its rimmed top. Lift up the soup bowl and look into the bowl, admiring the soup.

✔ **Touch:** Be aware of the feel of the bowl when you pick it up. A good lacquer bowl has a wonderful, smooth feel or sensation to it. (Plastic Japanese soup bowls can be quite pretty, but they lack the look of warmth and life that lacquer bowls have.) Sip the soup, feeling the warmth of it pass over your lips.

✔ **Smell:** After you release the lid, wonderful scents waft up. Appreciate the wonderful fragrance of the clear soup.

✔ **Taste:** Sip the soup, relishing the fresh flavors. Be aware of all four senses as you eat your soup. You're now enjoying soup with a full awareness of the experience.

Clear Soup with Tofu, Wakame, and Shiitake Mushrooms

My (Judi's) first taste of this ethereal soup *(Tofu to Wakame no Osumashi)* convinced me that the Japanese are on to something in their reverence for clear, flavorful soups. The soup is based on Primary Dashi *(ichibandashi),* a pale golden sea-flavored stock made from *dashi konbu* (dried kelp) and *katsuobushi* (dried bonito flakes).

Just the right amount of diced tofu, reconstituted deep green *wakame* (dried seaweed, see Chapter 3), and fresh shiitake mushrooms float in the soup. *Wakame,* after it's reconstituted, has a delicate, almost sweet flavor and a delightfully chewy texture similar to fresh shiitake mushrooms. It's a kick to watch the ready-to-use *wakame* soften and instantly plump up when it hits the hot soup. A dime-sized piece of lemon zest is the traditional garnish.

Preparation time: *10 minutes*

Cooking time: *18 minutes*

Yield: *4 servings*

2½ cups Primary Dashi (see the following recipe)

¼ teaspoon salt

1 teaspoon sake

1 teaspoon light-colored soy sauce

7 ounces soft or silken tofu, rinsed and diced into ½-inch pieces

½ cup (1 ounce) rinsed, stemmed, and thinly sliced fresh shiitake mushrooms

2 rounded tablespoons (5 grams) ready-to-use dried wakame

1 scallion, thinly sliced

4 dime-sized pieces of lemon zest

1 Place the Primary Dashi over medium heat. After it's hot, season it with the salt, sake, and soy sauce. Taste, and if you like, add more salt, not soy sauce, which will darken the color of the soup.

2 Add the tofu and mushrooms to the soup. Heat the soup back up (the tofu cools it off). After it's hot, add the *wakame.* Immediately turn off the heat.

3 Ladle the soup into 4 bowls, garnishing each with a generous pinch of scallions and 1 piece of lemon zest. Serve immediately.

Per serving: Calories 50 (From Fat 12); Fat 1g (Saturated 0g); Cholesterol 12mg; Sodium 856mg; Carbohydrate 7g (Dietary Fiber 1g); Protein 3g.

Primary Dashi

Yield: *2½ cups*

4-inch square piece of dashi konbu

3 cups water

1½ cups (½ ounce) loosely packed katsuobushi (dried bonito flakes)

1 Wipe off the *dashi konbu* with a damp paper towel. Cut a few slits in the edges of the piece to help release flavors. Add the *dashi konbu* and the water to a pot. Place it over medium heat. Bring just to a boil and then remove the *dashi konbu*. Add a splash (2 tablespoons) of cold water to stop the boil. Discard the *dashi konbu.*

2 Add the *katsuobushi*. Bring the stock back just to a boil. Turn off the heat. Let the stock rest for 1 or 2 minutes. Strain the stock through a cheese-cloth-lined strainer (a paper towel or coffee filter works in a pinch). Don't squeeze or press on the *katsuobushi,* or the Primary Dashi stock will become cloudy. If it's a little cloudy, which happens, don't worry. The soup will still taste delicious. You can make the Primary Dashi a day in advance and keep it refrigerated.

Go-With: *Any of the sushi recipes in this cookbook go well with this soup, but pressed sushi is especially good because the soup and pressed sushi both have an elegant look.*

Miso Soup with Manila Clams

Miso Soup with Manila Clams *(Asari no Misoshiru)* is a big hit in Japan, and for good reason. The nutty flavor of miso (fermented soybean paste) finds a perfect partner in the sweet flavor of clams. If you can't find Manila clams (asari, sometimes called Japanese littleneck clams), which are about 1½ inches across, choose another type of clam, preferably small ones.

A rich and diversified world of miso is waiting to be enjoyed (see Chapter 3). You can use any salty (not sweet) miso, red or white, you like for this soup, however, we favor *shinshu* miso, which is a pale salty miso. Don't allow the soup to boil, or the subtle miso flavors will change unfavorably.

Preparation time: *10 minutes*

Cooking time: *15 minutes*

Yield: *4 servings*

1 pound (20 to 24) Manila clams or other very small clams	*¼ cup shinshu miso*
4 cups water	*4 tablespoons thinly sliced scallions (see Chapter 3)*

1 Submerge the clams in cold, lightly salted water for several hours in the refrigerator, allowing them to release any sand. Drain and then scrub the clams well under running water. Discard any clams that don't shut when touched, which indicates that they're dead.

2 Place the clams and the 4 cups water in a pot, bringing them to a boil over high heat. Skim off any foam forming on the surface of the stock. Reduce the heat to low and then simmer the clams for 4 to 5 minutes, until open. Discard those that don't open.

3 Dissolve the miso in ¼ cup of the hot clam stock in a small bowl. Pour the dissolved miso into the pot of clam stock, stirring gently for a moment or two, being careful not to knock the clams out of their shells. Add the scallions. Remove the soup from the heat.

4 Ladle the soup into 4 bowls, dividing the clams equally. Serve immediately.

Vary It! *Mussels taste delicious in place of the clams.*

Go-With: *This is the perfect soup to serve with seafood sushi, especially the Marinated Tuna Tokyo-Style Scattered Sushi in Chapter 9.*

Tip: *Miso soup with clams is best served right away; however, you can gently reheat it if you're careful not to knock the clams out of their shells.*

Per serving: Calories 71 (From Fat 14); Fat 2g (Saturated 0g); Cholesterol 23mg; Sodium 781mg; Carbohydrate 4g (Dietary Fiber 1g); Protein 11g.

Japanese Chicken Soup

I (Mineko) created this easy, chicken-flavored miso soup for people who didn't feel like using Primary Dashi (see the recipe earlier in this chapter) as the basis for their miso soup. If you don't prepare your own chicken stock from scratch, buy low- or no-sodium chicken stock because red miso is quite salty. You may use soft, regular, or firm tofu, but firm tofu is less likely to lose its shape in the hot soup. Don't allow the soup to boil, or miso's subtle flavors will change.

Preparation time: *5 minutes*

Cooking time: *10 minutes*

Yield: *4 servings*

3½ cups unsalted chicken stock, skimmed of fat

¼ cup red miso

Salt

7 ounces (half of a 14-ounce package) tofu, rinsed and diced into ½-inch pieces

3½ ounces (1 package) enoki mushrooms, rinsed and stem ends trimmed

⅓ cup finely sliced scallions, cut on the diagonal

1 Pour the chicken stock into a pot and place over medium-high heat. When the stock is hot, lower the heat to medium. Put the miso paste in a small strainer and dip it into the hot stock. Using chopsticks or a spoon, stir the miso in the strainer until it dissolves into the stock. (Or you can dissolve the miso with 2 tablespoons of the hot stock before adding the dissolved miso to the pot.) Add salt to taste.

2 Gently slip the tofu into the hot soup. Simmer over medium heat 1 minute or so, just long enough to warm the tofu through. Add the mushrooms and scallions to the pot. Immediately turn off the heat.

3 Divide the soup among 4 bowls. Serve immediately.

Vary It! *Serve this soup without the tofu, adding more enoki mushrooms and scallions, toward the end of a dish-by-dish meal. Or instead of all enoki mushrooms, use an assortment of mushrooms, such as fresh shiitake, oyster, or himeji mushrooms.*

Per serving: *Calories 98 (From Fat 17); Fat 2g (Saturated 0g); Cholesterol 0mg; Sodium 930mg; Carbohydrate 9g (Dietary Fiber 4g); Protein 9g.*

Chilling Out with Salads

To excite and refresh your palate during a sushi meal, it's nice to serve something cold, such as one of these four salads.

 ## Asian Pear Salad with Wasabi Vinaigrette

Juicy Asian pears possess a mildly sweet flavor and firm, crunchy texture even when they're ripe, characteristics that make them a perfect choice for this salad and its punched-up wasabi vinaigrette. Asian pears can range in size from roughly ½ pound to 1 pound. A ¾-pound pear yields about 2 cups slivered pears. Refrigerate the pears before slicing them so that the salad is nice and cold.

Special sushi tools: *Japanese mandoline (see Chapter 2) or a sharp knife*

Preparation time: *15 minutes*

Yield: *4 servings*

1½ pounds (2 large) Asian pears	½ cup Wasabi Vinaigrette (see the following recipe)
1 tablespoon fresh lemon juice	
4 large butterhead lettuce (Boston or Bibb) leaves	4 small sprigs parsley, preferably Italian

1 Using a Japanese mandoline or a very sharp knife (dull knives bruise the fruit), sliver the Asian pears. (For more on cutting techniques, see Chapter 7.) Toss the slivered pears with the lemon juice for flavor and to help slow down oxidization, or discoloration, of the fruit. Refrigerate the slivered pears if not serving them right away, up to an hour or so.

2 Rinse and shake most of the water off the lettuce. Set each damp leaf on a salad plate. Top with one-fourth of the slivered Asian pear and then a parsley sprig on top for garnish. Drizzle just a little of the Wasabi Vinaigrette over the pears and around the sides of the lettuce leaf. Pass the remainder of the dressing. Serve immediately.

Wasabi Vinaigrette

Yield: *½ cup*

¼ cup rice wine vinegar	1 teaspoon wasabi paste
2 tablespoons extra-virgin olive oil	½ teaspoon sugar
1½ teaspoons soy sauce	Salt to taste

Stir all the ingredients together until well combined. Refrigerate, covered, up to a day or so, at which point the wasabi flavor begins to soften, or fade.

Vary It! *Serving the pears with their skins on makes for a pretty presentation, especially if you use both yellow and brown Asian pears.*

Per serving: *Calories 121 (From Fat 60); Fat 7g (Saturated 1g); Cholesterol 0mg; Sodium 287mg; Carbohydrate 15g (Dietary Fiber 5g); Protein 1g.*

Shredded Daikon and Carrot Salad with Sweet Citrus Dressing

People in Japan celebrate New Year's over the course of three days, January 1 through 3. Family and friends visit back and forth between houses, so food for these days must be the do-ahead variety and quickly set out when company comes. This New Year's salad *(namasu)* is a Japanese coleslaw of sorts. The first day, it tastes of refreshingly sharp daikon radish. The second day, the carrot's sweetness has taken the edge off the daikon sharpness. The third day, this salad tastes positively effervescent. The colors of the salad, orangy red and white, symbolize happiness in Japan.

Preparation time: 30 minutes

Yield: 4 servings

2 cups (½ pound) slivered daikon radish (see Chapter 7)

1 cup slivered carrots

1 teaspoon salt

¼ cup rice wine vinegar

1 tablespoon sugar

3 tablespoons fresh orange juice

1 tablespoon fresh lime juice

1 tablespoon orange zest

4 hollowed-out orange shells (optional)

1½ teaspoons lime zest

1 Place the daikon radish and carrots in a glass or plastic bowl. Sprinkle with the salt, tossing the ingredients gently but well. Let rest 30 minutes to 1 hour, allowing the daikon radish time to render a lot of juice. Strain the daikon radish and carrots, squeezing them gently to render more juices.

2 Prepare the dressing by stirring the vinegar and sugar together until the sugar dissolves. Stir in the orange and lime juices and the orange zest. Pour this dressing over the daikon radish and carrots and toss. Cover and refrigerate the salad until served.

(continued)

(continued)

3 To serve, divide the salad mixture among 4 small plates, or, if desired, serve each portion in a hollowed-out orange shell. Garnish each with lime zest.

Tip: *Man, oh man, does this salad taste good, but does it ever smell strong, given a little time, because of the daikon's pungent flavor! Be sure to cover it well, or when you open the refrigerator door, you'll be in for an olfactory punch!*

Per serving: Calories 60 (From Fat 18); Fat 2g (Saturated 0g); Cholesterol 0mg; Sodium 591mg; Carbohydrate 10g (Dietary Fiber 1g); Protein 2g.

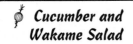
Cucumber and Wakame Salad

This light, refreshing salad is called a vinegar salad *(sunomono)* because it contains no oil. It possesses just the right amount of thin, crunchy cucumber in proportion to delightfully chewy *wakame* seaweed, to tease your palate into wanting more. Buy ready-to-use, already cut-up, dried *wakame* that needs just a few minutes to soften and come back to life. Use a good rice wine vinegar (see Chapter 3) because it's the dominant taste in this salad.

Special sushi tools: Japanese mandoline (see Chapter 2) or sharp knife

Preparation time: 20 minutes

Yield: 4 servings

½ cup high-quality rice wine vinegar	2 Japanese cucumbers
2 tablespoons sugar	1 cup water
1 teaspoon soy sauce	1 teaspoon salt
¼ ounce (10 grams) dried, ready-to-use wakame	1 tablespoon slivered fresh gingerroot (optional)

1 Stir the vinegar, sugar, and soy sauce together until the sugar is dissolved. Refrigerate this dressing until needed, up to 3 or 4 days.

2 Cover and soak the *wakame* in cold water until it softens, about 5 minutes. While the *wakame* is soaking, slice the cucumbers into very thin rounds, using a Japanese mandoline or a sharp knife. Drain the wakame and set it aside briefly.

3 To soften the cucumbers so that they absorb the rice vinegar dressing, soak the sliced cucumbers in the water seasoned with the salt for 5 minutes. Drain the cucumbers, gently squeezing out any excess moisture.

4 To serve, toss the softened wakame and cucumbers with one-fourth of the dressing. Place one-fourth of this salad in each of 4 small, shallow plates or bowls. Drizzle over a little more dressing and garnish with slivered gingerroot, if desired. Serve chilled or at room temperature.

Vary It! *Serve this salad cold with flaked crabmeat or boiled shrimp, placing the shellfish in one side of the bowl, or tossed with the wakame and cucumbers.*

Tip: *Make the dressing and soak and drain the wakame and cucumbers well in advance, refrigerating them until needed. Assembling and serving the salad then takes only moments.*

Per serving: *Calories 43 (From Fat 1); Fat 0g (Saturated 0g); Cholesterol 0mg; Sodium 270mg; Carbohydrate 10g (Dietary Fiber 2g); Protein 2g.*

Stand-Up Hearts of Romaine Salad

It's almost embarrassing to call this a recipe because it's really about the super-crisp texture of the heart, or center leaves, of a head of romaine lettuce, and the lettuce's upright presentation. Friends and family just love crunching away on the crisp lettuce like it's finger food.

Preparation time: *5 minutes*

Yield: *4 servings*

1 heart or head of romaine lettuce	5 tablespoons Miso Dipping Sauce (see Chapter 10)

1 If using a head of romaine lettuce, strip it of its loose outer leaves, saving these outer leaves for another use. Cut the heart of romaine leaves off the root end, rinse them, and then submerge them in cold water for 10 to 15 minutes to refresh the leaves.

2 Take the leaves out of the water and shake them gently to remove most of the water, leaving them just a little damp. Stand the leaves up in a pretty container or in 4 smaller individual containers. Serve with the Miso Dipping Sauce (you find the recipe in Chapter 10) on the side in 4 individual bowls.

Vary It! *Serve one-fourth of a heart of romaine, quartered lengthwise, on a plate, drizzling the dressing across the top of each one.*

Per serving: *Calories 39 (From Fat 4); Fat 0g (Saturated 0g); Cholesterol 0mg; Sodium 207mg; Carbohydrate 6g (Dietary Fiber 2g); Protein 2g.*

Eat your sea veggies

The Japanese know their seaweeds like people in the United States know salad greens. They use more seaweed products than any other country in the world, consuming over 100 different kinds. Seaweeds are sold in Japan fresh, salt cured, and dried. They're used in broths, soups, salads, simmered dishes, and sushi; as garnishes for sashimi (raw fish); and, believe it or not, in sweets and eaten as snacks. Put on your snorkeling mask and meet two other deep-sea beauties:

✔ *Hijiki:* Translates as black seaweed, which it is when cooked and dried.

Hijiki is loaded with vitamins and minerals, as are all seaweeds, but this dark beauty is one of the best natural sources of calcium you can find. Its strong flavor, a bit like licorice, is a favorite of the Japanese, especially when sautéed and simmered with pieces of deep-fried tofu (*abura-age,* see Chapter 3).

✔ *Ao-nori:* Dried, flaked nori. It's sprinkled on top of rice and other foods for a light taste of the sea. Sprinkle it on the rice of inside-out rolls as a fun green coating.

Selecting Smashing Side Dishes

Each of these side dishes is distinctly different and incredibly popular. Add one or two to your menu, along with a hot soup and cool salad, for a well-rounded sushi feast. Serve any of these side dishes with your sushi or as an appetizer, whichever way you prefer.

Putting a chill on veggies

In a little over 15 minutes, you can prepare both of the popular sushi side dishes in this section. The Chilled Seasoned Tofu is a sit-down dish, but Edamame, or boiled soybeans, is like popcorn, eaten sitting down or walking around. Keep a package of Edamame in your freezer for a last-minute snack for company — or you!

 Chilled Seasoned Tofu

Chilled Seasoned Tofu *(Hiyayako)* is a hot-weather favorite in Japan, but it's a favorite year-round in sushi bars and sushi lovers' homes worldwide. Custardlike tofu soaks up the flavor of the soy sauce it's served with, so use the highest-quality, naturally brewed soy sauce you can get (see Chapter 3). Try not to nick or mar any of the tofu edges so that each portion comes to the table with perfect lines. (This attention to detail is part of the Japanese culinary ethos of serving beautiful food!)

Preparation time: *8 minutes*

Yield: *4 servings*

14 ounces (1 package) soft or silken tofu, drained and rinsed	*4 teaspoons thinly sliced scallions, rinsed and patted dry (see Chapter 3)*
1 teaspoon finely grated fresh gingerroot	*4 teaspoons soy sauce, or to taste*

1 Cut the tofu block into 4 pieces. Place each piece on a small plate.

2 Top each piece with ¼ teaspoon of the grated gingerroot and 1 teaspoon scallions. Serve with soy sauce on the side, 1 teaspoon per serving.

Vary It! *Cut the tofu into ½-inch cubes instead of serving it in 4 large pieces.*

Go-With: *Chilled Seasoned Tofu is yummy with sliced avocado, broiled eggplant, or steamed asparagus.*

Per serving: *Calories 60 (From Fat 17); Fat 2g (Saturated 0g); Cholesterol 0mg; Sodium 370mg; Carbohydrate 3g (Dietary Fiber 0g); Protein 8g.*

 **Edamame**

As a testament to their growing popularity, edamame, or soybeans in their pods, are now found in freezer sections all across the country. They're fun to eat because you get to pick them up with your fingers, stripping the two or three soybeans out of the pod into your mouth with your teeth. The pods are discarded. After one or two edamame, you'll become addicted! Adjust the salt in this recipe to your taste.

Preparation time: *2 minutes*

Cooking time: *6 minutes*

Yield: *1 pound soybean pods, 8 servings*

6 cups water	*1-pound package edamame*
1 teaspoon table salt	*1 teaspoon sea salt, or more*

1 Bring the water to a boil over high heat and then add the 1 teaspoon table salt. Add the edamame and bring the water back to a boil. Boil them for 1 to 2 minutes — no more. You want the pods to retain some texture.

(continued)

(continued)

2 Drain and add the sea salt to the edamame. Serve hot, at room temperature, or cold, sprinkled with more salt, if you like. Provide a bowl for the discarded pods.

Tip: *Nip off the stem ends of the soybean pods after you boil them, making it easier to strip the soybeans out of the pod.*

Per serving: Calories 44 (From Fat 18); Fat 2g (Saturated 0g); Cholesterol 0mg; Sodium 292mg; Carbohydrate 3g (Dietary Fiber 1g); Protein 4g.

Steaming-up shellfish

We know that you'd rather spend your time making sushi, so here is a quick hot mussel side dish that would seem positively French if it weren't for the sake, which makes it positively Japanese!

Sake-Steamed Mussels

Hot mussels take to hot sake like cold oysters take to champagne — one brings the other's flavor into focus. Black-shelled mussels or green-lipped mussels (see Chapter 4) both taste delicious steamed in sake.

Preparation time: *5 minutes*

Cooking time: *8 minutes*

Yield: *4 servings*

1 pound live mussels (the smaller the better)	¼ cup thinly sliced scallions
1 teaspoon salt	2 teaspoons minced fresh gingerroot
½ cup sake	1 lemon or lime, cut into wedges

1 Put the mussels in a bowl and sprinkle them with the salt. Rub the salt all over the shells and then rinse them well under running water. Pull off any threads (called the *beard*) hanging out of the shell (refer to Figure 4-2 in Chapter 4). Throw out any mussels that aren't shut, or don't shut when you handle them, because that indicates that they're dead.

2 Place the mussels, sake, 2 tablespoons of the scallions, and 1 teaspoon of the minced gingerroot in a pot or frying pan set over medium heat. Cover and bring the sake to a boil. Lower the heat and steam the mussels until they all open, about 6 to 8 minutes. Discard any mussels that fail to open.

3 Divide the mussels and their broth among 4 bowls. Strain the sake stock through a dampened cheesecloth-lined strainer if the broth seems gritty (you can use a paper towel or coffee filter to strain the sake stock in a pinch). Pour one-fourth of the sake broth into each bowl. Sprinkle the remaining 2 tablespoons scallions and the remaining 1 teaspoon minced gingerroot among the 4 bowls. Serve hot with lemon or lime wedges.

Vary It! *Manila clams are traditionally steamed in sake, but any other small clam can substitute nicely.*

Go-With: *Drink sake — what else? — with it!*

Per serving: *Calories 106 (From Fat 23); Fat 3g (Saturated 1g); Cholesterol 32mg; Sodium 908mg; Carbohydrate 6g (Dietary Fiber 0g); Protein 14g.*

Diving into the Drinks

The only concern when choosing what to drink with sushi is that you don't want the beverage to overshadow or bury the delicate tastes of the sushi. Truest to sushi tradition is hot green tea. Sparkling water, served with a slice of lemon, is always good with sushi.

If you drink alcohol, you may prefer sake, an ice-cold beer, or white wine with your sushi. I (Judi) love sushi with champagne!

Discovering green tea

Sushi purists drink only green tea with sushi. The tea is favored for its delicate yet pleasantly astringent taste. The higher the quality of green tea leaves, the better the cup *(yunomi)* of tea. We like *sencha,* a steamed and dried, good-quality green tea, for sushi dinners. You don't add sugar or milk to this tea. Here's how to make green tea for 4 people:

1. **Put 2 tablespoons green tea leaves in a teapot, preferably with a built-in strainer.**

2. **Bring 3 cups of good-tasting water to a boil.**

3. **As soon as the water boils, pour it over the green tea leaves.**

4. **Let the tea steep 1 minute, no longer.**

5. **Pour off all of the tea at once (through a strainer, if your pot has no strainer); don't let it sit on the leaves.**

For a second pot of tea, pour hot water on the damp leaves in the pot. Brew as directed in the preceding steps.

Sipping sake

Sake is a fermented rice wine, and sushi is vinegared rice. Some sushi connoisseurs argue that neither the sake nor the sushi is enhanced when enjoyed together. This lack of enhancement isn't very important to the leagues of sake and sushi fans, who happily enjoy the two together. But, always serve sake with sashimi (raw fish), everyone says — always!

Sake, unlike most wine, is best drunk within 6 months of being bottled (some bottles are dated). How much the rice is refined, or polished, contributes to the sake's quality (the more refined, the more delicate and smooth the taste). The difference in tastes between sakes can be subtle. Within each of the four popular types of sake explained in this section are many styles of sake, ranging from dry to sweet, making it difficult to recommend one main type of sake for a particular sushi recipe. Add to this the fact that, for some sake connoisseurs, dishes are selected to complement their favorite sake, not the other way around. Solve this sake dilemma by starting with one type of the four types of sake mentioned here. Then, with your favorite type in mind, begin to try different styles and brands within that type.

Good sake ranges from clear to pale gold in color, tasting very dry to noticeably sweet, with a broad range of fragrances, from ricelike to fruity or herbal, depending on the region it comes from and other factors. Its alcohol content is similar to wine, about 15 percent. Although sake, especially premium sake, is preferred chilled by most sake lovers, drinking warm sake during cold weather is much enjoyed in Japan. Ultimately, enjoy sake whichever way you prefer.

Here are 4 popular types of sake:

- ✔ *Junmai-shu:* This pure rice (no alcohol added) sake, in which about 70 percent of the rice grain remains, is rich in flavor and body and goes well with a wide variety of sushi dishes.

- ✔ *Honjozo-shu:* This sake is similar to *Junmai-shu,* with a little alcohol added. It's a good choice for warm sake.

- ✔ *Ginjo-shu:* This sake is made with rice in which about 60 percent of the grain remains. Made with or without a little alcohol, this sake is generally lighter in body, with a fruitier fragrance than other sakes, and it's popular with women.

✔ *Daiginjo-shu:* This extremely smooth, very fragrant, and light-tasting sake is made with the best sake rice, with about 50 percent of the grain remaining. Made with or without a little alcohol, this sake is expensive and much sought after.

Some like it warm

It's not true that only inferior sakes are served warm. My (Mineko's) father always liked his sake warm in the winter. Warm does not mean hot (which would kill the taste and fragrance of the sake), but just a little warmer than body temperature, 100 to 105 degrees. To warm sake the traditional way (see Figure 13-1), follow these steps:

1. **Pour sake into a *tokkuri* (ceramic sake pitcher, see Chapter 14 for resources).**

2. **Put a small pot of water on to boil.**

3. **After it comes to a boil, turn down the heat and place the *tokkuri* in the hot water.**

   The water should come about halfway up the bottle.

   Within 3 to 6 minutes, depending on how cold the sake was, the sake will be just warm enough.

To determine how warm the sake is, lift up the *tokkuri,* wait a few seconds, and touch the indentation on the bottom. The bottle should feel warm, not so hot that you can't touch it. If it's too hot, take the bottle out of the water and let it cool down before serving it. Unless you've boiled it, the quality shouldn't suffer too much.

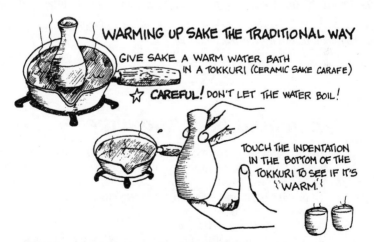

WARMING UP SAKE THE TRADITIONAL WAY

GIVE SAKE A WARM WATER BATH IN A TOKKURI (CERAMIC SAKE CARAFE)

☆ CAREFUL! DON'T LET THE WATER BOIL!

TOUCH THE INDENTATION IN THE BOTTOM OF THE TOKKURI TO SEE IF IT'S "WARM."

Figure 13-1: Warming up sake the traditional way.

Some like it cool

Sake should be served cold, but not ice cold, or its fragrance and flavor are hidden. Sake can be refrigerated and then set out for a few minutes or so to lose the chill. The exception to this guideline is cold Saketinis!

Saketini

We like to use sake as you would use vermouth: to flavor the vodka for this drink. Keep your vodka bottle in the freezer, ready to make ice-cold Saketinis. Saketini fanatics even keep their martini glasses in the freezer, ready to go! You can use whatever ratio of vodka to sake you like. The cucumber stick, amazingly, flavors the drink.

Preparation time: *2 minutes*

Yield: *1 Saketini*

2 ounces high-quality vodka, chilled	2 to 3 slices pickled ginger
1 splash (1 or 2 tablespoons) sake	1 cucumber stick

1 Pour the vodka and a splash of sake into a martini shaker or other covered container and add the pickled ginger and a few ice cubes. Shake briskly.

2 Pour the Saketini into a martini glass, straining out the pickled ginger and ice. Serve with a cucumber stick.

Vary It! *If you like the taste of pickled ginger, shake the vodka and sake and then pour the drink over the pickled ginger you've put in the martini glass.*

Per serving: *Calories 152 (From Fat 0); Fat 0g (Saturated 0g); Cholesterol 0mg; Sodium 1mg; Carbohydrate 1g (Dietary Fiber 0g); Protein 0g.*

Enjoying beer and wine

In Japan, beer is enjoyed as a refreshing drink before eating, especially during hot summer months. Then it's on to whatever seems right with the meal, perhaps sake, wine, or more beer. Japanese beers are light and crisp, perfect for sushi's delicate flavors, as are light American beers.

Light, refreshing white wines and crisp, dry champagnes are the best-of-the-grape for sushi. White wines, such as Sauvignon Blanc, Pinot Grigio, a dry Gewürztraminer, or dry Riesling, go well with sushi. But, a little spicier and fuller-flavored white wine, like an Austrian Gruner Veltliner, is also good. The exception to this white wine rule comes into play when you're serving fuller-flavored creative sushi *(sosaku-zushi),* such as our Portabella Sushi Rice Cakes with Balsamic Sauce and Wasabi Oil in Chapter 12. Here the flavors hold up to a bolder wine, and vice versa. A Pinot Noir or Merlot would do nicely for a recipe such as this.

Indulging in Sweet Conclusions

The Japanese don't have a tradition of eating sweets with their meals, sushi or otherwise. Pieces of perfectly ripe, beautiful fresh fruit, yes. Decadent desserts, no. But sushi has such a light taste and texture that rich, creamy desserts hit the spot for us! Some of the desserts in this section are cold, such as the Fire and Ice Cream Sandwiches and the Oranges in Plum Wine. Some meal-ending treats are hot, such as the Sake Brownie Soufflés. And some are in between, such as the Crystallized Ginger Crème Brûlée. Whichever you choose, it's bound to be a delicious adventure.

Fire and Ice Cream Sandwiches

The burn in these ice cream sandwiches that comes from a substantial punch of wasabi paste is tempered by the sweetness of the vanilla ice cream. Serve a stack of these ice cream sandwiches at your next party.

Preparation time: *10 minutes, plus about 2 hours for the ice cream to freeze in stages*

Yield: *10 ice cream sandwiches*

½ pint (1 cup) high-quality vanilla ice cream, slightly softened

20 chocolate wafers

2 teaspoons to 1 tablespoon wasabi paste

1 Spoon the ice cream into a bowl. Stir 2 teaspoons of the wasabi paste into the softened ice cream until it's completely incorporated. Taste and add 1 more teaspoon wasabi if it's not hot enough for you. Put the ice cream back in the freezer to firm up, about 1 hour. (Use a metal bowl and the ice cream will set up faster.)

2 Scoop up about 1 tablespoon of wasabi-flavored ice cream and gently squish it between 2 chocolate wafers. Make a few sandwiches and put them on a plate, not touching each other. Place them in the freezer to harden the ice cream, about 1 hour. Make the remaining sandwiches the same way. You can serve them now, or later.

(continued)

(continued)

3 If serving the sandwiches later, individually wrap the sandwiches in plastic wrap. Serve that day, while the chocolate wafers are still crisp. They still taste good the next day or two, but the chocolate wafers soften.

Vary It! *Stir chocolate chips into the wasabi ice cream. Serve the ice cream in bowls by itself, or with chocolate wafers or other crisp cookies on the side.*

Per serving: *Calories 111 (From Fat 50); Fat 6g (Saturated 3g); Cholesterol 24mg; Sodium 117mg; Carbohydrate 14g (Dietary Fiber 0g); Protein 2g.*

Oranges in Plum Wine

We make this dessert more than any other because it's so easy, beautiful, refreshing, and well liked by everyone we serve it to. You can make it as much as a day ahead.

Preparation time: *15 minutes, plus 30 minutes to marinate the orange segments*

Yield: *4 servings*

4 large navel oranges	2 tablespoons orange zest
1 to 2 tablespoons sugar	4 mint sprigs
1 cup plum wine	

1 Rinse and dry the oranges. Peel the oranges with a sharp knife, being careful to avoid leaving any white pith, which is bitter, on the fruit.

2 Slice the oranges into segments, between their membranes, holding them over a bowl to catch the juices as you do so. Drop the segments into the juice. Squeeze any remaining juice out of the orange membranes. Taste the juices and add the sugar, as desired. Pour the plum wine over the oranges and marinate them for 30 minutes or so in the refrigerator to soften the flavors.

3 Serve the oranges in the plum wine juice, garnished with orange zest and mint leaves in 4 individual bowls. Or serve the oranges in one large bowl and let guests help themselves.

Vary It! *Use just pink grapefruit or a combination of grapefruit and oranges. Instead of cutting the fruit in segments, peel and slice the fruit into rounds.*

Per serving: *Calories 191 (From Fat 4); Fat 0g (Saturated 0g); Cholesterol 0mg; Sodium 1mg; Carbohydrate 35g (Dietary Fiber 5g); Protein 2g.*

Honeyed Yogurt with Strawberry Sauce

When you drain yogurt, it gives off a tart liquid, smoothing out the flavor of the yogurt, which becomes the consistency of softened cream cheese. The yogurt becomes perfect up against the bright flavor of ripe strawberries. Although you can use no-fat or lowfat yogurt, the taste and texture will not be as satisfying as using regular yogurt. Sushi is lean food, so a little fat in this recipe is appreciated. If fresh strawberries are out of season, frozen strawberries will do.

Preparation time: _15 minutes, plus draining the yogurt overnight_

Yield: _4 servings_

1½ pounds plain yogurt	1 tablespoon sugar, or more to taste
1 tablespoon salt	4 teaspoons honey
2 quarts water	4 fresh mint leaves
2 pints ripe strawberries	

_1_ Place a large strainer, lined with dampened cheesecloth (or a coffee filter or paper towels), over a bowl. Scoop the yogurt into it, folding the cheese-cloth over it. Cover with plastic wrap and refrigerate overnight, or at least 6 to 8 hours, to give off liquid. By 8 hours, the yogurt is about as thick as it will get.

_2_ Stir the salt into the water. Add 1 pint of the strawberries, swirling them gently to help clean them. Scoop them out of the water with your hands and rinse them off under running water, removing any saltiness. Drain them well on paper towels.

_3_ Trim the strawberries and then puree them in a food processor or blender with 1 tablespoon or more sugar, to your taste. Strain the sauce. (You can do this a day ahead and refrigerate the sauce.)

_4_ Divide the sauce among 4 dessert plates. Using a large, wet spoon, scoop up one-fourth of the drained yogurt and place it in the center of the sauce. (Shaping the yogurt into an oval by using 2 large wet spoons looks very pretty.) Drizzle the honey over the yogurt and sauce. Garnish with the remaining 1 pint strawberries, either whole or sliced, using as few or as many as you like, and with a sprig of fresh mint. Serve immediately.

Vary It! _Flavor the strawberry sauce with rum or kirsch (a cherry brandy). Or make the sauce out of raspberries, mixed berries, mangoes, peaches, kiwis, or pineapple._

Per serving: _Calories 181 (From Fat 55); Fat 6g (Saturated 4g); Cholesterol 22mg; Sodium 80mg; Carbohydrate 27g (Dietary Fiber 3g); Protein 7g._

Crystallized Ginger Crème Brûlée

The combination of an ultrarich, cold custard under a thin, crisp candy crust is heaven sent. We've taken the classic crème brûlée and bumped up the flavor with an Asian twist, crystallized ginger. Crème brûlée is a custard that is baked in the oven, chilled until firm, and finally covered with a thin crackling crust of caramelized sugar. If you bake the custard in the morning and have the sugar and ginger mixture ready to go, then all you do at the last minute is caramelize the sugar crust mixture, which takes just a few minutes.

Preparation time: *15 minutes*

Cooking time: *40 minutes*

Yield: *8 servings*

1½ cups heavy cream

½ cup whole milk

4 egg yolks, lightly beaten

¼ cup plus ⅓ cup sugar

½ teaspoon vanilla

3 tablespoons (about ¾ ounce) finely minced crystallized ginger

1 Preheat the oven to 325 degrees. Select a 4-cup shallow gratin dish or other heatproof dish (such as a 9-inch nonmetallic pie pan).

2 Pour the cream and milk into a heavy saucepan. Place the pan over medium heat and bring almost to a boil. While the cream mixture heats up, whip the egg yolks with the ¼ cup sugar until thickened, about 3 or 4 minutes.

3 Trickle the hot cream mixture into the thickened yolks, stirring constantly. (If you add too much hot cream and milk too fast in the beginning, the eggs will scramble!) Stir in the vanilla. Pour this custard through a strainer into the gratin dish. Sprinkle half of the minced crystallized ginger over the custard. Lower the oven temperature to 300 degrees. Put the gratin dish in a baking pan in the oven. Fill the pan with hot water halfway up the side of the gratin dish. Bake for 30 to 35 minutes, until the custard is just set. Take the custard out of the water bath and cool to room temperature. When cool, cover with plastic wrap and refrigerate the custard until cold.

4 To caramelize the top, turn on the broiler and set the gratin dish on a baking sheet. Stir the remaining ginger into the remaining ⅓ cup sugar. Sprinkle this mixture as evenly as possible over the cold custard.

5 Place the gratin dish on a baking sheet and broil about 4 inches from the burner until the sugar begins to caramelize, turning the dish if necessary to melt all the sugar, about 1 minute. You don't want the custard to get warm, so take care not to broil the sugar much longer. Some cooks put the gratin dish in an ice bath (a larger pan of ice) under the broiler to keep the custard cold.

6 Let the custard sit for 3 or 4 minutes, allowing the sugar crust to cool and harden. To serve, crack the crust all over with the back of a spoon. Scoop out some of the custard and cracked candy crust for each guest.

Tip: *You can caramelize the crust an hour or two ahead and refrigerate the dish, well wrapped in plastic wrap, without much loss in crispness to the sugar crust. But don't push it any longer than 2 hours, or the crust softens.*

Tip: *Kitchenware stores sell small butane torches just for culinary uses such as melting sugar on top of crème brûlée. The torch gives you more control, so the sugar melts evenly and has less chance of burning. Plus, it's fun to use!*

Per serving: *Calories 259 (From Fat 176); Fat 20g (Saturated 11g); Cholesterol 170mg; Sodium 29mg; Carbohydrate 19g (Dietary Fiber 0g); Protein 3g.*

Sake Brownie Soufflés with Matcha Sugar

The finishing touch — pouring cold sake into the hot soufflés — is what transports these boxed fudge brownie soufflés into dessert paradise. No one will ever guess that your soufflés are out of a box! The *Matcha* Sugar was a last-minute inspiration on our part. Its unexpected lime green color delights everyone, and the taste and fragrance of *matcha* (powdered green tea) are very complementary to chocolate.

Preparation time: *10 minutes*

Cooking time: *35 minutes*

Yield: *6 brownie soufflés*

1 box (1 pound 3.8 ounces) Betty Crocker Fudge Brownie mix	*½ cup vegetable oil*
	2 large eggs
¼ cup plus 6 tablespoons sake	*Matcha Sugar (see the following recipe)*

1 Preheat the oven to 325 degrees. Very lightly grease six 1-cup heatproof ramekins or small heatproof dishes. Beat the boxed brownie mix, ¼ cup of the sake, the oil, and eggs together until well blended. Divide the brownie mix among the 6 ramekins.

2 Bake the brownies in the center of the oven for 35 minutes, or until puffed and almost dry in the center.

3 Take the puffed-up brownies out of the oven and sprinkle each with just a touch of Matcha Sugar. Serve immediately, giving each guest a shot (1 tablespoon) of the remaining cold sake to pour into their hot brownie or to sip — their choice!

(continued)

(continued)

Matcha Sugar

Yield: *1 generous teaspoon*

1 teaspoon sugar   ½ teaspoon matcha

Stir the sugar and *matcha* together. Keep tightly covered if not using right away.

Vary It! *Sprinkle the Matcha Sugar over fresh fruit, or French toast in the morning.*

Go-With: *Vanilla ice cream, naturally, is a good accompaniment.*

Tip: *You can bake the brownies ahead and reheat them in the microwave for 30 seconds or so, but they won't be as puffy and impressive.*

Per serving: *Calories 542 (From Fat 200); Fat 22g (Saturated 3g); Cholesterol 76mg; Sodium 323mg; Carbohydrate 82g (Dietary Fiber 6g); Protein 8g.*

Chapter 14

Hosting a Smashing Hand Roll Sushi Party

· ·

In This Chapter

▶ Preparing for your sushi party

▶ Letting the good times roll!

· ·

*G*athering friends, making sushi, and having a good time are what this chapter is all about. Our hand roll sushi party is the easiest sushi party of all because guests have a ball putting together their own hand rolls, filled with what they like to eat. Best of all, you can do most of the preparations ahead.

This chapter explains how to host a hand roll party for eight people, but you can shrink or expand it to fit your own plans. We suggest that you read through this chapter to see what simple steps are involved to pull this party off smoothly. After you have fun hosting this satisfying hand roll party, we bet that you'll be ready to party with the blow-out sushi menus we suggest in the "Over-the-top sushi parties" sidebar at the end of this chapter.

If you haven't done so, read Chapters 4 through 7, which cover the basics of making great sushi rice, shaping hand rolls, properly cutting ingredients, and selecting and handling seafood, before putting on your party hat. That way, when you open your front door, you'll feel more like a guest than a host!

Getting Your Sushi Party in Order

You can get most of the shopping done and prepare parts of this party days in advance, or you can shop early that day, dig in a couple of hours before the party, and do everything in one swoop. Break the shopping and preparations up as we advise later in the chapter, and you can be confident that party day will be hassle-free. The following sections give you a quick countdown of things you can do ahead.

Planning the menu

The hand rolls make a meal, but your guests will appreciate something special to snack on and drink before dinner. Add a soup or side dish, and you really have a party! Refer to Chapter 13 to decide what you want to serve with the hand rolls.

Lots of great drinks go with sushi, from sparkling water and hot green tea for younger guests and those who don't drink alcohol, to sake, Saketinis, beer, wine, and even champagne!

Consider setting out a bowl of edamame (boiled soybeans in their pods) and Miso Soup with Manila Clams, kept warm in a slow cooker, so guests can serve themselves before or during the meal. Or, start the party off with easy-to-make Hard-Boiled Quail Eggs with Matcha Salt, and offer a slow cooker of Japanese Chicken Soup. If the party is a sit-down affair with the hand roll ingredients in the center of the table (as described later in this chapter), pass the quail eggs and then sit down to soup. Don't forget dessert! We're crazy about Fire and Ice Cream Sandwiches for this hand roll party. Recipes for this dessert, and all the other dishes mentioned here, are in Chapter 13.

Making a grocery list

Making a detailed grocery list of the drinks and ingredients you need to pick up, noting what day you'll pick them up, will ensure your party gets off to a good start. Granted, shopping takes time, but after you have everything home, setting the table and preparing the food take only two to three hours. Don't forget to refer to Chapter 13 for the ingredients needed for your choice of drinks and other dishes.

The ingredients offered in this gorgeous hand roll sushi party satisfy a broad range of tastes. But feel free to improvise. For example, if you or your guests don't like raw fish, double up on the cooked salmon or roast beef. Among the ingredients you'll be buying are the items you need to make the spicy soy mayonnaise, salt-grilled salmon, and tricolor vegetable curls, which we provide instructions for later in this chapter.

Your guests select their own fillings, so you want a little extra of each ingredient. That's why we allow ten pieces of some items instead of eight, and somewhat more of other ingredients than normally needed to put on a party for eight people. Most people eat about four hand rolls.

✓ **Wrappings:**

- 16 sheets nori

- 16 butterhead (Boston or Bibb) lettuce leaves or red-leaf lettuce leaves

✓ **Fillings:**

- 4 cups short- or medium-grain rice (see Chapter 5)

- 1 pound sashimi-grade tuna (suitable for eating raw)

- 10 slices (4 to 5 ounces) smoked salmon, or gravlax

- 2½ ounces (½ cup) *masago* (smelt roe), or *tobiko* (flying fish roe)

- ½ pound fresh salmon fillet (see the cooking instructions later in this chapter)

- 10 sticks (6 to 8 ounces) *kani kama* (imitation cooked crabmeat), leg style, or ½ pound cooked crabmeat, shredded

- 10 cold cut slices, about 10 ounces (roast beef, turkey, or ham, preferably roasted or baked without sugar or excessive seasonings)

- 2 Japanese cucumbers

- 1 medium carrot (2½ to 3 ounces)

- 1 large ripe but still firm avocado

- 1 medium sweet yellow pepper (about 8 ounces)

- 1 small daikon radish or jicama (about 8 ounces)

- 1 package (2 to 3 ounces) pickled mountain burdock (*yamagobo*)

- 1 package (about 2.2 ounces) daikon radish sprouts (*kai-ware*) or other sprouts

- 20 fresh *shiso* leaves (Japanese basil)

- 1 bunch Italian parsley or watercress

✓ **Condiments:**

- 1 bottle (at least 10 ounces) soy sauce

- Mayonnaise

- Thick chili sauce

- 1 small red onion (5 to 6 ounces)

- 4 to 5 scallions

- 5 to 6 ounces goat cheese or cream cheese

- 6 ounces pickled ginger, in a container or jar
- 1 can wasabi powder (1 ounce) or 1 tube of wasabi paste (1½ ounces) (see Chapter 3)
- ¼ cup white sesame seeds
- 2 lemons or limes

Shopping in shifts

Dashing about at the last minute to buy ingredients isn't much fun, nor does it guarantee that you'll find all the ingredients you need. So we break the shopping up over the course of three days.

Days in advance

On your first shopping expedition, you can buy any pantry items needed for the party, such as nori, short- or medium-grain rice, rice vinegar, wasabi powder, sesame seeds, and soy sauce (see Chapter 3 for more information about sushi staples).

Don't forget to order, by phone or in person, sashimi-grade tuna for pick-up or delivery on the day of your party. Refer to Chapter 4 for information on where to buy sashimi-grade fish and shellfish, and information on selecting, handling, and storing raw seafood.

The day before the party

You need to wait until the day before (or the day of) the party to purchase the fresh vegetables, smoked salmon, masago, kani kama, and goat cheese. Refrigerate all these ingredients when you get home from the store. Bring the seafood home on ice in a cooler.

The morning of the party

Because you've done most of the shopping already, party day shopping will be a breeze. All you have left to do is pick up the sliced roast beef (or turkey or ham), fresh salmon, and tuna and bring the raw fish home on ice, in a cooler.

Preparing a few items the day before

Make the day of the party hassle-free by preparing some of the hand roll ingredients a day in advance. Cover and refrigerate all these ingredients.

✔ Salt-scrub both Japanese cucumbers (see Chapter 3) and cut one into 3-inch matchsticks.

✔ Cut the yellow pepper into ⅓-inch-thick strips.

✔ Peel the daikon radish and cut half of it (4 ounces) into 3-inch matchsticks, saving the other half for tricolor vegetable curls.

✔ Rinse and cut the pickled burdock in half lengthwise.

✔ Rinse and pat dry the lettuce and then wrap it in paper towels before storing it in a plastic bag.

✔ Rinse and pat dry the daikon radish sprouts and trim off their roots. Wrap them in a paper towel before storing them in a plastic bag.

✔ Rinse and pat dry the bunch of Italian parsley or watercress. Wrap it in a paper towel before storing in a plastic bag.

✔ Peel and thinly slice the red onion. Rinse the sliced red onion as described in Chapter 2.

✔ Rinse, thinly slice about ½ cup of scallions, and then rinse them again as described in Chapter 3.

You can make a cup of spicy soy mayonnaise a couple days before the party. This condiment is so simple and good that you'll be making it for sushi, as a crab dipping sauce, or for any reason at all. Here's how you whip it up:

1. **Stir together 1 cup mayonnaise, 4 teaspoons thick chili sauce (or to taste), and 4 teaspoons soy sauce.**

2. **Refrigerate, covered, until needed.**

Completing preparations the morning of

You've already done lots of the preparations required for your hand roll party, so today will be a breeze. All you need to do is set the buffet table or dinner table, make the sushi rice, and finish up the food.

Finishing the food prep

Prepare the sushi rice (see Chapter 5) the morning of the party and keep it covered with a damp cloth in a cool, draft-free place. The rice takes 1½ hours to prepare, most of it spent letting the rice soak and cook, so you can use this time to set the table and prepare other ingredients, as follows:

✔ Reroast the nori (see Chapter 3). Cut the reroasted sheets of nori in half, forming 4-x-7-inch half sheets. Keep the nori sealed in a plastic bag to stay crisp until dinner.

✔ Cut the tuna into sticks ⅓ inch thick and 3 inches long. Cover and refrigerate them.

✔ Reroast the sesame seeds (see Chapter 3).

✔ Drain the pickled ginger and put it in a small bowl.

✔ Slice the lemons or limes into wedges.

✔ Crumble or slice the goat cheese, and put it in a small bowl.

Now it's time to prepare the salt-grilled salmon. Pan-grilling (or broiling) fish with salt to bring up its flavor is a traditional method of preparing fish in Japan. Here's how:

1. **Cut the salmon fillet into 4 or 5 thin slices.**

2. **Sprinkle the salmon slices with ⅛ teaspoon of salt.**

3. **Pan-grill (or broil) the salmon over high heat until lightly browned on both sides and cooked through, about 3 minutes per side.**

4. **Cool, cover, and refrigerate the salmon until dinnertime.**

Next, prepare a few handfuls of tricolor vegetable curls, an easy and pretty filling and garnish. Here's how:

1. **Prepare a large bowl of ice water.**

2. **Rinse and then peel the carrot.**

3. **Using a vegetable peeler, peel thin ribbons of the carrot, the remaining half (4 ounces) of daikon radish, and one Japanese cucumber.**

   Vegetable ribbons in different widths and lengths look pretty, but the wider the ribbons, the more spectacular they look.

4. **Put the vegetable ribbons in ice water for at least 15 minutes.**

   They'll look like they're dancing as they curl up! Keep them in the water, refrigerated, up to several hours. Drain them well before stacking them on one or two platters as fillings and garnishes.

Setting the table

First decide whether you want to serve the meal buffet style or as a sit-down dinner. If you prefer buffet style, designate one table (a card table or coffee table will work) for the hand roll ingredients and one table for dining. If you don't have space for guests to sit down at a table, offer dinner trays to hold their dinner plates, a soy sauce bowl, and their drink. If you want to host a sit-down dinner, make sure that you have enough space to put all the hand roll ingredients, except the rice, on platters in the center of your table. Then provide all guests at their seats their own bowl full of rice, a small bowl for soy sauce, a napkin, and chopsticks.

After you arrange the table or tables, pull out the platters, dishes, and utensils you need.

You don't need special dishes to host a sushi party, but after you get into sushi, you may crave different sets of Japanese bowls, tea cups, and other tableware — see the "Finding great tableware for your sushi party" sidebar in this chapter for a list of resources.

Gather a big bowl (or eight small bowls) for the rice and eight of the following: dinner plates, small bowls for soy sauce, napkins, and chopsticks (or forks for your chopstick-challenged guests). Disposable chopsticks are fine, especially because they're considered polite for company. You can buy disposable chopsticks at big grocery stores or Japanese or Asian markets. A nice but not necessary touch, before or after dinner, is to offer your guests damp, wrung-out white washcloths *(oshibori)* for their hands.

You also need platters for the ingredients:

- ✔ Present the wrappings (nori and lettuce) on separate platters.

- ✔ Serve the prepared sushi rice in one big bowl, or eight individual bowls.

- ✔ Be sure to designate one platter for the raw fish (including sticks of tuna, smoked salmon, and *masago* in its own bowl). It's important to keep raw fish separate from cooked seafood and meats. When it's time to eat, fill the platter with ice cubes or packed, crushed ice, cover it with plastic wrap, and serve the raw fish on top of it.

You and your guests should be aware of the health concerns regarding eating raw fish (see Chapter 4). Those with shellfish allergies should be told that *kani kama* (imitation cooked crabmeat) can contain crab extract.

✔ Place the salt-grilled salmon and *kani kama* on their own platter (preferably over ice).

✔ Serve the roast beef on its own plate (preferably over ice).

✔ Vegetarians appreciate your keeping the veggies separate from the fish and meats.

✔ Use one large platter to hold small bowls of all the condiments, except the soy sauce, which should be in a small pitcher, figuring 2 tablespoons soy sauce per person.

✔ Arrange the cucumber, avocado that's been peeled and sliced lengthwise (⅓ inch thick) at the last minute, sweet yellow pepper, daikon radish, pickled burdock, daikon radish sprouts, and shiso leaves on a platter.

Garnish platters with tricolor vegetable curls and parsley.

Looks are important to the enjoyment of food, so spend a little time deciding the prettiest layout for the hand roll ingredients. The ingredients themselves are very colorful and appetizing-looking, so something as simple as a bouquet of seasonal flowers in the center of the table is fine. Figure 14-1 shows one of the ways we like to display the ingredients, all laid out and ready to roll!

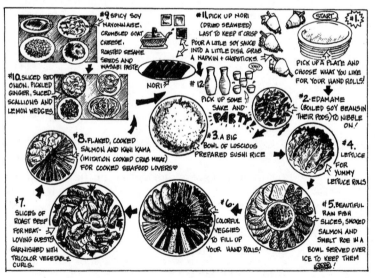

A HAND ROLL SUSHI BUFFET READY TO ROLL!

Figure 14-1: A hand roll sushi party buffet ready to go!

Finding great tableware for your sushi party

Here are three great sources for Japanese tableware:

✔ **Sur La Table:** This chain of kitchenware stores, which has many locations, offers a choice selection of small dishes, plates, chopsticks, and lacquer soup bowls. Call 1-800-243-0852 or visit the Web site at www.surlatable.com.

✔ **Utsuwa no Yakata:** This chain of Japanese tableware stores has lots of dishes, tea sets, and utensils to choose from. Call 1-800-269-5099 or visit its Web site at www.utsuwa.com.

✔ **Sara:** This small boutique offers handcrafted, exquisite tableware — a collector's dream. The store is located at 952 Lexington Avenue in New York City. Call 212-772-3243 or visit the Web site at www.saranyc.com.

Getting the Party Underway!

When it's time to eat, put all the prepared ingredients out on the buffet table (refer to Figure 14-1).

If your guests are new to the hand roll scene and seem a little perplexed as to how to roll 'em up, this is your chance to shine and show them how! Suggest that guests take a plate and help themselves to the wrap and fillings of their choice. Be sure to point out the different condiments for them to choose from, and suggest that they put about 1 teaspoon of wasabi and a generous pinch of pickled ginger on their plate. Explain that they'll spread the wasabi inside their hand rolls and eat the pickled ginger to refresh their palates between sushi rolls. The following list describes the hand roll process in a nutshell so that you, in turn, can describe to your guests how to make nori and lettuce hand rolls (Chapter 6 provides more details).

To make nori hand rolls, follow these steps:

1. **Place a piece of nori in the palm of your hand, shiny side down.**

2. **Using chopsticks or a fork (if guests use their fingers, they'll have a sticky mess on their hands), place about ¼ cup of sushi rice on the nori, spreading the rice out on a diagonal (refer to Figure 6-8 in Chapter 6).**

3. **Add whatever fillings or condiments you choose**.

A classic mistake that sushi beginners make is putting too much rice or too many fillings on the nori or lettuce, so tell your guests to go easy on the ingredients the first roll or two.

4. **Fold the bottom left corner of the nori over the fillings and then continue rolling to the right until you have a cone-shaped roll (refer to Figure 6-8 in Chapter 6)**.

5. **Clue them in that they should dip the top, or lip, of the hand roll — not the bottom of the roll — in soy sauce while they're eating it**.

Eat each hand roll immediately, while the nori is crisp.

Over-the-top sushi parties

When you're ready to move on to blow-out sushi parties that push your sushi skills to new levels, keep these menus in mind:

✔ **Blow-Out Sushi Party for 8:** The menu for this lovely party includes more-formal sushi foods, fit for special occasions.

Start the party with Saketinis and Sake Steamed Mussels (see Chapter 13 for both recipes).

For the main course, serve an assortment of sushi, including Avocado and Tapanade Finger Sushi (Chapter 11); Gorgonzola Cheese and Spicy Sprouts Battleship Sushi (Chapter 11); Tuna, Cucumber, and Black Sesame Seed Pressed Sushi (Chapter 9); and Crabmeat and Avocado Pressed Sushi with Wasabi Mayonnaise (Chapter 9). Offer the Asian Pear Salad with Wasabi Vinaigrette (Chapter 13) as a refreshing salad that guests may munch on as they eat their sushi.

Top off the meal with Crystallized Ginger Crème Brûlée (Chapter 13).

✔ **Bigger, Bolder, Blow-Out Sushi Party for 8:** When you're ready to pull out all the stops, challenging yourself, this is the sushi menu for you.

Kick things off with a traditional Japanese drink, such as cold or warm sake, and with bowls of Clear Soup with Tofu, Wakame, and Shiitake Mushrooms (Chapter 13).

Shift gears with an assortment of sushi, including Tuna Sliced Rolls (Chapter 9); Shrimp Tempura Rolls (Chapter 8); Avocado, Cucumber, and Pickled Daikon Radish Sliced Rolls (Chapter 10); Sweet Tofu Pouch Sushi (Chapter 10); and Stand-Up Hearts of Romaine Salad (Chapter 13).

Satisfy your guests' sweet tooth with Oranges in Plum Wine (Chapter 13).

You wrap lettuce rolls much the same way:

1. **Place a piece of lettuce in the palm of your hand.**

2. **Using chopsticks or a fork (if guests use their fingers, they'll have a sticky mess on their hands), place about ¼ cup of sushi rice on the lettuce, spreading the rice out in the center of the lettuce leaf.**

3. **Add whatever fillings or condiments you choose.**

4. **Fold the left side of the lettuce leaf over the fillings and then continue rolling to the right until you have a roll.**

5. **Dip and enjoy!**

Chapter 15

Demystifying the Sushi Bar Experience

*T*here's a time and place for sushi at home, and a time and place for sushi at a sushi bar. In this chapter, we take you on a tour of a first-rate sushi bar, exemplifying the best experience possible, where the sushi chef understands the traditional phrases and requests. (Each sushi bar is different, but the bare-bones experience in a good sushi bar should be the same no matter where you go.) We explain in detail what to expect from the moment you sit down at the sushi bar, or counter, until you pay the bill.

Even if you feel like a fish out of water, relax and enjoy yourself when you get there. As an elegant Japanese woman said to me (Judi) on one of my first visits, when I dropped a beautiful piece of sashimi (raw fish) in my soy sauce dish, "Even a monkey falls down out of the trees." Go with a friend who's experienced at ordering and eating sushi, and you'll pick things up very quickly. Then keep going back to your favorite sushi bar. Soon you may be receiving special items — such as true wasabi — reserved for the bar's best customers (see the sidebar "Wasabi and wannabes," later in this chapter).

See the "Two menus to order at a sushi bar" sidebar in this chapter for menus to help you order, and refer to the Cheat Sheet at the front of this book for crowd-pleasing items to eat at a sushi bar, as well as useful Japanese expressions to use. Chapter 17 tells you more about sushi manners, and Chapter 4 describes raw fish items not to miss at a sushi bar.

Getting the Best Seats in the House

The best seats in a sushi bar, if you're there for the sushi chef's expertise and the action, are at the sushi bar itself, or counter. Not all sushi bars take reservations, but if they do, make a reservation at the counter. You can order the same sushi and sashimi at a table that you do at the counter, but it's more personal and fun to order directly from the sushi chef. When you arrive at the sushi bar, the host or hostess will greet you with a bow and gesture to your seat.

If you're lucky, you'll be seated at one of the prized posts along the sushi counter. A great seat at the sushi counter is in front of the refrigerated glass case, where you can see the offerings of the day (not all cases are glass all the way around the bar). When you sit down, your view is of the refrigerated fish case, filled with live shellfish and shimmering blocks and fillets of fresh fish, and of the sushi chef standing behind it.

Each sushi chef takes care of five or six customers sitting in front of his area. But the very best of the best seats at the counter are the five or six seats in front of the *itamae,* or head sushi chef. Sushi chef's clothing doesn't necessarily reflect who's the *itamae,* so you'll need to do a little detective work. Here's how you know whether your guy is the head guy:

- ✔ He's probably not the one running back and forth to the kitchen fetching stuff, nor is he the one closest to the kitchen.

- ✔ He probably is the one giving orders to the other sushi chefs, standing behind the most impressive display in the cold case, and he's in the most prominent place.

Sushi chefs behind their counter prepare food for the sushi counter guests, as well as guests at any tables in the restaurant. If you're sitting at a table, your experience will be much like a Western restaurant experience, where the wait staff takes all your orders for drinks and food, including your sushi bar orders, and gives them to the kitchen or a sushi chef. In bigger sushi bars, the head sushi chef may not prepare sushi for the tables, unless they're special orders.

The sushi chef at your counter seat will say hello and bow when you sit down. Just say hello back. If, at any time during your meal, the sushi chef bursts into a cheer of "*Irasshai!*" turn around and look at the front door. The chef is shouting "Welcome!" to indicate that a good customer has come in.

Surveying Your Place Setting

When you sit down at the counter, you'll find the following dishes and utensils set out for you:

- ✔ **Disposable chopsticks:** Open the chopsticks package, keeping the paper sleeve as a chopstick rest if one is not provided. Split apart the wooden chopsticks and lay them down on their rest, always together, never separated. If chopsticks are too difficult for you to use comfortably, ask for a fork (see Figure 15-1 for help with chopsticks).

- ✔ **A cruet of soy sauce *(shoyu)* and a very small saucer in which to pour it as a dipping sauce:** Fill the saucer with just a touch — 1 tablespoon at most — of soy sauce because that's all you need. Drowning delicate sashimi and sushi in soy sauce ruins their subtle flavors.

- ✔ *Oshibori:* This item is a towel that looks like a tiny washcloth. It will be either hot or cold depending on the weather. Use it to wipe your hands, fold or roll it back up, and put it back in the dish it was delivered in. You may keep it and use it throughout the meal, or request a clean one from the wait staff whenever you want.

Deciding on a Drink

Shortly after you're seated, you'll be asked what you want to drink. You don't want the lingering taste of one sushi dish affecting the taste of another, so your drink should refresh as well as cleanse your palate. (Refer to Chapter 13 for more information on drinks.) Naturally sparkling waters are always good, and light beers, crisp white wines, and champagne go nicely. Some sushi bar patrons even think that whiskey is the ticket. Ultimately, it's about what you like to drink, but two classic drinks are associated with sushi: sake and green tea.

Traditionally, if you drink alcohol, your first drink at a sushi bar is sake, hot or cold, depending on the season. Sip it as you eat your first small plate of sashimi or other non-sushi appetizer. Premium sake is superb when it's cold. Other sakes can be enjoyed cold or warm. Sake is said to help you relax and build an appetite.

The Japanese don't traditionally drink sake while eating sushi or any rice dish. Sake is made from rice and is more redundant than complementary to rice's flavor. You may want to move on to green tea when your first sushi dish appears. It has just the right balance of green, leafy flavor and acidity to refresh your palate throughout the meal. Best yet, it's usually free. The waiter will continue to pour green tea into your *yunomi* (tea cup) throughout the meal. Regardless, lots of people drink sake straight through their sushi meals these days, or they choose to drink beer or wine instead of sake to begin with.

If you're with someone, etiquette dictates that you pour your companion's drink and that person pours your drink. Put another way, pouring your own drinks isn't polite. Lift your glass for your companion to fill. Put your glass down (no sipping first) and then fill your companion's glass. Now that you know what's correct, you can relax and break this rule when it feels right to you, especially as the meal progresses.

Placing Your Order with the Chef

A sushi counter is supposed to be an informal, lively place, bustling with activity and conversation. Sushi chefs, known as great entertainers as well as creative, skilled cooks, help create this type of atmosphere. They delight in performing for an audience. That's you and your neighbors. He's happy to talk to you. He's your own personal chef. Have a good time!

A sushi meal is composed of many small dishes that add up to one satisfying meal. Depending on your appetite, the size and the richness of the dishes you order, and your budget, you may want as few as three or as many as six dishes during a sushi meal. A daily menu may be available for you to look at, but sometimes sushi bars just post the selections on a menu board on the wall. These tips should help you decide what to order:

✔ The sushi chef looks to you for direction. Tell him what you'd like, and he'll acknowledge your order with "hai," meaning yes. Your order is in line in his head, perhaps behind several others. But the wait is never long, usually just minutes. Also tell him when you've eaten enough, and he'll see that you get your bill (see the section "Finishing Up Your Sushi Meal," later in this chapter).

✔ Sushi tradition calls for diners to ask the chef, "What's good today?" Sometimes he says, "Everything is good," but he may say, "We just got this or that," giving you interesting seasonal choices. If you ask for seared bonito with gingerroot and he apologizes, saying "So sorry, out of season," rejoice! You've come to the right kind of place — one that honors the seasons.

✔ Here's one sure-fire way to get the sushi chef on your side: When he asks how you'd like something prepared, say, "The best way — your way." He'll laugh, and you'll be in for a treat. That approach works for us every time.

✔ Usually, if you're sitting at the counter, you don't order off the restaurant's standard, or set, menu. You tell the sushi chef what you'd like to eat or ask for his recommendations. But if there's a daily menu of sashimi or sushi specials, you do place those orders with him. Order drinks and food items that aren't related to sushi or sashimi that the sushi chef prepares for you, such as edamame (boiled soybeans in their pod), from the wait staff.

✔ If the menu is printed only in Japanese, which would be rare in the United States, ask the sushi chef or the wait staff for assistance. (See the Cheat Sheet for help with Japanese names of fish, types of sushi, and common expressions.)

✔ Some seasonal fish is bought at market prices, which fluctuate daily. If cost is a factor, sit at a table, where you can ask the wait staff about prices, or order off the regular sushi menu. It's impolite to ask the sushi chef directly, in front of the other patrons, the cost of his dishes.

✔ Great sushi can be ordered off set menus at a good price when you ask for the restaurant's combination sushi plates. You should order these when seated at a table, leaving the sushi counter for those who want to order sushi dish by dish.

✔ Traditionally, you start your sushi bar meal with sashimi, or a simple raw fish sushi preparation, such as Tuna Finger Sushi (Chapter 9). Or, ask the sushi chef what he recommends as an appetizer. (See the "Two menus to order at a sushi bar" side-bar in this chapter for advice on how to start to your sushi bar experience).

Two menus to order at a sushi bar

Don't know what to order at a sushi bar? Consider the following menus, keeping in mind that seafood is seasonal and sashimi-grade seafood isn't always available. Order each course individually, not all at once. You also may want to try edamame (eh-dah-mah-meh), which are boiled soybean pods, as a delicious appetizer.

Menu #1: Crowd favorites

✔ **Maguro no nigiri-zushi** (mah-goo-roh noh nee-gee-ree-zoo-shee): Raw tuna finger sushi.

✔ **Ebi no nigiri-zushi** (eh-bee noh nee-gee-ree-zoo-shee): Cooked shrimp finger sushi.

✔ **Anakyu** (ah-nah-kyooo): Anago (saltwater eel) and cucumber hand roll.

✔ **Ikura no gunkan-maki-zushi** (ee-koo-rah noh goon-kahn-mah-kee-zoo-shee): Salmon roe battleship sushi.

✔ **Kappa-maki** (kahp-pah-mah-kee): A cucumber roll.

Menu #2: More exotic sushi

✔ **Suimono** (soo-ee-moh-noh): Clear soup, meant to warm up the appetite.

✔ **Tai no nigiri-zushi** (tah-ee noh nee-gee-ree-zoo-shee) Raw red snapper, or sea bream, finger sushi (see Chapter 9).

✔ **Amaebi no nigiri-zushi** (ah-mah-eh-bee noh nee-gee-ree-zoo-shee): Raw, sweet shrimp finger sushi. Ask the sushi chef to grill the heads for you to enjoy, too.

✔ **Chu-toro no nigiri-zushi** (chooo-toh-roh noh nee-gee-ree-zoo-shee): Raw, fatty tuna finger sushi.

✔ **Uni no gunkan-maki-zushi** (oo-nee noh goon-kahn-mah-kee-zoo-shee): Sea urchin roe battleship finger sushi.

✔ **Umejiso no temaki** (oo-meh-jee-soh noh teh-mah-kee): Pickled plum and shiso leaves hand roll. This is a traditional finish to a sushi meal.

✔ The fish case on the counter holds so many different creatures of the sea that knowing what to order can be difficult. You can choose from live abalone, sea urchin, octopus, flounder, red snapper, tuna, and yellowtail. If all else fails, point at what you think you might like to try, and ask the sushi chef how he would prepare it for you. Let him know whether you'd like a mild-tasting fish, such as *tai* or red snapper, or a bolder-tasting fish, such as *hamachi* (Japanese yellowtail) or *aji* (Spanish mackerel).

✔ Most finger sushi *(nigiri-zushi)* and battleship sushi *(gunkan maki-zushi)* are served in pairs. If you're with a friend who wants finger sushi, too, ask the sushi chef to split your orders between you, giving you each more variety. Ordering just one piece of finger sushi is also fine.

✔ *Omakase* means "chef's choice," allowing the chef to create dishes just for you. You'll be treated to the best sushi in the restaurant that day. But, beware, because it can be very expensive.

If you ask the chef to create a dish for you, let him know whether you have any allergies and any likes or dislikes. If you don't want any raw fish, just say so. He has plenty of other options, including cooked fish and shellfish, omelets, and vegetarian choices. Again, he's there to please you.

✔ If you think that the sushi chef is doing a great job for you, compliment him by offering to buy him a drink of his choice or offer him some sake from your *tokkuri* (sake carafe). He'll toast you, saying "kampai!" meaning "cheers!"

When you place an order for sushi, the sushi chef becomes a fireball of action, slicing fish, shaping the rice, and sometimes presenting you with the finished sushi so fast that you've barely finished ordering it.

Enjoying Sushi One Piece at a Time

When your food is ready, the sushi chef places your sushi orders on a plate on the counter in front of you. After you finish, the sushi chef may place your next sushi order on this same plate or replace it with a new plate and condiments. Condiments on sushi plates vary with the sushi dish. The most frequently used condiments are the following:

✔ **Wasabi:** This hot, usually horseradish-based paste is eaten with raw seafood and sushi dishes. For more information, see the sidebar "Wasabi and wannabes," later in this chapter.

✔ **Pickled ginger *(gari):*** Also called sweet pickled ginger, *gari* is small, paper-thin slices of sweetly pickled gingerroot, sometimes dyed a pale pink, that you eat to refresh your palate between bites of sushi.

✔ **Grated fresh gingerroot and thinly sliced scallions:** This tasty combination complements a variety of raw and cooked seafood sushi.

When you're ready to sample the first piece of sushi, keep these tips in mind:

✔ Finger sushi should be made to be enjoyed in one bite. Some sushi chefs are savvy enough to make them smaller for women than men; otherwise, we often have to take two bites. Use your fingers or chopsticks (see Figure 15-1) to pick up finger sushi, turn it over, and dip the fish or other topping — not the rice — in the appropriate dipping sauce. Battleship sushi, sushi rice balls, pressed sushi, and other sushi designed to be picked up and eaten with your fingers are always one or two, at the most three, bites in size.

A good sushi chef, if you ask him, will tip you off as to which sushi items need soy sauce. Some items come with a separate sauce, such as *hirame no nigiri-zushi* (flounder finger sushi with ponzu sauce), so you don't use soy sauce with this sushi. Ask him if you're in doubt.

✔ Hand rolls are meant to be eaten by hand immediately after they're made, while the nori is still crisp and easy to bite into. As it softens, the nori becomes chewy and more difficult to eat. Dip the lip of the hand roll, not the bottom, in soy sauce.

✔ Sliced rolls may be eaten by hand or with chopsticks.

✔ Always use chopsticks when eating sashimi (see Figure 15-1). Always lay your chopsticks back down, resting them on a chopstick holder or on top of the paper sleeve they came in, close together, never apart (see Chapter 17 for more on chopstick manners).

3 QUICK AND EASY STEPS TO USING CHOPSTICKS

1. GRASP ONE CHOPSTICK IN THE CROOK BETWEEN YOUR THUMB AND INDEX FINGER, RESTING IT ON YOUR RING FINGER.

2. GRASP A SECOND CHOPSTICK BETWEEN YOUR INDEX AND MIDDLE FINGERS AND HOLD IT IN PLACE WITH YOUR THUMB. MOVE THE TOP CHOPSTICK UP AND DOWN USING YOUR INDEX AND MIDDLE FINGERS.

3. NOW YOU'RE EATING WITH CHOPSTICKS!

Figure 15-1: Chopsticks 1-2-3.

Hesitancy is the enemy of enjoying adventurous, new-to-you sushi. Pick up the morsel of sushi, dip it in its sauce, and pop it in your mouth. You're going to be pleasantly surprised by all kinds of new tastes, textures, and flavorful combinations.

Wasabi and wannabes

Very little true wasabi makes its way into homes or sushi bars in the United States. This is because true wasabi, wasabia japonica, is a water-loving rhizome that is very tricky to grow commercially. The little mounds of complimentary wasabi paste on sushi plates in sushi bars are usually a horseradish-based paste, sometimes with a little mustard thrown in, meant to mimic true wasabi (see Chapter 3 for more wasabi information).

Wasabi (correctly pronounced wah-sah-bee, not wah-SAH-bee, as it's commonly mispronounced), a member of the mustard family, grows naturally in cold streambeds in the mountains of Japan. It's grown commercially in several countries,

including the United States, in Oregon. When grated into a smooth paste, the pale green pulp possesses a peppery, watercress-like, smooth-hot taste that blossoms into a sweet, fragrant finish.

To add to its mystery, when wasabi is ground, its complex flavors stay in full bloom only a short while. It's a very special moment when a sushi chef gives you a piece of true wasabi and a small sharkskin grater, specifically for wasabi, to grate your own wasabi while you eat sushi. This special little wooden paddle has a strip of sharkskin attached to it that's just the right roughness to grate wasabi into a paste (refer to Figure 3-3 in Chapter 3).

Finishing Up Your Sushi Meal

Tell the sushi chef when you've eaten enough. He'll give your sushi bar tab to the wait staff, who will add the drinks and cost of any items you ordered from the kitchen to the your bill. If you were pleased with the food and service, add 15 percent to 20 percent to the bill. Some customers discreetly tip the sushi chef, also. You'll probably receive a small piece of fruit, perhaps a slice of juicy orange or a piece of perfectly ripe melon, compliments of the house, before or when the wait staff brings you your final bill. Although dessert is not a traditional end to a sushi meal, most sushi bars offer a few desserts. Lastly, be sure to say "domo," or "thank you," to the chef as you leave if you've enjoyed his food (see the Cheat Sheet for other useful Japanese expressions).

Please be aware that lingering at the sushi counter over a drink when you're through eating is not appropriate if others are waiting to eat. The sushi counter is for socializing while you eat. To socialize after dinner, please move to a real bar. The sushi chef is just that — a chef — there to create beautiful sushi for his waiting guests.

Part V
The Part of Tens

The 5th Wave   By Rich Tennant

"I think you meant to ask for more 'wasabi', not, 'Kemosabe'."

In this part . . .

*W*e bet that you flipped to this part of *Sushi For Dummies* first. Everybody loves this part of all *For Dummies* books. Fun, informative stuff is what you find here. We don't want to hold you up, so read on about how to have a good time making sensational sushi at home and how to eat sushi with the manners of a sushi connoisseur!

Chapter 16

Ten Tips for Creating First-Rate Sushi at Home

I (Mineko) have found, over the years, that the following tips really help sushi beginners. A sushi novice cherishes these simple truths because, armed with these tips, you can march into your kitchen knowing that your sushi-making experience will be a fun-filled, satisfying, and very tasty adventure!

Adopting a Relaxed Attitude

This first tip is the most important one of all. Well-trained sushi chefs spend at least seven to eight years perfecting their craft. Each day, they stand behind their sushi bar, waiting to take your order and make exactly what you want, using the beautiful seafood and other exotic ingredients that fill the bar's cold cases. They create extraordinary sushi dishes, bordering on works of art, not just because they can but also because they want you to come back! Don't forget the amount of time these sushi chefs have spent perfecting their art, and remember that sushi preparation (like anything) has a learning curve. You don't have to knock yourself out making sushi — after all, it's only for you and friends, not for paying customers (although you certainly do want your friends to come back!). Remember, sushi can be sloppy-looking and still taste good if you've taken care preparing the vinegared rice and other ingredients. So just relax and enjoy making sushi, using your developing skills and the ingredients you have on hand.

Keeping Sticky Rice Out of the Bedroom

You can enjoy making sushi all the time if you stay ahead of the sticky rice, maintaining as clean a kitchen as possible. Pick up the sticky, cooked rice grains as they get stuck or dropped about, rinsing your hands frequently if you need to, or you'll find sticky rice clinging to your fingers, clothes, counters, and floors — even tracked into the bedroom. (We speak from experience!)

Moistening Your Hands

Sushi rice sticks to absolutely everything, including your hands, unless you moisten your hands before handling the rice. Keep a bowl of water, seasoned with a splash of rice vinegar, by your side when making sushi. That bowl is your first line of defense against a really sticky rice mess. You dip your hands in the vinegared water as you handle the cooked rice. When things get out of control (and they will) and rice completely covers your hands, rinse those hands off and start over. Be sure to also moisten all pieces of equipment that touch the rice, like knives and sushi molds.

Keep your hands moist, but don't make them dripping wet. You don't want soggy rice, and you don't want crisp sheets of *nori* (dried seaweed) getting wet. After dipping your hands in the vinegared water, your fingers drip with water. Some cooks slap their hands together to get rid of this water. We prefer a damp, wrung-out towel folded by our sides to tap our fingers on, removing excess water.

Resisting the Urge to Overstuff

All beginners are tempted to put way too much rice and filling in their sushi rolls. What happens? The rolls don't roll up, or they do roll up but then split open, ingredients squishing out all over the place. The rolls still taste good (refer to the first tip in this chapter), so go right ahead and eat them. They just don't look so hot. Think less is more — less is beautiful — and use a little less of everything. That way, when you make the next roll, it'll stay together and look marvelous!

Pressing Ever So Gently

King Kong wouldn't make a very good sushi chef — he'd be way too rough on the sushi rolls. Sushi rice is soft and easily smashed. You want each plump little rice grain discernible but stuck to its neighbor (go with us here . . . the first time you make sushi rice by our tried-and-true method, as we explain in Chapter 5, you'll see what we mean). Use a gentle, even, overall pressure when you use a bamboo mat to roll up your rolls. Press too hard with your fingertips or with your whole hand, and the roll comes out an odd shape, not round. The roll still tastes good but won't win any beauty contests.

Moistening Your Sharp Knives

After you roll up your sushi roll with a bamboo mat, you slice the roll into bite-size pieces. Easier said than done if your knife is dull or dry. A dull knife pulls through the roll, leaving you with ragged, pulled-out-of-shape pieces. They'll still taste good (check out the first tip in this chapter for some reassurance), but they'll fall short in presentation. So use a sharp knife.

For additional defense against torn rolls, keep the knife moist as you go. Sticky rice is the culprit, again. The rice sticks to dry knives just like it sticks to your dry fingers. Moisten the knife before each slice, wiping it on a damp, wrung-out towel set by your side. If the knife gets too sticky for the damp towel, rinse the knife off and then wipe it on the damp towel.

Chilling Out with Raw Seafood

You can tell avid sushi cooks by the way they keep a cooler in their car. They know — and now you know — that raw seafood suffers, and can become unfit to eat, if it's not kept constantly cold. So pack a cooler with ice and take it with you when you set out to get seafood, and pick up the seafood as close to dinnertime as possible. (See Chapter 4 for more about seafood.)

We love raw fish as much as the next sushi lover, but we also recognize that the sushi bar specializes in raw fish — the home cook doesn't. So don't think that to make sushi at home you must use raw seafood. Most Japanese don't. They use cooked seafood, lots of vegetables, and sometimes cooked meat or poultry in their sushi.

Tucking In Your Sushi Rice

Freshly prepared sushi rice is moist and pleasantly chewy, with a faintly nutty flavor and vibrant vinegar-dressing overtones. The rice can stay perfectly yummy, covered with a damp towel and left in a cool place in your kitchen, for a full day. Put sushi rice in the refrigerator, and it quickly dries and flattens out in taste. So don't be tempted — don't stick the rice in the fridge! (To see how to make perfect sushi rice, check out Chapter 5.)

The Cold Fish/Warm Rice Dilemma

Select your do-ahead recipes with care. Fish, meats, and poultry must be kept in the refrigerator, and sushi rice, which you can make hours ahead of serving, must be kept out of the refrigerator. In a nutshell, make do-ahead recipes based on vegetables, or keep the toppings and items that must stay cold in the refrigerator, pulling them out at the last minute and adding them to the prepared sushi rice. You can check out the do-ahead recipes in Chapter 10, or you can shirk do-ahead and ask your friends to work together, throwing a last-minute hand-roll sushi party, like ours in Chapter 14. By the time the vinegared rice is ready (about 1½ hours) you have all the other ingredients ready to go!

Breaking the Rules in the Name of Leftovers

The sushi dinner party is over, and you have leftovers. With the exception of perishables, like raw fish (which must be thrown out if it sits at room temperature for any length of time), you can save sushi in the refrigerator for tomorrow's snack. We know, we've told you too many times not to refrigerate prepared sushi rice or sushi dishes. But we're talking about leftovers here. And we just can't stand to throw them out — especially pieces of sliced rolls.

Place the pieces of sliced rolls on a dish, cover them with wax paper and then a moist towel, and cover the whole thing with plastic wrap. Don't skip a layer — it's the combination of the three layers that works! The next day, you can enjoy the sliced sushi cold, or you can toast the sushi in a toaster oven.

Chapter 17

Ten Tips for Minding Your Sushi Manners

*F*iguring out how to eat sushi politely can be confusing at first, but if you remember the tips in this chapter, you're sure to display good sushi manners in a Japanese friend's home or at a sushi bar. See Chapter 15 for more on sushi bar manners.

Don't Rub Chopsticks Together

Don't rub disposable wooden chopsticks *(waribashi)* together after splitting them apart. Making a performance out of rubbing them together shows bad manners. It implies that the chopsticks have splinters and are cheap, insulting your host. If you must, or the disposable chopsticks really do splinter when you snap them apart, rub them together discreetly, not in view of all.

Do Place Chopsticks Together

There's chopstick etiquette for proper placement and use just as there's etiquette for knives and forks. Don't cross your chopsticks when you set them down, any more than you'd cross your knife and fork when you set them down. Lay your chopsticks down tightly together, below your plate, and directly in front of you. The points should face to the left if you're right-handed, or the opposite way if you're left-handed. And heaven forbid you stick chopsticks in food — especially a bowl of rice! That's a definite no-no! This is done only at funerals, where the deceased's personal chopsticks are placed upright in a full bowl of rice, offering the person sustenance for the journey into the next world.

Don't Look for a Spoon

As unusual as it sounds, the Japanese don't use spoons. They sip their soups out of small soup bowls. Sometimes soups are served in lacquer bowls with lids. You remove the lid (which keeps the soup warm), lift the bowl, and sip out of it. Any small, solid ingredients are eaten with chopsticks while holding up the bowl. If the heat of the soup causes the lid to stick, don't panic. Simply squeeze both sides of the bowl gently with your fingers and the lid will pop loose. If it's too difficult for you to drink soup without a spoon, go ahead and ask for one. But give it a try the Japanese way, at least once.

Do Flip Chopsticks Over

If the sushi bar or dinner host doesn't provide serving utensils, go ahead and flip your chopsticks over and use the blunt, clean ends to pick up some tasty bit of sushi from a communal platter or bowl or from a friend's plate, if the friend is willing to share! Set the items down on your plate and flip the chopsticks back to their original position to eat with them. Doing this is hygienic and shows that you care for yourself and others at the table.

Don't Overload on Soy Sauce

Don't drench your sashimi (slices of raw fish) or sushi (vinegared rice items) with soy sauce. Soy sauce is meant to enhance flavors, not smother them. Just as it's polite to taste your food before you salt it, it's polite to limit the use of soy sauce, letting the hosts or sushi chef's mastery of flavors be your guide. Just lightly dip your sashimi or sushi in your soy sauce.

Do Dip the Fish in Soy Sauce

There's a practical reason for dipping the fish or other finger sushi topping — instead of dipping the sushi rice ball — into the soy sauce or other dipping sauce. The rice ball falls apart, making quite a mess. Plus, the rice absorbs too much soy sauce, drowning out the delicate tastes of the sushi rice. Doing so also insults the host or sushi chef who took time to season the way he felt was right.

Don't Put Wasabi in Soy Sauce

Unless you're absolutely crazy about wasabi and can't help yourself, don't mix wasabi in your soy sauce when eating sushi. If you want to do the proper thing, ask your host or sushi chef to put extra wasabi in the sushi itself. Eating sashimi is the exception. When eating sashimi, you can mix a bit of wasabi in soy sauce without being improper.

Do Eat Sushi with Your Fingers

Finger sushi started out about 200 years ago as a street snack meant to be picked up and eaten with your fingers. You can use chopsticks to eat sushi, but fingers are still perfectly acceptable. But always use chopsticks, *not* fingers, when you eat sashimi. Chapter 15 tells you how to handle chopsticks like a pro.

Don't Forget to Use the Washcloth

We're not talking about a washcloth or small towel that's in your host's bathroom. We're talking about *oshibori,* which is a small hot or cold (depending on the weather) wrung-out towel you'll receive in a sushi bar to cleanse your hands with, before and sometimes after you finish your meal. *Oshibori* is set in front of you when you sit down. Pick it up out of its little basket or tray, wipe your hands, fold it up, and put it back in the basket. If you like, keep this first *oshibori* to wipe your fingers during the meal. Sometimes you'll see the Japanese wiping their face with their *oshibori,* which is perfectly acceptable. Wiping your hands and face with an ice-cold towel is refreshing if it's a particularly hot summer day. Conversely, if it's been very cold, a warm towel on your face feels great!

Do Ask the Sushi Bar Wait Staff for Food and Drink

When you sit down at the sushi bar in a sushi or Japanese restaurant, the wait staff will bring you just about everything but the sushi. They'll bring you your first *oshibori,* or washcloth, for your hands, and a cup of complimentary tea. You'll place your orders for sushi with the sushi chef in front of your section of the sushi bar, but you ask the wait staff for any drinks, like sake, wine and beer, and items such as soups, salads, and desserts that are on the restaurant's Japanese menu. The exception to this rule is if you'd like the sushi chef to prepare a special dish, perhaps a salad, to go with his sushi that's not on the menu. If you need more soy sauce, extra plates, clean dishes, or another *oshibori,* ask the wait staff. Tell the sushi chef when you've finished your meal. He's been keeping track of your sushi dishes and will have the wait staff add them to your bill.

Metric Conversion Guide

. . . .

*N**ote:* The recipes in this cookbook were not developed or tested using metric measures. There may be some variation in quality when converting to metric units.

Common Abbreviations

Abbreviation(s)	What It Stands For
C, c	cup
g	gram
kg	kilogram
L, l	liter
lb	pound
mL, ml	milliliter
oz	ounce
pt	pint
t, tsp	teaspoon
T, TB, Tbl, Tbsp	tablespoon

Volume

U.S Units	Canadian Metric	Australian Metric
¼ teaspoon	1 mL	1 ml
½ teaspoon	2 mL	2 ml
1 teaspoon	5 mL	5 ml
1 tablespoon	15 mL	20 ml
¼ cup	50 mL	60 ml

(continued)

Volume *(continued)*

U.S Units	Canadian Metric	Australian Metric
⅓ cup	75 mL	80 ml
½ cup	125 mL	125 ml
⅔ cup	150 mL	170 ml
¾ cup	175 mL	190 ml
1 cup	250 mL	250 ml
1 quart	1 liter	1 liter
1½ quarts	1.5 liters	1.5 liters
2 quarts	2 liters	2 liters
2½ quarts	2.5 liters	2.5 liters
3 quarts	3 liters	3 liters
4 quarts	4 liters	4 liters

Weight

U.S. Units	Canadian Metric	Australian Metric
1 ounce	30 grams	30 grams
2 ounces	55 grams	60 grams
3 ounces	85 grams	90 grams
4 ounces (¼ pound)	115 grams	125 grams
8 ounces (½ pound)	225 grams	225 grams
16 ounces (1 pound)	455 grams	500 grams
1 pound	455 grams	½ kilogram

Measurements

Inches	Centimeters
½	1.5
1	2.5
2	5.0

Inches	Centimeters
3	7.5
4	10.0
5	12.5
6	15.0
7	17.5
8	20.5
9	23.0
10	25.5
11	28.0
12	30.5
13	33.0

Temperature (Degrees)

Fahrenheit	Celsius
32	0
212	100
250	120
275	140
300	150
325	160
350	180
375	190
400	200
425	220
450	230
475	240
500	260

Index

FOR DUMMIES

Helping you expand your horizons and realize your potential

PERSONAL FINANCE & BUSINESS

0-7645-2431-3

0-7645-5331-3

0-7645-5307-0

Also available:

Accounting For Dummies
(0-7645-5314-3)

Business Plans Kit For
Dummies
(0-7645-5365-8)

Managing For Dummies
(1-5688-4858-7)

Mutual Funds For
Dummies
(0-7645-5329-1)

QuickBooks All-in-One
Desk Reference For
Dummies
(0-7645-1963-8)

Resumes For Dummies
(0-7645-5471-9)

Small Business Kit For
Dummies
(0-7645-5093-4)

Starting an eBay Business
For Dummies
(0-7645-1547-0)

Taxes For Dummies 2003
(0-7645-5475-1)

HOME, GARDEN, FOOD & WINE

0-7645-5295-3

0-7645-5130-2

0-7645-5250-3

Also available:

Bartending For Dummies
(0-7645-5051-9)

Christmas Cooking For
Dummies
(0-7645-5407-7)

Cookies For Dummies
(0-7645-5390-9)

Diabetes Cookbook For
Dummies
(0-7645-5230-9)

Grilling For Dummies
(0-7645-5076-4)

Home Maintenance For
Dummies
(0-7645-5215-5)

Slow Cookers For
Dummies
(0-7645-5240-6)

Wine For Dummies
(0-7645-5114-0)

FITNESS, SPORTS, HOBBIES & PETS

0-7645-5167-1

0-7645-5146-9

0-7645-5106-X

Also available:

Cats For Dummies
(0-7645-5275-9)

Chess For Dummies
(0-7645-5003-9)

Dog Training For
Dummies
(0-7645-5286-4)

Labrador Retrievers For
Dummies
(0-7645-5281-3)

Martial Arts For Dummies
(0-7645-5358-5)

Piano For Dummies
(0-7645-5105-1)

Pilates For Dummies
(0-7645-5397-6)

Power Yoga For Dummies
(0-7645-5342-9)

Puppies For Dummies
(0-7645-5255-4)

Quilting For Dummies
(0-7645-5118-3)

Rock Guitar For Dummies
(0-7645-5356-9)

Weight Training For
Dummies
(0-7645-5168-X)

Available wherever books are sold.
Go to www.dummies.com or call 1-877-762-2974 to order direct

FOR DUMMIES®

A world of resources to help you grow

TRAVEL

0-7645-5453-0

0-7645-5438-7

0-7645-5444-1

Also available:

America's National Parks
For Dummies
(0-7645-6204-5)

Caribbean For Dummies
(0-7645-5445-X)

Cruise Vacations For
Dummies 2003
(0-7645-5459-X)

Europe For Dummies
(0-7645-5456-5)

Ireland For Dummies
(0-7645-6199-5)

France For Dummies
(0-7645-6292-4)

Las Vegas For Dummies
(0-7645-5448-4)

London For Dummies
(0-7645-5416-6)

Mexico's Beach Resorts
For Dummies
(0-7645-6262-2)

Paris For Dummies
(0-7645-5494-8)

RV Vacations For
Dummies
(0-7645-5443-3)

EDUCATION & TEST PREPARATION

0-7645-5194-9

0-7645-5325-9

0-7645-5249-X

Also available:

The ACT For Dummies
(0-7645-5210-4)

Chemistry For Dummies
(0-7645-5430-1)

English Grammar For
Dummies
(0-7645-5322-4)

French For Dummies
(0-7645-5193-0)

GMAT For Dummies
(0-7645-5251-1)

Inglés Para Dummies
(0-7645-5427-1)

Italian For Dummies
(0-7645-5196-5)

Research Papers For
Dummies
(0-7645-5426-3)

SAT I For Dummies
(0-7645-5472-7)

U.S. History For Dummies
(0-7645-5249-X)

World History For
Dummies
(0-7645-5242-2)

HEALTH, SELF-HELP & SPIRITUALITY

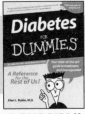

0-7645-5154-X

0-7645-5302-X

0-7645-5418-2

Also available:

The Bible For Dummies
(0-7645-5296-1)

Controlling Cholesterol
For Dummies
(0-7645-5440-9)

Dating For Dummies
(0-7645-5072-1)

Dieting For Dummies
(0-7645-5126-4)

High Blood Pressure For
Dummies
(0-7645-5424-7)

Judaism For Dummies
(0-7645-5299-6)

Menopause For Dummies
(0-7645-5458-1)

Nutrition For Dummies
(0-7645-5180-9)

Potty Training For
Dummies
(0-7645-5417-4)

Pregnancy For Dummies
(0-7645-5074-8)

Rekindling Romance For
Dummies
(0-7645-5303-8)

Religion For Dummies
(0-7645-5264-3)

Available wherever books are sold. Go to www.dummies.com or call 1-877-762-2974 to order direct

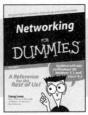